LEGENDARY WESTERNS

Peter Guttmacher

MetroBooks

MetroBooks

An Imprint of Friedman/Fairfax Publishers

© 1995 by Michael Friedman Publishing Group, Inc.

Library of Congress Cataloging-in-Publication Data
Guttmacher, Peter.
    Legendary westerns/Peter Guttmacher
        p. cm.
    Includes bibliographical references and index.
    ISBN: 1-56799-172-6 (hardcover)
    1. Western films–History and criticism. I. Title.
PN1995.9.W4G88 1995
791.43'6278–dc20   95-12333
                                                        CIP

Project Editor: Elizabeth Viscott Sullivan
Editor: Ben Boyington
Art Directors: Jeff Batzli & Lynne Yeamans
Designer: Zemsky Design
Photography Editor: Wendy Missan

Color separations by Ocean Graphic International Company Ltd.
Printed in China by Leefung-Asco Printers Ltd.

For bulk purchases and special sales, please contact:
Friedman/Fairfax Publishers
Attention: Sales Department
15 West 26th Street
New York, NY 10010
212/685-6610 FAX 212/685-1307

ACKNOWLEDGMENTS

I would like to thank the following small-town compadre and big-city institutions for their guidance and support: Robin Rose Brownstein, C.T. Wemple, Ben Boyington, Elizabeth Sullivan, the Gene Autry Western Heritage Museum, the Margaret Herrick Research Library at the Academy of Motion Pictures Arts and Sciences, the Beverly Hills Library, the Santa Monica Library, and the Los Angeles County Library.

This book is dedicated to my ma, Ann Guttmacher.

Newfound friends Lieutenant John Dunbar (Kevin Costner) and Lakota chief Kicking Bird (Graham Greene) exchange a look that says, "This is going to be the most popular western ever made," as they survey the situation in Academy Award–winning Dances with Wolves (1990).

CONTENTS

INTRODUCTION

The West, a horse, a camera—that's how it all began...or so the story goes.

The year was 1877. The place, of course, was California. Governor Leland Stanford, founder of Stanford University and the man who hammered in the spike that joined the Central Pacific to the Southern Pacific Railroad, had made a friendly little wager of twenty-five thousand dollars concerning his horse, Occident. The bet wasn't about a race. It was about image and reality. The politico claimed that, contrary to appearances, at some point when his cayuse was at full gallop, all four of its thundering hooves would be flying off the ground at the same time.

The bet taken, Stanford hired British nature photographer Eadweard Muybridge to prove his point. Muybridge, who had been making an artistic if slightly scandalous name for himself by capturing bodies in motion (often nude young ladies descending staircases or picking flowers, among other Victorian niceties) through a series of still photographs, rigged twelve cameras with trip wires down a length of Stanford's dusty horse track. Occident was spurred and off he pounded through the trip wires. Once the film was developed (five years later, after Muybridge was tried and acquitted for the murder of his wife's lover), the truth was evident in black and white—a shot of Occident with four off the floor. Stanford won his twenty-five thousand dollars, and the photographs gave Muybridge an action sequence free from epidermal distractions.

To display his images, Muybridge created the Zoopraxiscope, a crude device that allowed him to project a seemingly fluid succession of sequence-of-motion paintings (based on his still photographs) from rotating discs reflected by highly polished mirrors onto a screen. The photographer then took his creation across the continent to Thomas Alva Edison, who had been experimenting with his own "moving pictures." The great inventor, so taken with the ramshackle device and especially the horse shots, borrowed a few of Muybridge's ideas, added some refinements of his own, and came up with the film-projecting Kinetiscope (a box containing a twenty-second loop of film that ran past an electric light and was viewed by squinting through a tiny hole). Soon, Edison's Menlo Park, New Jersey, studios were cranking out the very first movies this young nation had ever seen, with the most popular ones set in the West. As the lights went down in theaters and tents across the country, a revolutionary popular entertainment was born, and ever since it has left all others in the dust. The rest is, er, horsetory.

If the birth of the western seems a little mythic, perhaps it's only fitting. After all, the western myth and filmmaking are joined in one of the few marriages made in heaven. Movies provide limitless possibilities for both telling the truth and embellishing it. And nothing feels quite as genuinely American as the West. With a stunning canvas of wide-open spaces to wrap around stories of history, morality, revenge, hardship, freedom, romance, and adventure, no other film genre has as vividly depicted America's ever-changing image of who we are, who we like to think we were, and who we hope to be. No other medium has woven life with legend so seamlessly and with both so much and so little showmanship.

And then there are the fans. Be honest. Who has never tried on John Wayne's inimitable walk or talk for size: "Well, pilgrim?" Who hasn't seen a good man clean up a bad town or watched him ride off into the sunset with a good woman (as Gary Cooper does in *The Westerner*, 1940) without a wistful moment of, "Boy, I've really got to make my life

> *While literary men seem to have neglected their epic duties, the epic has been saved for us, by the Westerns [and] by of all places, Hollywood.*
>
> **—Jorge Luis Borges**

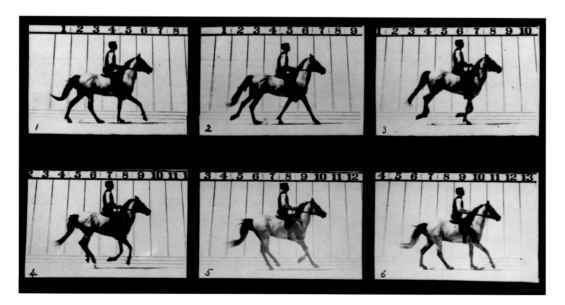

Notice all four hooves detached from terra firma at the same time in frame four? That's the fragment of Eadweard Muybridge's moving picture that won tycoon Leland Stanford his twenty-five-thousand-dollar wager and sent the western galloping into the twentieth century.

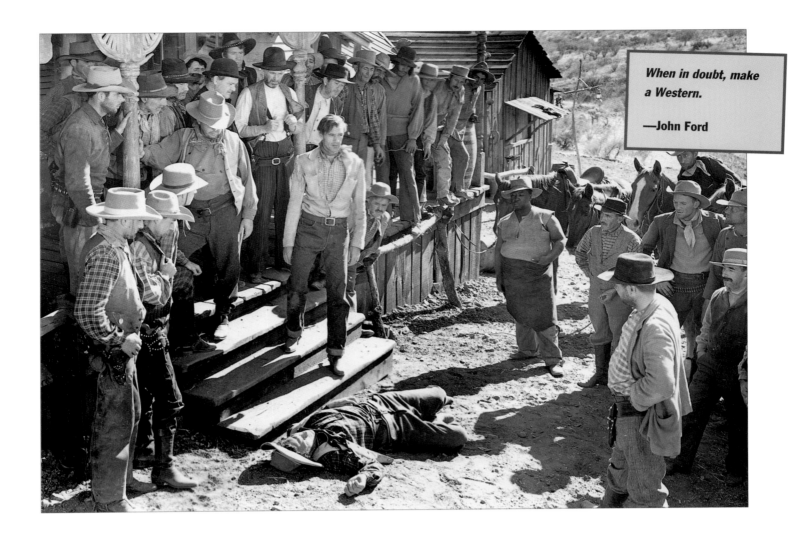

The western is one of the most vapid, infantile forms of art ever conceived by the brain of a Hollywood movie producer.

—Dwight MacDonald, The Miscellany

simpler?" Who would actually turn down the chance to thunder through Monument Valley on horseback (a scene and locale immortalized in so many of John Ford's films) at desert daybreak with the sweet scent of sage on the wind and the cactus in bloom?

Well, friends, the folks who forged this trail made sure there was room for all of us. Whether you're after heroes or antiheroes, sidewinders or schoolmarms, saloon girls or tough-as-nails cattlewomen, soft-hearted bad men or hard-hearted good men, colorful characters or stark portraits, splendor or squalor, honor or infamy, you've come to the right roundup. From seminal silents and ham-handed horse operas to contemporary stories of true grit, from larger-than-life historical epics to psychological dramas so archetypal that Carl Jung would have pulled up a front-row seat, westerns have drawn a bead on us. For almost a century we've never really been out of their sights, and now they're back with a vengeance. *Dances with Wolves* grossed $183,243,347 of our hard-earned dollars. Clint Eastwood swept the 1993 Oscars with his unforgivably good *Unforgiven*.

Cole Hardin (Gary Cooper) may have just felled one varmint on the dusty streets of Langtree, Texas, but the real sidewinder to watch out for is Judge Roy Bean (Walter Brennan), right behind him in The Westerner (1940).

The *Posse* is out, and the *Young Guns* and the *Bad Girls* are back in town. Stars all over Hollywood are going *Maverick* in what could only be called *The Cowboy Way*.

But we've got some ground to cover. It's a genre as big as Texas out there—big enough to hold the likes of John Wayne, Henry Fonda, Jimmy Stewart, Kevin Costner, Barbara Stanwyck, and Gary Cooper in one hand and Humphrey Bogart, Dustin Hoffman, Bob Hope, Boris Karloff, Montgomery Clift, Jane Fonda, and Marlene Dietrich in the other. So saddle up and we'll take a turn through some of the finest films Hollywood has to offer, big and small. We'll mosey behind the scenes and through a page or two of history. We'll expose Indians that weren't and cowboys that were. We'll toss off some legendary lines and draw the line at your knowledge of the best of the West. Lawmen, publicity men, stuntmen, legendary horses, little-known horses' asses, singers, slingers, swingers, desert rats, divas, shootists, and shoots—they're all waitin' on us up ahead, and we're not gettin' any younger just talkin' about it.

Let's ride!

Chapter One

THE
MAKERS
OF
THE
MYTH

Western movie history is made as the Indians thunder 'round the circled wagon train (in a scene that will resurface in many more films) in James Cruze's original, silent, epic "oater," The Covered Wagon *(1923).*

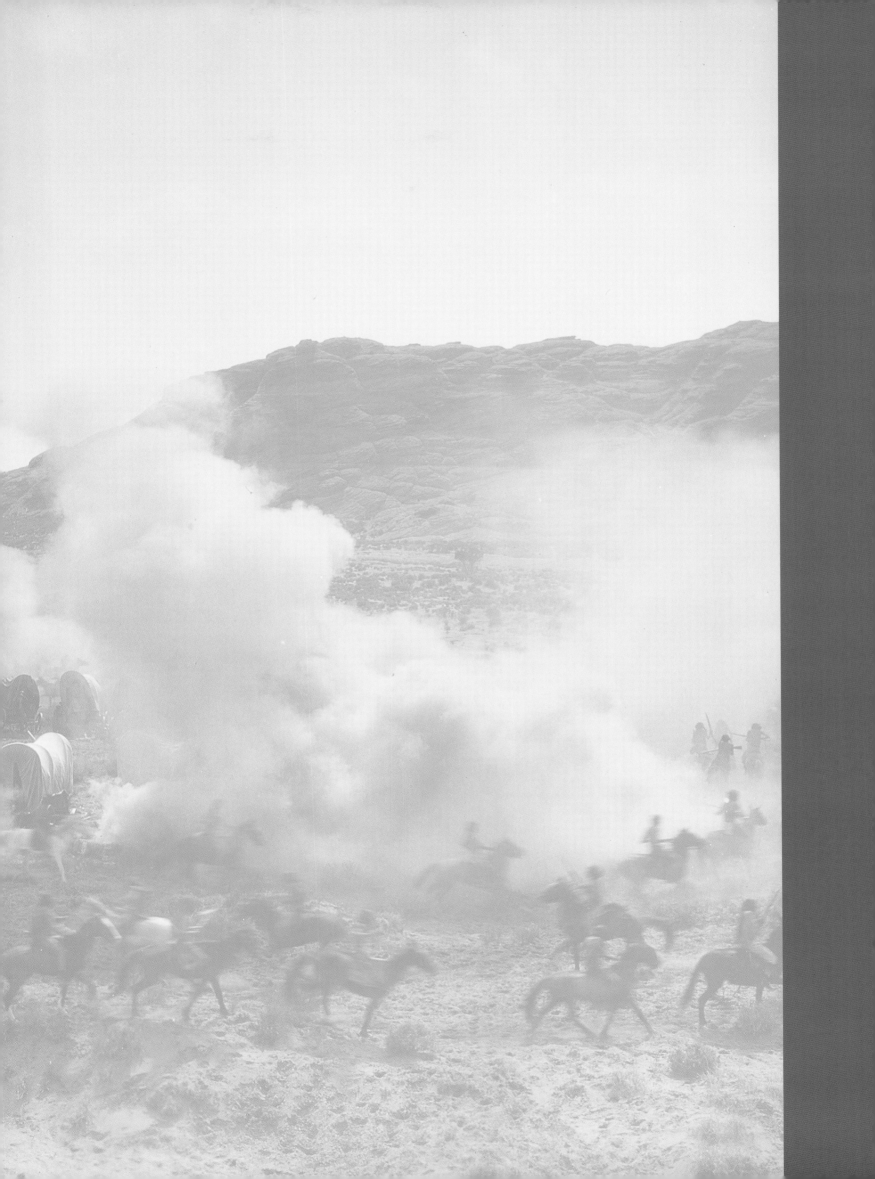

THE WEST IS DEAD! LONG LIVE THE WEST!

> *I knew the railroad was coming. I saw men already swarming into the land. I knew the derby hat, the smoking chimneys, the cord-binder and the thirty-day note were upon us in a restless surge. I knew the wild riders and the vacant land were about to vanish forever, and the more I considered the subject, the bigger the forever loomed.*
>
> —Frederic Sackrider Remington, painter and sculptor

In 1893, Harvard historian and professor F.J. Turner announced the death of the "western frontier"—there were no more wide-open spaces. Removed as he was, sequestered on the East Coast, and wrong as he was by today's standards, he did have a point, or so it seemed. More than fifteen million immigrants had landed on American soil within the space of

Don't be buffaloed by their clean-cut good looks: these hombres are ornery. Meet (clockwise from top left) Bob, Bill, Grat, and Emmett: the infamous Dalton Brothers—the type of outlaw legends that dime novelists and Hollywood producers alike made the most of in their books and films.

a century. Once ashore, this steady stream of humanity had taken John L.B. Soule's (often misquoted as Horace Greeley's) famous advice (first printed in an 1851 editorial in the *Terre Haute* [Indiana] *Express*) and wagon-wheeled along the westward Overland and Oregon trails. The end of the Civil War had turned that stream into a torrent, pouring people into the territories and young states along the way to California and points north. Some immigrants sought fortune, religious freedom, or fertile land. Some were on the run from the law. Some just needed a fresh start. All faced the challenge of their lives. It was no shirker's job forging the metal of the western edge of the melting pot, and it brought out the best and worst in those who made the journey. It also made those travelers seem to loom a little larger than life—a trait the American public liked to see when looking at themselves.

Readers had thrilled to the adventures of James Fenimore Cooper's woodsy hero Natty Bumpo in books like *The Last of the Mohicans* (1826). Francis Parkman had introduced them to Indian life on the Great Plains in *The Oregon Trail* (1849). Samuel Langhorne Clemens (a.k.a. Mark Twain) had given a similar journey a comic flair in the rollicking travelogue *Roughing It* (1872). And Bret Harte's colorful stories of outlaws, gamblers, and prostitutes from California's gold camps, which appeared in *Overland Monthly*, a magazine published in the late 1860s and 1870s, garnered him fans across the country.

These exploits out west took America's mind off the chaos of Reconstruction, fueling the hunger and bolstering the bravery of those considering the crossing. The tales supported Manifest Destiny, America's sense of divine right to expansion, and these westward adventures were most effective when they were, at least partially, based on fact. The early exploits of such daring souls as Davy Crockett, Daniel Boone, and Jim Bowie had already been told and retold into the realm of folklore. The burning ambitions of frontier Indian-fighters like generals Nelson Miles, George Crook, and George Armstrong Custer (who traveled with his own publicity man) had assured these men places in history and infamy. As mechanized publishing hit its stride, dime novels overflowing with full-fledged, larger-than-life outlaws like the Robin Hood–esque Frank and Jesse James, the Younger and Dalton brothers, William Bonney (Billy the Kid), John Wesley Hardin, Belle Starr, George Leroy Parker (Butch Cassidy), and Harry Longbaugh (The Sundance Kid) captured the country's attention.

Initially targeted to kids and working stiffs, these adventure rags quickly became a sensation. These five- to twenty-five-cent newspapers (approximately one hundred pages) and magazines (sixteen to thirty-two pages) originated in 1860 with Ann Stephen's "Maleska: The Indian Wife of the White Hunter." Like most western stories published before 1875, this tale was a colorful account of adventurers and what they learned through their wilderness experiences in a primitive paradise. The West of the imagination proved even more profitable with Edward Ellis' immensely popular *Seth Jones: or Captives of the Frontier* (1860). The story, with its

Daniel Boone–ish hero, sold 600,000 copies for Beadle and Adams Publishers. Three publishers specializing in this American mix of journalism and fiction soon had more than one hundred separate series on the newsstands.

As the real West's population filled new and often lawless towns, as local barons decided that their wealth was worth killing to ensure, as pioneers turned against one another—rancher against sodbuster, cattleman against sheepman—dime novelists kept up with the times. Stories shifted their focus from individual acts of heroism on the killing ground to dangerous journeys, stands against bad men, and frontier corruption. They chronicled the real lawmen, gamblers, and gunslingers for the adventure-hungry folks back home.

Frontierswoman Martha Jane Canary (Calamity Jane) was glamorized in the dime novels of Edward L. Wheeler and was even written into romances with the wholly fictitious character Deadwood Dick. (Wheeler never mentioned that Jane's association with the U.S. Army may well have been one of the oldest professional nature.)

RIGHT: Whole lotta shootin' goin' on! Dime novels, like some western movies, tended to vilify their bad guys more than just a little and to beautify their cowgirls quite a bit more. BELOW: This tough customer is that rose of the prairie, Martha Jane Canary, a.k.a. Calamity Jane.

Gunfighter, scout, and lawman James Butler (Wild Bill) Hickock had first achieved notice in an 1867 interview in *Harper's New Monthly Magazine*, in which he had beefed up the number of men he had killed in a Nebraska shoot-out from three to ten. By 1867, Hickock was starring in dime novels like *Wild Bill, the Indian Slayer*. Fur-trapping, Indian-fighting frontier guide Kit Carson, who had already been made the highly sanitized hero of two novels and three biographies, was further embellished in the 1879 dime novels *The Fighting Trapper* and *Kit Carson to the Rescue*. Carson had even savored the uncomfortable celebrity of finding one of his literary tributes among the bloody Apache plunder taken from a recently raided wagon train.

Exploiting these exploits took a certain directorial vision, and nobody's vision was more keen than that of Edward Zane Carroll Judson (Ned Buntline), who had put mountain man and supreme scout Jim Bridger (possibly the first white man to see the Great Salt Lake) to pen. On July 1, 1869, Buntline met former Custer scout, friend to Wild Bill Hickock, buffalo hunter, stagecoach driver, and showman in his own right William Frederick (Buffalo Bill) Cody.

This encounter changed the West of the imagination forever. Buntline's *Buffalo Bill, King of the Border Men* canonized Cody so successfully that it was made into a play in 1872. Following the show's success, Buntline convinced Cody to star in the sequel, *The Scouts of the Prairie*. Buffalo Bill soon wintered onstage in New York and worked as a scout for celebrities on the plains in the summer. He also got some directorial ideas of his own.

On May 19, 1883, at the Omaha Fairgrounds, Buffalo Bill opened his "Wild West, Hon. W.F. Cody and Dr. W.F. Carver's Rocky Mountain and Prairie Exhibition," a spectacle featuring daredevil Pony Express riders, a simulated attack on the Deadwood stage, cowboy shoot-'em-ups, and a simulated Indian hunt complete with wild horses, elk, deer, mountain sheep, and buffalo. The show was a sensation, and it kept Bill busy for the next thirty years. Future performances would feature reenactments of the battles of Little Big Horn and Wounded Knee, sharpshooter Annie "Little Sure Shot" Oakley, rodeo star Buck Taylor, Sitting Bull, Geronimo, Teddy Roosevelt's Rough Riders, and even scenes from China's Boxer Rebellion. Cody's mythic western entertainment traveled widely throughout America and Europe, and was even blessed by the pope. At a performance at Queen Victoria's Golden Jubilee in 1866, the careening Deadwood stage contained the kings of Greece, Belgium, Saxony, and Denmark, with the Prince of Wales riding shotgun.

The West of the imagination was gaining ground. Behind the lens, photographer Camillus S. Fly's tintype portraits of living legends like Wyatt Earp, Bat Masterson, and Geronimo were all the rage. Edward Sheriff Curtis' photographs gave much deserved dignity and no small amount of romance to American Indian life while Andrew J. Russell chronicled the adventurous westward expansion of the Union Pacific Railroad. On the canvas, Frederic Remington's western scenes derived as much from nostalgic feeling as they did from accurate depiction. Landscape master Albert Bierstadt went so far as to paint in Wagnerian-looking mountains that didn't even exist. Already surrounded by western words and images, the American public was primed for the coming of western film.

THE EARLY DAYS: SILENCE AND SAGEBRUSH

The Western was accepted with enthusiasm by a public anxious to learn quickly of its pioneer heritage, in order to acquire fundamental principles for its destiny.

—From *The Western*, by George N. Fenin and William K. Everson

Thomas Edison had been busy. By April 23, 1896, his moving images were flickering on the screen at Koster and Bial's Music Hall in New York City. His early films were minute-long documentaries and more or less a result of stationing his camera before an interesting person or event. Annie Oakley and Buffalo Bill Cody had been caught on film; so had calf branding, mule trains, railroad rides, a bucking bronco, and the Ghost Dance of the Sioux. One of Edison's first attempts at "setting a scene" was 1898's *Cripple Creek Barroom*: with a jug marked RED EYE in the foreground, and bricks and planks (looking as if they could use a fresh coat of stage paint) in the background, a top-hatted, mustachioed gambler leans against a bar while a motley assortment of cowhands (looking more like miners) mingle and drink whiskey behind him and a female bartender (who is displaying a five-o'clock shadow) serves the customers.

Another Edison short on a western theme, *The Great Train Robbery* (1903), directed by former Edison cameraman Edwin S. Porter, is generally considered to be the first narrative film. As

the true tale goes, on August 29, 1900, four members of Butch Cassidy's Wild Bunch had stopped the Number 3 train on Union Pacific's run for Table Rock, Wyoming. The men forced the conductor to uncouple the passenger cars and, after having blown the safe in the mail car, got away with about five thousand dollars in cash and a few hundred dollars' worth of watch parts.

Porter's movie shows similar events, using jump-cuts for the first time ever: from the bandits clobbering and hog-tying the telegraph operator, to the dastardly crime, to the operator's little daughter dramatically discovering and releasing her daddy, to the operator busting in on a dance hall to round up a posse, to the robbers divvying up the booty, to pursuit, to shootout, to justice. In the space of ten minutes—at a budget of $150 and shot on location not in Wyoming but in Delaware and on

OPPOSITE: Ladies and gentlemen! In the center ring, none other than one of the first entrepreneurs in show business— the one, the only Buffalo Bill Cody! BELOW: By the time Edward Sheriff Curtis went west on his commission from J.P. Morgan to photograph Native American tribes, old ceremonies had died out. This 1908 photograph is actually a posed shot of Slow Bull enacting a part of a rite of his tribe, the Ogalala Sioux.

the Lackawanna Railroad near Dover, New Jersey—this film garnered a fistful of firsts.

The Great Train Robbery contained the first (intentional) double exposure, the first stop-motion photography, the first pan shot, and the first film of anyone dancing to gunshots in the floor. A separate piece of the film that could be tagged before or after the feature showed the first close-up, in which a mean hombre (George Barnes) pointed his gun at the camera and blasted away. Audiences reportedly screamed and fainted from this special effect. They weren't the only ones: Porter had made good on his publicity release, which promised a body thrown from a train moving at 40 miles (64km) per hour.

The dummy was tossed from a bridge over the Passaic River and landed in front of a streetcar below—and caused quite a commotion.

The film was a hit. Theaters opened in cities across the country just to show it. Rural communities were treated to traveling road showings. Other budding film companies rushed to cash in on its popularity with hundreds of other films. Philadelphia's Lubin Co. created nearly an exact duplicate in what would be the first in the tradition of western remakes. Edison even parodied it himself in *The Little Train Robbery* (1905), which featured an all-child cast. *A Race for Millions* (1906) gave the western its first shoot-out on Main Street. Early French westerns like *The Cowboy Kid* (an appropriately European term, as the word *cowboy* originally referred to the English farmboys who came to America to fight as redcoats in the Revolutionary War) and *The Hanging at Jefferson City* were more violent and realistic, though their stabs at costuming made Porter's haphazard effort look accurate. Authentic locations were still a problem. The West was out there, and the filmmakers were everywhere but. In one of the first attempts at

capturing the true look of the West, former Oklahoma lawman William M. Tilghman crudely crafted the twenty-minute two-reeler *The Bank Robbery* (1908) in his home state. The cast included Al Jennings, who had recently been released from prison (after being arrested by Tilghman for robbing a bank). The film boasted authenticity but little else.

(NOT QUITE) THE REAL THING

God may have created man, but Bronco Billy Anderson created himself. The closest connection that former salesman Max Aronson had to anything western was posing as a cowboy for a cover of the *Saturday Evening Post*. But Aronson had acting aspirations, and when Edwin Porter was in search of western easterners for *The Great Train Robbery*, Gilbert Anderson (as Aronson had renamed himself) assured him that he could ride like a *vaquero*. He could not. He couldn't even get up on a horse.

Porter relegated Anderson to the role of an extra, but after witnessing the film's acclaimed release, Anderson was convinced that film—westerns, in particular—was where he wanted to make his future. He got a job with the Vitagraph Company as an actor and production assistant, and soon graduated to directing. Still hankering for westerns, Anderson moved to Chicago, and after hiring on with the Selig Company, he took a cameraman out to Colorado, hired a cast of locals, and made some westerns of his

OPPOSITE: Looking like a cross between Roy Rogers and Lon Chaney, early cowboy matinee idol Buddy Roosevelt soulfully stares in through a dusty window on the lone prairie in Ride 'Em High. *ABOVE: Before Sam Peckinpah ever wore a bandana, before Paul Newman and Robert Redford ever got into western gear, these gentlemen train robbers were known as The Wild Bunch. Seated left is Harry Longbaugh (The Sundance Kid); seated right is George Leroy Parker (Butch Cassidy).*

nearly five hundred one- and two-reel films. Each cost around eight hundred dollars to make and brought in up to fifty thousand dollars at the box office. (You do the math.) Although Anderson made the transition into feature-length westerns and eventually reaped an Oscar in 1957 for his contribution to the genre that he almost single-handedly established, his popularity faded by 1914, when an even bigger—and more realistic—gun arrived on the scene, another ersatz cowboy, William S. Hart. Unlike Bronco Billy, however, this cowboy did not make himself a star; he needed the help of one of filmdom's first great producers.

That money sack looks mighty heavy for a New Jersey boy to carry. Here's a scene from the first great western (made Back East), Edwin S. Porter's The Great Train Robbery *(1903).*

own. When the films neglected to get much attention from Selig, the young director formed the Essanay Company with his old friend George K. Spoor, which led to his directing some of the early films of Charlie Chaplin, Francis X. Bushman, Ben Turpin, and even a young Gloria Swanson.

Success sent Anderson farther west. In 1908, he moved to Niles, California, near San Francisco, to open Essanay's West Coast studio. He still wanted to make westerns, and he remained convinced that they could make money, but he was just as convinced that he needed to have a colorful, western character in order to sell them. With few actors available on the West Coast, let alone in Niles, Anderson resorted to casting the one person he could count on—himself.

Thus Bronco Billy Anderson was born. He adapted a story called "Bronco Billy and the Baby," by Peter B. Kyne, without buying it (only to have Kyne pay him a personal visit to collect what was owed), brushed up on his riding, perfected his rope twirling, tried to lose a little weight, and began work on *Bronco Billy's Redemption* (1908). In it he played a bad man gone good through the power of love, sacrificing his freedom for the sake of a sickly child. He was a little heavy in the saddle, a little flashily dressed, and a little lumpy to look at, but he was also big and burly, fumbled with his hat in front of the ladies (standard cowboy behavior), and lived by a code of his own.

The public responded enthusiastically, and Bronco Billy became the West's first film star, serial star, and B star all in one. In the next few years, Bronco Billy continued his derring-do in

Two Wagons West

As the movie business slowly moved west, two filmmakers were at the forefront, riding tall in the saddle. One would become a model for visionary directors to come, while the other would be an archetype for the perfectionist producer; both had been actors. David Wark (D.W.) Griffith had had a story refused by the Edison studios, but ironically had been given a leading part in one of Edwin Porter's films. Eventually joining New York's Biograph Company, he cut his teeth making eight silents each month (quite a few of them westerns) between 1908 and 1913, at a salary of fifty dollars per week. A sampling of his 1910 offerings alone includes *In Old California, A Romance of the Western Hills, The Gold Seekers, Ramona, In the Border States, That Chink at Golden Gulch, The Twisted Trail, The Thread of Destiny, A Man, A Rich Revenge, Over Silent Paths, Unexpected Help, The Broken Doll, The Two Brothers,* and *The House with the Closed Shutters.* And unlike most other directors—certainly unlike Bronco Billy—no two of Griffith's films were significantly alike.

At first, Griffith spent summers in New York and winters in Los Angeles. In 1913, though, he moved west, lock, stock, and film can (not to mention his stable of actors, which included Lillian and Dorothy Gish, Mary Pickford, Lionel Barrymore, Harry Carey, and Blanche Sweet). With an emphasis on acting and storytelling and a gift for panoramic sweep and depth of field, Griffith hardly ever used scripts, keeping story lines and even editing plans entirely in his head. He also perfected the art of mounting a story's suspense by cutting from scene to scene and from long shot to medium to close-up.

In Griffith's *Last Drop of Water* (1911), he gave westerns their first besieged wagon train and ensuing cavalry rescue. The last frames of this movie, depicting a lonely prairie grave in the foreground and diminishing wagons in the background, comprised one of the most starkly powerful endings a western had yet to receive. Griffith devoted a full two-thirds of *Fighting Blood* (1911), a story of the conflict between settlers and Sioux in the Dakota territory of 1899, to crafting suspense through battle and chase scenes. He increased tension symbolically with shots of cowering children inserted between scenes of settlers fighting off Indians from their cabin. He surprised the audience by stringing a long line of cavalry riding across the back of the screen only to then bring the front riders into close-up, suggesting the immense length of the regiment. And to increase the film's impact, he filmed the final rescue in sweeping panoramic shots from hills above the plain.

Ironically, Griffith turned his back on westerns after his early days. Some served as dry runs for later, greater films: *The Battle at Elderbrush Gulch* (1913) shared plot points, shots, and its two stars—Lillian Gish and Mae Marsh—with the famed *Birth of a Nation* (1915). The father of film artistry eventually abandoned the West, but he left his telltale mark on the medium and on the young directors he nurtured and influenced—Raoul Walsh, Erich Von Stroheim, King Vidor, and John Ford.

Thomas Ince was the western's first serious studio executive. He had been sent to Los Angeles in 1911 by a couple of bookmakers (not to be confused with publishers) to make "oaters" (the slang term for the short, quickly made western films that were becoming as plentiful as oats for a horse) at a movie studio the men had recently invested in. Ince discovered that the Bison Film Company's West Coast headquarters were little more than an abandoned grocery store/film-developing lab with a backyard stage and one backdrop of birds in flight. Luckily, Ince, possessed of almost inhuman energy, was detail-crazy and masterful with money, and was skilled in lighting, cinematography, dialogue writing, and self-promotion.

By 1913, Ince was turning out pictures at the phenomenal rate of one a week, and they were anything but standard. His first move was to rent out the entire Miller Brothers' 101 Ranch Wild West Show, with its real cowboys and Indians, trick riders, buffalo, livestock, wagons, guns, costumes, and sets for $2,500 a week. Next, he purchased 14,000 acres (5,600ha) at the mouth of Santa Ynez Canyon in the hills north of breezy Santa Monica, California—soon dubbed "Inceville." Presto—instant West.

Ince didn't have Griffith's creative genius, but he did have a genius for detail. Unlike Griffith (with whom Ince and comedy director Mack Sennett later formed the Triangle Corporation), Ince put everything on paper: his shooting scripts contained complete dialogue (and acting motivations) for each character (in silents, dialogue was very much for the actors' benefit alone); facial expressions; shot-by-shot descriptions of decor, furniture, and

lighting tints; and a numbered breakdown of the different sets. Ince was also less stereotypical in his treatment of American Indian characters than other directors; he promoted the performers and tried, unsuccessfully, to make stars of them. He promoted himself with more success, taking directorial credit for almost every "important" film of the roughly eight hundred he supervised. The real directors had to settle for assistant credits.

In time, though, Ince's scripts grew a little morbid for his audiences' tastes. How cheery is an outlaw girl who sells whiskey to Indians, repents, and falls in love with the minister she once tried to kill, then wanders off alone into the desert to die when scandal brews? Would this pick up your spirits? How about an opera diva whose husband suffers from tuberculosis, which forces her to join in the Arizona land rush to fund his recovery, only to find herself injured from a fall from her horse and forced to bear molestations from drunk cowboys at the saloon where she has to sing to survive? The filmmaker's resolution: after a bigamous marriage to a gambler, she finds out that her husband has died and all her suffering has been for nothing. She poisons herself.

Though his westerns faded from popularity by the early twenties, Ince left more than his organizational innovations as a legacy. He brought the western its next great hero, one who would rouse the genre to new popularity—a Shakespearean stage actor who would come to embody the unadorned West.

> I was an actor, and I knew the West. The opportunity that I had been waiting for years to come was knocking at my door....Rise or fall, sink or swim, I had to bend every endeavor to get a chance to make western pictures.
>
> —William S. Hart

(JUST ABOUT) THE REAL THING

William S. Hart was long in the tooth when he came to Tinsel-town in 1914. He had studied the Bard in England and had trod the boards in New York in such western fare as *Squaw Man*, *The Virginian*, and *Trail of the Lonesome Pine*. But there was much more to this eastern hombre. As a boy, Hart had traveled with his father, who built grain mills across the frontier West, and he had grown up in Dakota territory among the Lakota (Sioux) people, learning their language and a deep respect for their ways. He had been caught in the crossfire of a gunfight in Sioux City, and he had worked as a trail herd cowboy in Kansas. Once Back East, he felt like a "white Indian boy."

As an adult actor on tour, Hart saw his first western in Cleveland and was both transfixed by its power and disgusted by its inaccuracies. He made it his mission to bring the real West to the screen. Approaching his old roommate from Broadway's Hotel Harrington, the formerly struggling actor Thomas H. Ince, Hart put forth his case so convincingly that he won supporting roles as villains in a couple of two-reelers. Frustrated, he pressed friendship further for the chance to star in features and write some of his own material. Ince yielded and put his pal in *The Bargain* (1914) and *On the Night Stage* (1915), but Hart was disheartened by the experience, and after filming he headed back to New York.

A call came a couple of months later. *The Bargain* was such a hit that Ince had sold it to a much larger film company, Famous Players, for national distribution. William S. Hart's name was about to become a household word. Hart flew back to Hollywood and signed on to act in and direct his own films for a paltry $125 a week (most of Ince's players received much more). Even as Hart's films soared in popularity, garnering budgets of fourteen thousand dollars and more, he never spent much on his own salary. The picture was what counted.

And count they did. Hart demanded physical authenticity in every aspect of his pictures. His face might have looked a little plain, but he had believable grit and western skills. Above all, he dressed like a real cowboy, in a dust-covered, rumpled, well-worn frock coat; a rugged but colorful shirt; and an old Mexican sash under his gun belt—as

opposed to the Liberacelike outfits many of his successors wore, or the vague assemblages of clothing that made his predecessors look "like something between a Wisconsin woodchopper and a Gloucester fisherman." Hart's cowboys were usually bad characters with good intentions, often gentle to their horses or devoted to their sisters—as Hart was in real life. Often mistreating his heroines in the films' early parts, Hart's tough cusses would inevitably reform and prove themselves through sacrifice.

With as much emphasis on human drama as on their final explosions of action and violence, Hart's pictures were a boon to westerns even if they were a tad melodramatic. But Hart's intensity had to be taken seriously. His reverence for womanhood went so far that he felt compelled to propose to every unattached leading lady he ever had. That is, until one, Winifred Westover, took him up on it. He tried to backpedal, but she caught him and kept him.

As a director, Hart walked just as tall. He made the most of the landscape, refusing to water down blowing dust to make a tidier scene. His skylines—unlike the renowned John Ford's, which were often optimistically low on the screen, maximizing human freedom with an artfully enlarged horizon—

> **What remains of these films in my heart is that reliable manly spirit and the smell of male sweat.**
>
> —Akira Kurosawa, on William S. Hart

Is it life or just the movies? Thankfully, in William S. Hart's westerns, like this scene from On the Night Stage *(1915), it was often difficult to tell.*

Hell's Hinges—A Play-by-Play Synopsis, Complete with Subtitles! (Please, Try to Imagine a Piano Accompaniment)

A great example of the typical Hart picture is 1916's Hell's Hinges. *A young minister of dubious mettle ("a weak and selfish youth utterly unfit for the calling that a love-blinded mother has persuaded him to follow") is sent far from the temptations of the city to Placer Centre, a.k.a. Hell's Hinges ("a good place to ride wide of...a gunfighting, man-killing, devil's den of iniquity that scorched even the sun-parched soil on which it stood"). With the minister is his sister, Faith ("a different kind of smile, sweet, honest and trustful, and seeming to say, 'How do you do, friend?'").*

His supporters are few ("a scant handful of respectable people in a sin-ridden town...a drop of water in a barrel of rum"). And the town power broker, Silk Miller, is not in his corner ("mingling the oily craftiness of a Mexican with the deadly treachery of a rattler, no man's open enemy, and no man's friend"). He tries to get gunslinger Blaze Tracey (Hart, "the embodiment of the best and worst of the early west. A man-killer whose philosophy of life is summed up in the creed, shoot first and do your disputin' afterwards") to gun down the preacher.

Blaze may not have use for the preacher, but he is somehow thunderstruck by Faith ("One who is Evil, looking for the first time on that which is Good"). Even in the saloon where she has followed her wayward brother, she shines, stalwartly singing a hymn to drunken hecklers. In Blaze's mind's eye, her image transforms to a crucifix rising out of calm surf on a distant shore. He stops the town mob from running her brother out of town.

Meanwhile, Miller convinces his girl, a saloon strumpet named Poppy, to seduce the parson after plying him with more whiskey. Miller then leads Blaze to witness the debacle of the fallen preacher in his slattern's arms. Though disgusted by the spectacle, Blaze is falling for Faith ("I reckon God ain't wantin' me much, ma'am, but when I look at you, I feel like I've been ridin' the wrong trail").

Instead of shooting, Blaze rides for medical help for the drunk person. In his absence, Miller raises a mob and wakes the stuporous parson. Enraged by his own weakness, the parson slides all the way inside the whiskey bottle and accompanies the mob to burn down his own church. In the melee, he is shot and killed.

That night, Blaze returns to find Faith by her brother's newly dug grave amid the charred ruins of the church. In a reformed fury, he goes to the local saloon and shoots Silk down like the dog that he is. Blaze allows the girls to escape and, blasting the saloon lanterns, burns Hell's Hinges to the ground ("Hell needs this town, and it's goin' back, and goin' damn quick!"). As the sun rises on the stamped-out Sodom ("and then from the mothering sky came the baby dawn, singing as it wreathed the gray horns of the mountains with ribbons of rose and gold"), he finds Faith, and walks with her into a new day ("whatever the future, theirs to share together").

ABOVE, RIGHT: *Blaze Tracy saves the day and gets the girl in William S. Hart's* Hell's Hinges *(1916).*

---

were higher up, giving the land and situations more weight. Though he could ride and fight just fine (and still did his own action scenes at age fifty-nine), Hart didn't go in for a lot of stunts. Yet he choreographed great mob scenes and could set up a terrifying shot: in *Hell's Hinges* (1916), where he emerges oblivious and unharmed from the midst of an inferno with a burst of flame behind his head, he looks like an instrument of God's own retribution.

On a star level with Douglas Fairbanks (who'd done his share of adventure westerns) and Charlie Chaplin, Hart became an action hero to French film buffs, who for some reason dubbed him "Rio Jim." Following an incredible fight scene in Hart's *The Narrow Trail* (1914), French filmmaker Jean Cocteau was moved to expound (and perhaps hallucinate) the following:

A little masterpiece...in the center of a half-blinded and horrified crowd, the two figures circle...The camera draws back, moves nearer, rises higher. The naked bodies, slippery with blood, take on a sort of phosphorescence. Two mad creatures are at grips, trying to kill each other. They look as though they were made of metal. Are they kingfishers or seals, or men from the moon, or Jacob with the angel? Is it not some Buddha, this great naked figure which falls to its knees and dies there like a thousand little fishes in a lake of mercury? M. Ince may be proud of himself [for discovering and backing Hart], for a spectacle such as this seems to equal the world's greatest literature.

Will the Real Tom Mix Please Stand Up!

Tom Mix, "America's Champion Cowboy," lived a full life before bursting onto the western scene, but there's a limit to just how much a body can cram into one incarnation. At one point or another, Mix is said to have made the following claims about his personal, prescreen history:

* He was raised in a log cabin near El Paso, Texas.

* His dear old dad served in the 7th Cavalry (the one that Custer made so famous).

* His mother was of Cherokee blood.

* His great-grandfather had translated the Bible into Osage, an Indian language.

* He spoke Spanish and four Indian languages.

* He trained to be a soldier at the Virginia Military Institute.

* As a young man, he joined the famed Texas Rangers.

* He was wounded in action while serving as both a scout and courier for General Chaffee in the Spanish-American War.

* He took part in China's Boxer Rebellion and in the Philippine insurrection.

* He busted broncs for the British during the Boer War in the wilds of Africa.

* He acted as a wilderness guide for Teddy Roosevelt.

* He wore a tin star as the proud sheriff of Two Buttes County, Colorado.

* He was stood up before a firing squad in Mexico.

* He had to fight a pair of wolves, bare-handed.

* He enforced the law as U.S. Marshal in both New Mexico and Montana, and captured the cattle-rustling Shonts Brothers while he was at it.

* He sustained eighty injuries during his life on horseback.

The legendary Tom Mix with his horse, the talented Tony.

Though God of westerns Hart seems to have been, he was far from immortal. After forty films, his conflicts with Ince, his refusal to spank up his style with more entertainment value, and the fading popularity of his grave realism made 1925 his last year in the celluloid saddle. With the release of the $312,000-budgeted feature *Tumbleweeds*, a slightly disgusted Hart retired from the biz to a modest ranch. There, he played stud poker and otherwise hobnobbed with the likes of Wyatt Earp and Bat Masterson, pampered his horses (upon his death, he would leave fifty thousand dollars to the A.S.P.C.A), and coauthored western stories with his sister. Though Hart was coaxed to guide both Johnny Mack Brown and Robert Taylor through their later portrayals of Billy the Kid, and was brought back to sound-record a supremely moving introductory speech (a speech with which many said he wrote his own epitaph) to the rerelease of *Tumbleweeds*, his star had indeed faded. In his place rose another cowboy, just as striking but as different from Hart as night from day.

Thomas Edwin Mix was the West's consummate showman and its most popular film star. In fact, as impressive as his credentials were, it was hard to tell where the man ended and the myth began. What is probable is that he was born and raised the son of a teamster (horse-handling) in Pennsylvania. He knew horses, and at the age of ten, after seeing *Buffalo Bill's Wild West Show*, made it his life's ambition to be Buffalo Bill the second (a fact that may have almost ended his aspirations early, as he received his first bullet wound while he and a young friend were playing with an old single-shot pistol).

Mix got handier with guns as he grew. He saw military service, and lots of it. He tended bar in Oklahoma City, where he met the first of his five wives, and later did several stints as a law enforcer. Then Mix did what came most naturally—he joined the Miller Brothers' 101 Ranch Wild West Show as a livestock foreman. It wasn't long before he had talked himself into rodeo riding, where he became pals with the great Will "I never met a man I didn't like" Rogers and won the 1909 rodeo championship at Prescott, Arizona.

That same year, after settling down on a little ranch in the Cherokee territory of Oklahoma with his third wife, Olive, he had his first fateful encounter with the movie biz. Chicago's Selig Polyscope Company was looking for a place to shoot a documentary called *Ranch Life in the Great Southwest*. Tom's place was available. At first, Mix was hired on to handle the horses and cowboys, maybe even ride a little bit, but it soon became apparent that he had both star quality and burning ambition. Between 1910 and 1917, while William S. Hart and Bronco Billy Anderson were kings of the range, Mix made nearly one hundred films for Selig, many of them forgettable "oaters." There were comedies like *Why the Sheriff Is a Bachelor*; there were more somber tales like *Pony Express Rider*; there were oddities like *Sage Brush Tom*, in which cowboys decide to stage a western version of *Quo Vadis*. Some of these movies, like *Mr. Haywood, Producer*, were even about making westerns. And make them he did—all the while learning to write and direct as well as act and show off his undeniable flair for tricks and stunts.

By 1917, Mix had moved to the big leagues and was signed to Fox Studios. Though he wrote, directed, produced, and starred in his first flick, *Six-Cylinder Love*, he soon after gave over the creative reins to directors like Sydney Franklin and the young John Ford, and went to work on his screen image. Fox didn't want a Hart clone (though most studios were not above packaging performers with names like Neal Hart, William Fairbanks, and Art Mix), and the unique marketability of Mix's rough-and-ready derring-do eventually dawned on the studio. Mix evolved into something the western had never seen—a pure, white-suited supercowboy who was all action and almost no trail dust.

Amen. Mix's tobacco-, alcohol-, profanity-, and gratuitous violence–free cowboy rose to stellar heights (almost as tall as the ten-gallon hat that seemed to tower on top of his bulldoggish face). He was larger than life, dressing more like a circus rider than the real thing he was. Hand-tooled Mexican boots, gloves, embroidery–emblazoned shirts, pants snaked with gold braids—all were standard attire. He never shot a villain if he could tackle him from horseback or lasso him instead. Why sneak up to a campfire when he could dangle from a rope running from his faithful horse, Tony, to the top of a cliff, in order to eavesdrop on some bad guys' conversation?

Mix used a stunt double less than any other western star. His pictures were frantically fun action fests and not always anchored in the Old West, or even the United States for that matter. Stunts executed from trains, cars, planes, horses—anything with speed—were Mix's meat, and audiences ate it up. He took them away from worries about World War I to some of the West's most beautiful locations (he'd been around enough to know), with a special fondness for national parks and the Colorado Gorge. And no penny pinching either: by 1925, Mix was bringing down $17,500 a week. He deserved it. Like Rin Tin Tin for Warner, his Bs were keeping Fox's A pictures afloat. And the studio was wise enough not to let him stray from what he did best (Mix switched from his western duds to period costume only for a disastrous remake of Douglas Fairbanks's *Dick Turpin*).

> **I Yam What I Yam, and That's All That I Yam—The Mixmaster, on his screen persona:**
>
> I ride into a place owning my own horse, saddle and bridle. It isn't my quarrel, but I get into trouble doin' the right thing for somebody else. When it's all ironed out, I never get any money reward. I may be made foreman of the ranch and I get the girl, but there is never a fervid love scene.

Mix lived as large as he filmed. His residence was a Hollywood mansion complete with English butler. Outside blazed the towering neon letters "T.M." (No tours were going to miss this house.) He collected silver-trimmed custom autos and thousands of western artifacts—more than enough to fill the Tom Mix Museum in Dewey, Oklahoma. After sixty Fox features, he took a vacation from film in the early thirties to take Tony on tour with the Sells Floto Circus, at a salary of ten thousand dollars per week. In 1925, he also took Tony on a tour of Europe, where his faithful mount became the first horse to climb the circular staircase at the Paris Opera House.

Mix returned in 1932 to make nine talkies for Universal. One of these, *Rider of Death Valley*, which showed the National Monument in all its geological glory, included thirty horsemen galloping through sand dunes; the pathos of Tom having to force Tony to desert him in the desert (after which the horse galloped into town to do a Lassielike dance to bring cowboys to the rescue); and the pith of an exchange between Mix and his leading lady, the six-year-old Edith Fellows (Mix: "How do you do, young lady?" Fellows: "I'm not a lady." Mix: "You're the first female I've heard admit that."). He was soon back on the road.

In 1935, at the age of fifty-five, he left the silver screen for good, traveling with the *Tom Mix Wild Animal Circus*, and marrying his fifth and final wife, a trapeze artist. Tom did get to be Buffalo Bill after all: he had made three hundred of his own pictures; his films were the prototype for countless clean-living B pictures; and he was the archetype for numerous serial cowboys to come. In 1940, the rough rider took a curve too fast in his sports car on an Arizona highway, making the full and final transition from life into legend.

If Tom Mix was in a film, a picture-perfect ending like this fond farewell from horseback in **The Texan** *(1920) was par for the course.*

THE (TOO) REAL THING

The western's early legends didn't all have Pepsodent smiles and sports cars. Emmet Dalton of the famed Dalton Gang, after having served fourteen years of a life sentence, left the pen to produce and star in a film about his own family, *The Last Stand of the Dalton Boys* (1912), and also starred in 1918's *Beyond the Law*. Legendary lawman Wyatt Earp (of OK Corral and Doc Holliday fame) turned up on the set of the Douglas Fairbanks film *Half Breed* in 1919 and was put into a crowd scene. Having settled down in nearby Pasadena, California (rumor has it he secretly wanted to be L.A.'s police chief), a liquored-up Earp would drop in on John Ford's sets whenever his religious wife was out of town, just to put in his two cents.

Truly, as the days of the real cowboy had dwindled, cow-hands, rodeo riders, Wild West show performers, and roustabouts gravitated to Hollywood as extras, stuntmen, and often actors. A job working on your horse was always better than setting boot to sod. And you could make five dollars a day plus a box lunch risking your neck for the camera as easily as risking your neck for nothing. Besides, there was all that downtime between takes.

These former cowboys developed a closed society, playing poker and drinking mescal and tequila from coffee cups (throughout Prohibition) at a Hollywood café called the Watering Hole. They creased their Stetsons to show one another what part of cattle country they hailed from. They waited for work at the horse barn on Sunset Boulevard or at the bull pen on the Universal lot.

A still from James Cruze's premier epic, **The Covered Wagon** *(1923).*

They thought Hart was an eastern ham; Mix was beneath their contempt. They passed the word that Cecil B. De Mille deliberately staged unexpected accidents to make his movies more racy. They liked John Ford, Irish and eastern though he was, for the genius and tough son of a bitch he also was.

Ford (who we'll encounter a couple chapters down the trail) had been instrumental in carving the careers of two coots whom these cowboys much admired: the Will Rogers–esque Ed "Hoot" Gibson, a.k.a. "the Hooter," and the no-nonsense Harry Carey. Carey, who got his start with D.W. Griffith's stock company, had moved on with Ford to immortalize "Cheyenne Harry." Gibson had worked his way from Wild West shows and a 1912 cowboy competition championship to playing supporting characters in Tom Mix movies, doing stunts for Harry Carey, and, in Ford's hands, embodying the sloppily dressed, slightly chunky, mobile-faced Every-cowboy. When originally asked if he'd take five dollars to let himself be dragged by a horse, Gibson quipped, "Make it ten, and I'll let him kick me to death."

Art Accord was even more beloved. Art was a pistol and, many claimed, the greatest western horseman Hollywood had ever seen. This physical titan from the Show-Me State made films only in the winter months, when the rodeo shut down. Accord, who had served with distinction in World War I, was voted the best cowboy of 1916:

he could bulldog a steer to the ground in twenty-four seconds, and had even hung on to a bucking bronco as it sliced him through six strands of barbed wire. Problem was, he was just as pugnacious off-screen as on: one day he arrived on Hoot Gibson's set, shouting, "Gibson, I can whip your ass." He swung at the Hooter and broke his hand on a post, after which Gibson said, "Good, you son of a bitch," and proceeded to pummel Accord mercilessly. Accord's fuse burned too short, however, and after getting hooked on booze and drugs, he disappeared into Mexico, where he was stabbed to death in 1931.

Other cowpokes from bedrock backgrounds had their place in the early days. Steely-eyed Colonel Tim McCoy was the star who beat out even John Wayne when it came to playing a cavalry officer in Mike Todd's *Around the World in 80 Days* (1956). And the Colonel was the real McCoy: he had run away to Wyoming at age sixteen, living there among the Arapaho and Shoshone people. In World War I, he was a cavalry captain supervising cowboys from Montana and Wyoming. After the war, McCoy served as Wyoming's agent of Indian affairs and was the first man to research the Custer massacre at Little Big Horn from an Indian perspective.

Hollywood got wind of McCoy, hiring him on to wrangle as many Indians as he could for James Cruze's premier epic, *The Covered Wagon* (1923). McCoy showed up at the train depot with five hundred braves, plus their squaws and papooses. The gods were pleased enough to grant him a new job as the film's technical adviser, with the bonus of writing his own prologue, which would include his Arapaho pals, to narrate before the show. The men behind the camera couldn't help but notice his ramrod-straight military bearing, flashing eyes, commanding presence, granite jaw, and genuine ability to draw a gun with lightning speed. By 1926, MGM whiz-kid producer Irving Thalberg signed Colonel Tim to star in a series of westerns that stressed Indian life. McCoy's work for MGM, Universal, and Columbia (most notably, the film *End of the Trail*, 1932) produced the most pro-Indian films ever made until recent times.

Ordained minister Fred Thompson got down from the pulpit, got up on a horse, married western screenwriter Frances Marion, and hit the celluloid trail. He achieved a popularity almost as great Tom Mix's, and like Mix did his own stunts. He was versatile enough to be a hero or bad man (he played both in *The Sunset Legion*, 1928) and his hoss, Silver King, would change costumes to match Thompson's moral alignment—when Fred was dastardly, the animal would wear black right along with him. Unfortunately, pneumonia took the ex-preacher's life before his star had finished rising.

Buck Jones was decency personified: having lied his way into the army at age fifteen, he signed on to the reliable old Miller Brothers' 101, and was later hired by Fox as a backup for the temperamental Tom Mix. Once, swarmed by a sea of young autograph hounds along with his good pal William "Hopalong Cassidy" Boyd, Jones responded to Boyd's telling the "little bastards" to get lost, with the following caution: "Careful, Bill. Without these little bastards, you don't have anything."

For the good of his career, Hopalong was lucky he didn't let that comment slip while on the set. But before long, real cowboy behavior had been all but replaced by the West of the filmmakers' imaginations. Studios seemed bent on sanitizing their rough-hewn heroes out of existence. In 1919, the Fox film company even set rules down for Buck Jones and all other elevated stuntmen to follow.

As Hollywood tiptoed its way into the talkies, the names of the B and serial silent stars were legion: Buddy Roosevelt, who had earned twenty-two dollars a week as one of the sinners in Hart's *Hell's Hinges;* George O'Brien, who was, as one of the ads boasted, "not a sheik or a caveman, or a lounge lizard" but "a man's man and an idol to women"; Buster Crabbe, who swung his way from the desert to Tarzan's jungle; Charles Starrett, who was the first western hero to wear a white hat consistently. The list goes on. Some, like twenty-year-old Bob Steele, a.k.a. the Whirlwind Kid, lasted all the way from silents to the sixties television series *F Troop.* Others didn't die, they just faded away....

By the twenties, the twin trails from the real West and the West of the imagination had merged for better or worse at Hollywood and Vine. But the genre needed a boot in the backside to be elevated from B to A status in the minds of the filmgoing public. Contrary to sound-phobic Hollywood expectation, talkies would rejuvenate the western and slowly but surely give it back some of the grit it had lost along the way. It would take time for it to do so, but like the noon stage, it was bound to get there.

The Four Commandments

1. Your hair must always be neatly combed, unless you are in a fight. Have it cut, washed, and oiled once a week to give it proper gloss.

2. Your teeth require polishing and cleaning by a dentist once every two months, and careful attention daily. Open your mouth a little wider when you smile so that your teeth are seen more.

3. The new suits of clothes, shirts, and collars you are having made should be worn so that you will get in practice of wearing those kind of clothes and will not appear strange in them before the camera.

4. Give attention to your fingernails so they are clipped not too close and are always clean.

Chapter Two

BETWEEN A ROCK, A HARD PLACE, AND A CAMERA

John Ford was right on track with his first superwestern, the silent classic The Iron Horse (1924). Here, frozen in time, is the glorious joining of the Union Pacific and Central Pacific railway lines, thus forming the United States' first transcontinental railroad.

It's hard to get away from yourself in a landscape that seems both to highlight and dwarf human presence. But in the final year of the twenties and the first few years of the thirties, getting away from yourself and the widespread Depression-era problems was just what most audiences wanted to do. Clear answers were needed—and so were heroes.

Hollywood was eager to provide—and cash in, of course. Still, there were many cold feet in the film business when it came to the momentous transition to sound. Early attempts at talkies had been known as "squeakies" because of the crude sound-recording equipment; the technology's weight and bulk didn't make location work any easier. Still, slowly but surely, sound edged its way in. Buck Jones had left Fox to finance his own part-sound, western/flyboy combination adventure, *The Big Hop* (1928). It featured sound effects, but no dialogue or music. Unfortunately for Jones, his risk did not pay off—*The Big Hop* landed with a crash, and Jones was broke: fifty thousand dollars in the hole.

Warner Brothers waded into sound with Rin Tin Tin growling his way through *Land of the Silver Fox* (1928). For a while, the studios hedged their bets, releasing both sound and silent versions of the same pictures in case the talkies ended up being just so much static. Then, in January 1929, Fox released the icebreaker: Raoul Walsh's *In Old Arizona* was chock-full of western sounds, including bawling cattle, thundering hooves, the crack of gunshots, even cowboy ballads. It also earned actor Warner Baxter an Academy Award (a first for a western) as O. Henry's gentlemanly outlaw, the Cisco Kid. The critics loved it, and audiences flocked to see it.

> **Clever talk and a domineering manner have little to do with being man at his best.**
>
> **—Eastern philosophy, courtesy of Confucius**

Still, the public wanted more than talk (and many of the early sound westerns were endlessly talky). They wanted good men in bad situations. Loquaciousness didn't get American hero Charles Lindbergh from New York to Paris in 1927; guts did. Paramount's first sound western, the all-talking (in some of its posters, "TALKING" almost dwarfed the movie's title) *The Virginian* (1929), tried to accommodate—and found success in the lanky, laconic form of one Gary Cooper (a Lindbergh type if there ever was one).

"Coop" had gotten his big break with a supporting role in *The Winning of Barbara Worth* (1926), but it was Victor Fleming's adaptation of *The Virginian* that made him a star. Owen Wister's 1902 novel of the same title had been a trendsetter, the first shoot-'em-up story to be elevated above the dime-novel level. Its theme of honor was so popular that after visiting Wyoming in 1911, Wister's daughter had remarked, "Everybody in the West seems to have read *The Virginian*....It was written as fiction but has become history." For westerners who had taken these drawling portraits to heart, life was already imitating art. Or, as one cowboy noted, "Well, maybe we didn't talk that way before Mr. Wister wrote his book, but we sure talked that way after...."

The Virginian had twice been adapted for the silent screen. But for its talkie debut, Coop was perfect for the part—tight-lipped and taciturn. Paired off against the garrulous veteran stage actor (and villain, in this case) Walter Huston (John's father), he played a southern transplant who, while at first impassive about the rampant cattle-rustling around him, is spurred by his love for a schoolteacher (Mary Brian) to face down the rustlers' ringleader, Trampas (Huston). It was one of the first sound walk-downs or shoot-outs on Main Street and the first time the classic western warning "When you call me that, smile" was ever spoken on the silver screen.

Sound revitalized the western. Universal's 1930 serial *The Indians Are Coming* (starring Colonel Tim McCoy) ensured the health of the rock-'em-sock-'em B western, which did much to promote the genre's health in general. MGM's entré into serious sound westerns was King Vidor's *Billy the Kid* (1930), starring Johnny Mack Brown. To ensure the film's veracity, Metro hired on William S. Hart as a technical adviser (Hart gave Brown one of Billy the Kid's six-guns for the role).

> **A man's gotta do what a man's gotta do.**
>
> **—Western philosophy, courtesy of John Wayne**

Nobody walked taller (or funnier) than the Duke (John Wayne). Here, as Texas border town sheriff John T. Chance, he takes no chances as he saunters out of his office in the Howard Hawks hit Rio Bravo *(1959).*

Giants of the Plains, Part I: Along Came Coop

Unaffected, quiet, humorous, stalwart, and true, Gary Cooper was the living archetype of all that was good (if a little stiff) in the American character. Seeming to play no more and no less than himself, he came to embody the best of the West.

The same man whom poet Carl Sandburg dubbed "one of the most beloved illiterates this country has ever known" was also one of its richest. In 1939 the U.S. Treasury Department tagged Cooper as the nation's top wage-earner, at $482,819 for 1939. (And why not? Living up to a whole country's expectations is a big job.) He had the guts to pal around with Ernest Hemingway on safari in Africa, yet the modesty to admit to a much younger actor, "I only have two or three tricks at best, and that's not enough, is it?" Here's a little background on how this complex yet simple man came to a theater near you.

Roots: Born Frank J. Cooper in Montana in 1901. His father, a British-trained former barrister and gentleman farmer, is a judge on the Montana Supreme Court.

Education and Job Experience: As a kid he works as a ranch hand in his home state. He travels to Europe to attend English public school before returning to enroll in Iowa's Grinnell College for two years. Following his folks to Los Angeles on Thanksgiving Day 1923 with the vague idea of one day going into advertising as a commercial artist, he sketches cartoons for local Hollywood papers, sells real estate, solicits door-to-door for a family photographer, and draws advertisements on the curtains of vaudeville houses, all the while saving around four hundred dollars to fund an art school education in Chicago.

Break into Show Biz: Young Frank is walking toward the intersection of Hollywood and Vine one day when he bumps into two old cowboy pals from his Montana days. They're working as movie stuntmen, and they guide Frank to Slim Talbot and a five-dollar-a-day job falling off horses. (Coop later returns Talbot's favor, making Slim his stunt double in many films.) Between 1925 and 1926, he makes his money as a supernumerary cowboy or Indian in Tom Mix silents and Zane Grey serials.

The Turning Point: Learning that Mix makes $1,700 a week compared to his measly $50, Frank vows that his supernumerary days are numbered and works to polish his image. He studies makeup, poses for portraits with both a western and a steamy Rudolph Valentino look. He makes his own short audition reel, where he rides from a long shot into close-up and says simply, "Hello." After starting to

carry his short film and publicity pictures with him everywhere, a buddy introduces him to casting director Nan Collins, who becomes his first agent. She tells him to ditch the Valentino look and change his moniker to anything but Frank Cooper (there are several in town already, and one is wanted for murdering his wife). In picking a new label for her boy, she selects the name of her Indiana hometown: Gary.

Luck?: Gary dates producer Sam Goldwyn's secretary. Goldwyn spots him through his office window while casting about for believable-looking cowboys for supporting roles in The Winning of Barbara Worth. *He calls the hombre in and screens his audition film. The men don't like it much, but the ladies in the studio's secretarial pool love it. Gary is given a small role and stands in for the absent Abe Lee in the role of a western mining engineer who helps eastern mining engineer Ronald Coleman. Lee never shows for filming, and Gary gets his role. Critics claim he steals scenes from Coleman. Paramount snatches him away for a whopping $125 a week.*

The Making of a Heartthrob: The star machinery was in full gear. Though his characters were known for their moral code (and Coop did sweat out stage fright in his early love scenes), this young Hollywood buck didn't balk at off-screen romance. Neither did his handlers. His affair with "IT Girl" Clara Bow led to his being dubbed the "IT Boy." His carefully selected one-minute performance in her film Wings *(1927), as an air cadet doomed to die, brought in a flood of female fan mail. And his much-publicized romance with his Mexican costar Lupe Velez in* Wolf Song *(1929) finalized his arrival as an official hot property. And then* The Virginian *came to town...*

ABOVE: A might dustier than Tara....Gone With the Wind director Victor Fleming lensed this early, all-talking western, The Virginian *(1929). That's Gary Cooper in the fancy pants.*

James Cruze's seminal 1923 silent settler epic, *The Covered Wagon* (which had cost an unprecedented $800,000 to produce but raked in $4 million at the box office) had given audiences a taste of the megawestern. John Ford had nurtured that appetite further with his 1924 railroad epic films, *The Iron Horse*. Cecil B. De Mille, who was never to be outdone when it came to epics, provided the dramatic, six-reel talkie *The Squaw Man* (1931), which boasted itself as the first feature shot entirely in Hollywood. The film's tragic story follows a nobleman who flees romantic scandal in England into the wilds of Wyoming. There he marries an Indian maid who kills his rustler enemy and then herself, conveniently releasing him to return home to society to lead a civilized life.

By the mid-1930s, westerns were ready for anything. The glitches had been ironed out of the equipment, the Bs were alive and well at Saturday matinees, the epics were on the roll, and morality (a lot more of it than had actually existed in the Old West) was moving into western territory.

WHITE HATS VS. BLACK HATS: NOW, LET'S SEE WHAT YOU'RE MADE OF, PART I

Here's the situation, hoss. Say you've made a name for yourself as a man who stands up for what's right, so they pin you with a tin star. Keeping your town from becoming a rattlers' nest isn't exactly a Sunday picnic. You bury a lot of men in the process. Then one day, your luck runs out.

Not only has the one man you managed to send to prison (instead of Boot Hill) been released, he's hired on—along with his three murderous brothers—to help the local cattle baron burn out the sodbusters who've moved to your territory. And his first job is to put a bullet hole in that star of yours if you interfere.

It'll be four against one, hoss. The farmers can't shoot. Your deputy's drunk. The local authorities have been bought off. And when you stand up in church to ask your friends and neighbors for help, the answer is stony silence. Do you...

    A) Put in for an immediate transfer?

    B) Accept a "beefy" gift toward a little unplanned paid vacation?

    C) Do some creative re-zoning with the farmers?

    D) Hide in someone's root cellar until things blow over? Or...

    E) Defend the law, the town, and your honor?

    If you answered E, continue.

Lines are drawn in the dust and you'd better choose your side—or go inside and stay there. Heroes might set themselves against odds that seem suicidal by today's standards. They might always be the last to draw, a code almost unheard of in the real West, where if you wanted to live you walked into a shoot-out with your gun good and drawn. But these heroes you could depend on, and that's just what townsfolk, homesteaders, sodbusters, peasants, miners, and immigrants did...again and again, God bless 'em.

Farmers were the easiest target. The real West's early ranchers resented farmers tremendously. In the middle of the nineteenth century, open range had been the name of the game. You grabbed a big piece of land; you fought off the elements, the Indians, and whoever else came along; and you let your cattle wander. Not a problem when your nearest (white) neighbor was 20 or 30 miles (32 or 48km) away. Who needed a fence? Then came the settlers with their land grants to parcel it up. Barbed wire wrapped the prairie.

Legitimate as the grievances of some may have been, the ends rarely justified the means (burning, trampling, and killing). In one of Coop's early films, the cards were stacked even higher against the sodbusters—their town was run by the childishly sentimental yet ruthless Judge Roy Bean (Walter Brennan, in an Oscar-winning role).

William Wyler's *The Westerner* (1940) brings Cole Hardin (Cooper) to the real frontier town of Vinegaroon, Texas, where western history's colorful Roy Bean presides as "The Law West of the Pecos." Ol' Roy is as apt to buy a fellow a drink just for showing respect to the object of his obsession, actress Lillie Langtry (for whom both the real and the movie Bean renamed the town), as he is to take a dislike to a passing stranger, shoot him, and clean out his pockets as a fine for carrying a concealed weapon.

OPPOSITE: Worlds collide as an English nobleman, Lord Henry Kerhill (Paul Cavanaugh), takes a shine to an Indian maiden, Naturich (Lupe Velez), in Cecil B. De Mille's 1931 extravaganza, The Squaw Man. Though Lord Henry weds Naturich, she obligingly kills herself by the final reel, allowing him to return to civilized society with their half-breed baby. ABOVE, RIGHT: You don't sell out your friends. That's what Billy the Kid (Johnny Mack Brown at right) would like Pat Garrett (Wallace Beery at left) to understand in King Vidor's Billy the Kid (1930), the early film incarnation of this legendary relationship.

Cole, just passin' through town on the way to California, finds himself mistakenly seized as a horse thief. Barroom becomes courtroom, and his horse is actually brought into the bar as evidence. Cole must bluff Bean about having known Langtry, and offers to give him a treasured lock of her hair or even introduce him to her—anything to avoid being summarily lynched. As Cole's stay continues, he grudgingly gains an affection for the garrulous old coot but becomes all too aware of Bean's wicked ways. As he says to Roy, "When I was young I had a pet rattlesnake. I was fond of it, but I wouldn't exactly turn my back on it."

One of Bean's wickedest ways is his hatred of the farmers who have moved into town. He sends his cronies to cut their fence wire, trample their struggling crops, drag one man through his own corn, and hang another for shooting one of their marauding steers. But the farmers are plucky, and the pluckiest is Jane Ellen Matthews (Doris Davenport), who defiantly tells Bean, "You can pester us, rob us, and kill us, but you can't stop us. 'Cause there'll always be more and more of us. And we'll stay on our farms in spite of you and your courtroom and your killers."

Cole soon finds himself lovestruck, and he steps over that line in the dust onto the side of right. Trying to mediate between the two sides, he uses the leverage of Bean's hunger for Cole's lock of Lillie's hair ("the greatest woman in the world. The fairest flower that ever bloomed") to negotiate a removal of cattle from the farmers' land. But at the height of the farmers' celebration, Bean reneges and his cowboys set fire to the cornfields. The houses burn, too, and Jane Ellen's elderly father is trampled to death.

After finding Jane Ellen clutching a charred Bible, Cole rides into action. He knows just where to find Bean: Lillie Langtry has come to play nearby Fort Davis, and the obsessive judge has bought out every ticket, donned his Civil War duds, and taken the best (and only) seat in the house. The curtain comes up to reveal Lillie's lanky replacement (Cole) and the shoot-out commences. Bean does get to meet Langtry, just before he dies from the wounds Cole has given him. Tragically, his men have mistaken the gunshots for the judge having a good time.

Producer Sam Goldwyn had a lot riding on *The Westerner*. The year before, Fox (*Jesse James*), Warner Brothers (*Dodge City*), and Universal (*Destry Rides Again*) had proved that big-budget westerns could be box-office manna. And John Ford had erupted back onto the scene after a thirteen-year and thirty-two-film absence from the genre with *Stagecoach*, an epic that would become one of the greatest westerns of all time. Goldwyn needed a gimmick.

Thanks to writer Niven Busch, *The Westerner*'s new angle was to make a traditionally secondary (and in this case, mentally skewed) character (Brennan as Bean) luminous in the story and highlight not just his evil deeds but his purer passion as well. Busch's conviction that "the single-mindedness of lonely people was a basic motivating power among the western frontier cultures" comes through blazing, as it does in his other fine films.

In reality, Lillie never met the judge, but she did visit her namesake town two years after his death. Perhaps in compensation for the film's slight embellishment, Cooper wrangled eighty-two-year-old Cal Cohen, who had actually tended bar for the judge, into the role of the bartender. Art director James Basevi and his researchers sifted though a sea of nineteenth-century western magazines to plaster Bean's bar with pictures of the real Lillie. Authenticity was okay by Brennan, too: Busch encountered him on the lot one day with his head cocked around at a weird angle. "Did you do something to your neck, Walter?" Busch asked. "Well, no," replied Brennan, "not my neck." The actor had read up on his role enough to add a twist of his own, which Busch promptly put in the dialogue: "I was hung once but my friends cut me down in time. Now, when I don't live right, the crick comes back."

Authenticity had its drawbacks, however. The seven thousand head of cattle (the biggest herd ever assembled for a feature) had

Aging sheriff Will Kane (Gary Cooper) clutches his quaking Quaker bride, Amy (Grace Kelly), in this publicity still from Stanley Kramer's thoughtful production of Fred Zinnemann's taut direction of Carl Foreman's cutting edge script, the legendary High Noon (1952).

to be driven from New Mexico to near Tucson, where the film was being shot. Coop, who had injured a leg early in the film, had to be lifted onto his horse; with director "Ninety-Nine Take" Wyler's notorious habit of shooting till a scene was perfect, it turned into a painful experience. Brennan died more times than he'd like to remember, too.

Killing Time

Right triumphed over much higher odds in one of the more Oscar-decorated westerns ever shot. Frederick Wiseman's *High Noon* (1952) was much more than a western. It was a timely parable of one man risking being outcast and destroyed by standing against a prevailing evil wind. Long-winded as that description might sound, it all boiled down to the very real communist witch-hunts of the 1950s.

It was the days of the House Un-American Activities Committee (HUAC), and Senator Joe McCarthy was taking potshots at "commie pinkos," Hollywood writers being some of his favorite targets. Carl Foreman was one of them, or knew he soon would be. If he was a cooperative witness (if he fingered his friends, he would be left in peace) he'd have to live with his con-

> High Noon...is the most un-American thing I've ever seen in my life. The last thing in the picture is ole Coop putting the United States marshal's badge under his foot and stepping on it. I'll never regret having helped run [Carl] Foreman out of this country.
>
> —John Wayne

Move Over, Rover:
A Hoss Has to Have His Horse

Chivalry, that ten-dollar term that so many gentlemen have aspired to, ultimately has its roots in the five-franc French word cheval, meaning "horse." Mistreating a mare or a stallion was something a gentleman would never do. (Bringing it into a saloon was probably frowned upon, too.) Desperate settlers may have slit open their horses' bellies to tuck in their youngest children when caught in blizzards on the pioneer trail. Augustus Macrae of the television miniseries Lonesome Dove (1989) may have shot his horse in the head to make it a supine shield to bad men's bullets. Former NFL quarterback Alex Karras may have had the temerity to slug one in the chops in Mel Brooks' Blazing Saddles (1974). But a real gentleman treated his animal right.

Marlon Brando took things to an extreme (as he is wont to do) when he aimed stormy, romantic speeches at his horse, serenaded it with a harmonica, and shared a carrot with it (each eating from opposite ends and meeting in the middle) in Arthur Penn's The Missouri Breaks (1976), but his passion had a precedent. No self-respecting B western star was complete without his trusty steed, and many took the appreciation of horseflesh to a kind of reverence.

William S. Hart started it off by giving his horse, Fritz, the first equine screen credit (My Friend Flicka, Black Beauty, and Mr. Ed would have approved), his own leading characters to play (Pinto Ben, 1915), and a kiss before dying (an act that gave cowboys the questionable reputation for romancing their horses instead of their sweethearts). Tom Mix graced his stallion, Tony, with a love interest all his own in Tumbling River (1927) and star status in three more: Tony Runs Wild (1926), Oh You, Tony (1924), and Just Tony (1922). (Tony outlived Tom by two years.)

Ken Maynard's Tarzan the Wonder Horse could dance, roll over, play dead, even use his sense of smell to warn Ken when danger was coming. Maynard put Tarzan through incredible stunts—hanging virtually upside down from the horse's neck while at full gallop to grab a wounded man, or riding the steed off a sixty-foot (18.3m) cliff into a lake (where the frightened Tarzan tried to climb onto his master's shoulders). Tarzan often got better reviews than Ken: For Lucky Larkin (1930), Variety noted that "Next to Nora Larkin, Tarzan is the best actor in the film."

The following is a list of western movie and series stars and the marvelous mounts they rode. Some were show-biz stars in their own right. Some were just the horses behind (or under) the men.

Rider	Horse
George O'Brien	Mike
Hoot Gibson	Mutt
Buck Jones	White Eagle
Fred Thompson	Silver King
Colonel Tim McCoy	Midnight
John Wayne	Duke
Tex Ritter	White Flash
Jack Hoxie	Scout
Buster Crabbe	Falcon
William "Hopalong Cassidy" Boyd	Topper
Clayton "The Lone Ranger" Moore	Silver
Rex Allen	Koko
Lash Larue	Rush
Roy Rogers	Trigger (who lives eternally taxidermed at the museum of his master's name)

science. If not, he'd merely live with the stigma of being blacklisted. His script for United Artists producer Stanley Kramer and director Fred Zinnemann reflected his feelings in the simple story of Will Kane: "Well, one more ceremony and Will's a free man...more or less. Marshal, turn in your badge."

Any movie that begins on that jovial a note has to be headed for big trouble. It's tantamount to Jimmy Stewart's buying luggage in the beginning of *It's a Wonderful Life:* he ain't goin' nowhere. So it is for Kane (an aging Gary Cooper), who has just gotten hitched to Amy (Grace Kelly in her first major film role), a beautiful Quaker from Back East, and is just about to turn in his badge and ride away from Hadleyville into domestic bliss. But a storm rolls into town, arriving in the form of Frank Miller, an outlaw whom Kane sent to prison (and who everyone says is crazy), now pardoned and back to gun Kane down. Waiting for Frank's arrival on the noon train are his former outlaw cohorts: his brother Ben Miller (Sheb Wooley), Jack Colby (Lee Van Cleef, of later Sergio Leone fame), and Jim Pierce (Robert Wilke).

The bulk of the film, counted off in about ninety stark black-and-white minutes on a seemingly ever-present on-screen crock, details Kane's torturous decision to stand against the killers, and his subsequent struggle to get some kind of backup. All desert him

When test audiences were less than enthusiastic (fueling studio fears that Coop was too old and Kelly too young to be a good match), more close-ups of Coop and the ubiquitous clock were added. Twenty minutes were trimmed: scenes between Jurado and Kelly and Jurado and Bridges were deleted. For audiences, it made all the difference—$4 million worth.

Unfortunately, unlike Kane, Foreman could not drop his badge disdainfully in the dust when the film was over (or pick up his Oscar as Cooper did). His badge was taken from him. Called by HUAC to testify during the film's last week of shooting, he took the "diminished fifth" (refusing to implicate others) and was blacklisted and exiled to England. His metaphor for "Hollywood under the political gun" had proved all too true.

in his hour of need, including his swaggering deputy, Harvey (Lloyd Bridges), who resents being passed over for Kane's job; his old flame, Helen (the sensational Katy Jurado), a wealthy businesswoman who's had a bellyful of living with the small-town stigma of being a Mexican; the former sheriff (Lon Chaney, Jr.); the town judge; the mayor; the general populace; and even his blushing bride, who doesn't intend to sit ringside for his slaughter.

The vulnerability and tangible fear exuded by Kane is breathtaking. Cooper, who was going through a rough patch in his career (he had cut his usual fee of $275,000 a picture down to $60,000 and a piece of the profits) as well as suffering the beginnings of an ulcer, had agreed to let it show. Bags were highlighted under his eyes, the lines in his face accentuated. And with every shot, Wiseman reminded him not to hide Kane's unheroic tiredness and stress.

The environment was just as brutal. Wiseman and cinematographer Floyd Crosby wanted a gritty documentary feel (made popular by Italian directors Vittorio De Sica and Roberto Rossellini). To that end, Matthew Brady's harrowing Civil War photographs were studied for their brutal realism; no beautiful backgrounds were chosen; no filters were used, washing out the sky; and the lighting was kept flat to arrest any depth of field. Even the opening credits played against a silent, sun-blasted background.

The human environment wasn't any better. Each of the many townspeople whom Kane encounters has a vague yet undeniable loathsomeness. Even his one ardent supporter bitterly backs out when Kane can't round up any more deputies—the only offers come from a kid and an old drunk. And when it comes to the walkdown...well, Amy may surpise you.

Wiseman had gotten everyone on the picture for a song—a total salary of $35,000 for all but Cooper, and the neophyte Kelly for the unprincessly sum of a few C-notes a week. Music was punched up in postproduction. Though Tennessee Ernie Ford was a contender, Tex Ritter won the right to sing Dimitri Tiomkin's mournfully eerie "Do Not Forsake Me Oh My Darlin'," which returns again and again like a ghost to underscore Kane's desperation.

Introducing the Duke

Coop didn't corner the market on getting out of tight spots. Another more swaggering hombre who got his start while talkies were first squawking went on to be the only actor to eclipse Coop in western hero identification, filming nearly ninety westerns and "dying" in only four. John Wayne surpassed the realm of stardom and became an American icon of heroic machismo, before cancer took what tough guys could not.

By the time he faced down his own version of Coop's Hadleyville horror in Howard Hawks's 1958 *Rio Bravo* (supposedly made as an indignant antidote to the vulnerability of law enforcement and the despicability of the populace in *High Noon*), Wayne had been around the block more than a few times. He'd come up the hard way, from extra, to stuntman, to B movies star, to a shot at the big leagues, to bust, back to Bs, and finally to *Stagecoach* and on to stardom.

In *El Dorado* (1966), the centerpiece of a trilogy of films that included *Rio Bravo* and *Rio Lobo* (1970), a mature and somewhat mellowed Wayne plays Cole Thornton, a gunman who rides in under the hire of nabob Bart Jason (Ed Asner) to wage a range war against the peaceable MacDonald family. This time it's the new power (symbolized by Asner's gunless, gutless brute) that is threatening the old. In other words: sell out or die.

Cole finds that old friend (and equally fast gun) J.P. Harrah (Robert Mitchum) is the local sheriff and opts to break his engagement with Jason. On the way to tell the MacDonalds, Cole surprises their young lookout, killing him in self-defense. Leaving the area in disgust (with a bullet permanently lodged in his back from the lookout's spunky sister), Cole returns months later only upon learning that Jason has hired another legendary gun, Nelse McLeod (Christopher George), to do his dirty work, and that his

One of the highest-paid, highest-powered westerns ever filmed, Arthur Penn's Missouri Breaks *(1976) brought a serious-acting Jack Nicholson (right) together with a perniciously playful Marlon Brando (left) to create nihilistic fireworks.*

Giants of the Plains, Part II: What Becomes a Legend Most

Though his politics may have been just right of Barry Goldwater's, John Wayne's place will always be firmly in the center of millions of hearts and electronic hearths. He mellowed with age but had fiery beginnings. Here's a taste of the legend before he became vintage American male.

Roots: Born Marion Michael Morrison on May 26, 1907, in Winterset, Iowa. Father Clyde's (druggist and farmer) philosophy of "Keep your word. Never insult someone unintentionally. Don't look for trouble, but if it comes, don't quit," stayed with Marion (the actor taught it to Ron Howard in The Shootist, 1976).

Education: He learns some cowboy craft on horseback behind his father's harvesting machine, shooting snakes and rabbits. Moving to Palmdale, California, in 1917, and to Glendale in 1919, he gets saddled with the moniker "Duke" by local firemen who always see him with his dog of the same name. He does a little acting in high school and attends the University of Southern California on a football scholarship.

Experience: His football coach arranges a part-time job with Tom Mix. Duke has hopes of being Mix's athletic trainer, but ends up hauling props and furniture for thirty-five dollars a week. His football career is ended when he smashes his shoulder in a 1927 surfing accident. Young turk John Ford begins using him for bit parts and stunts in his early films.

Bonding: During the football film Salute (1929), Ford objects to Duke's three-point stance and, kicking the young man's arm out from under him, drops Duke face first in the dirt. Later that day, Duke angrily returns the favor, asking Ford to show him the correct stance near a mud puddle and then kicking him into it. Everyone on the set freezes, but Ford laughingly wipes himself off and invites Duke to join his select circle of poker-playing cronies.

Blowing It: Director Raoul Walsh sees Duke working shirtless on the Fox lot and wonders if he might fill the bill for the lead role in an early talkie The Big Trail (1930). With a little help from Ford, Duke gets a screen test. At first, flustered by the contempt of the professionals around him, Duke loses his temper—and it looks good on camera. So good-

bye, Marion Morrison, and howdy, John (because it sounds American) Wayne (after General Anthony Wayne). But Wayne is merely adequate, and the film is a financial flop.

Rebuilding It: Fox casts him in a basketball picture but later yanks him. Harry Cohn at Columbia blackballs him (perhaps because of romantic jealousy over Cohn's secretary). For the next nine years, Wayne is relegated to the B leagues of the smaller studios, where he makes countless westerns (including a humiliating stint as crooner Singin' Sandy Saunders, secret treasury agent) and makes enough money to marry Josephine Saena in 1933. He hones his riding, shooting, and roping skills with cowboy Jack Padgin. He also meets the man who will become the West's greatest stuntman, the legendary Enos Yakima Canutt. On their first set together, Yak and the Duke opt to sleep out in the open to avoid the commute back to Los Angeles. Around the fire, another lifelong friendship is forged. Soon Wayne is emulating everything about the tough former rodeo rider...including his weird walk.

Bonding II: Having kept in touch with Ford, Wayne is invited to Ford's yacht, the Araner, for an overnight cruise. There, the director tortures his protégé by showing him the script for Ford's comeback western, Stagecoach, and asking Duke's advice on who to cast as the male lead of the Ringo Kid. Duke miserably reads all 123 pages, suggests Lloyd Nolan, and drinks himself to sleep. In the morning, Ford aggravates Wayne's hangover by ribbing the actor about the stagnation of his own career. As they're about to disembark in San Pedro, Ford casually says, "Oh, Duke, I want you to play the Ringo Kid."

Blastoff: Over the next thirty-nine years, Duke made nearly one hundred more films, twenty of which were among the top grossers in Hollywood history. For fifteen of those years, he was the number one male movie star in the United States.

ABOVE: John Wayne in El Dorado (1966), one of a trilogy of westerns directed by Howard Hawks.

lovesick friend Harrah has drunk himself into a permanent stupor. The killer must now become the protector.

The rest of the film revolves around male bonding (interesting when you think that *El Dorado* was cowritten by a woman, Leigh Brackett): Cole, with the aid of a knife-throwing, Edgar Allan Poe–quoting drifter, Mississippi (James Caan), and Harrah's grizzled, old faithful deputy, Bull (the western character actor Arthur Hunnicutt), tries to sober up Harrah ("What the hell are you doin' here?" "I'm lookin' at a tin star with a drunk pinned to it!") to the point where the four can make a respectable stand against the opposing forces riding in.

It ain't easy. With the aging Cole's gun hand paralyzed from the shifting bullet in his back, Mitchum's leg injury and detox remedy (a mix of gunpowder, ipecac, cayenne, mustard, and God knows what else, courtesy of Mississippi) playing havoc with his innards, Mississippi's aimless aim (which is so poor that even with a scattershot pistol he can't hit anything), and Bull with his bow and arrow...the Magnificent Seven they're not—but they get by.

Perhaps most moving of all in *El Dorado* is George's respectful, well-mannered gunman, who literally saves Wayne's hide out of "professional courtesy" so that they can find out who's fastest later. They almost do.

Star line-ups don't get any more legendary than this. With apologies to Akira Kurosawa and his seven samurai: from left to right, Horst Buchholz (Chico), Brad Dexter (Harry Luck), Robert Vaughn (Lee), Charles Bronson (O'Reilly), James Coburn (Britt), Steve McQueen (Vin), and Yul Brynner (Chris) make up The Magnificent Seven *(1960).*

MALE CALL

Sometimes just a handful of good guys isn't enough—not when you're facing a murderous cadre of Mexican banditos, for example. Why settle for two or three stars for your ticket dollar when you can get a magnificent seven for the same price? The first western to be based on a film by the renowned Japanese director Akira Kurosawa (*The Seven Samurai,* 1954, which was itself inspired by American westerns), *The Magnificent Seven* (1960) was a new twist and a new location (Mexico) on an old formula. By 1960, with the increasing popularity of television as the shoot-'em-up medium of choice, major studios were reining in their western output. From the year before, Columbia had gone from 7/36 (seven westerns out of thirty-six total features) to 1/35. Fox had gone from 7/34 to 7/39, MGM from 3/24 to 1/19, Paramount from 4/17 to 1/24, Universal from 3/11 to 2/12, Warner Brothers from 5/19 to 3/17, and United Artists from 8/35 to 6/29.

Actor Yul Brynner first got his mitts on the rights to direct the western remake of Kurosawa's Oscar-winning epic (Best Foreign Film 1955). Anthony Quinn was set to costar. When Brynner sold the rights to United Artists, Quinn was out (and suing for breach of contract) and a new supporting ensemble of up-and-comers was rounded up (and hurriedly, for a Screen Actors Guild strike was in the wind).

Steve McQueen, Robert Vaughn, Charles Bronson, James Coburn, and Eli Wallach—all household names within a matter of years—were looking for their big break. This was it.

The story: emmissaries from a sleepy Mexican farming village head north to offer all their worldly possessions for a little ballistic protection from bandit chief Calvera (Wallach) and his forty men, who annually strip their village of most of its food as the band retreats into the mountains. Yul Brynner, as the exceptionally cool-headed, philosophical, articulate, and graceful Chris, gathered his group together at twenty dollars a man (usual wages for most were over five hundred dollars).

Soon seven down-on-their-luck gunfighters were thundering south (to Elmer Bernstein's famous score, which would eventually serve as Marlboro Cigarettes' trademark jingle). Together they teach the passivist peasants how to shoot and stand up for themselves, Western style, and along the way become charmed by the goodness and simplicity of village life. James Coburn's taciturn Britt, who could win a showdown with the draw of a throwing knife, but uttered no more than a dozen lines in the whole film, admires the local señoritas (once they are brought out of hiding). The dandified Lee (Robert Vaughn), a man who has lost his nerve somewhere along the way, secretly struggles to get it back. Harry Luck (Brad Dexter) is convinced the Mexican village is a cover for a gold or opal mine. O'Reilly (Charles Bronson) is adopted as a surrogate father by local niños. Vin (Steve McQueen) observes it all with an amiable alienation. And Chico (Horst Buchholz), a former village boy himself, has followed them down to share in their glory.

Glory there is, along with plenty of time for contemplating the lives they have chosen (which makes them fight all the harder for the village). In one cantina confab in which the ever-cool Chris attempts to dampen the ambitions of the hot-headed young Chico, the following perspective on a gunfighter's life is passed on:

> **Chris:** *After a while you call bartenders and faro dealers by their first name: 200. Rented rooms you live in: 500. Meals you eat in hash houses: 1,000. Home: None. Wife: None. Kids: None. Prospects: Zero. Suppose I left anything out?*

> **Chico:** *Yeah. Places you're tied down to: None. People with a hold on you: None. Men you step aside for: None. Insults swallowed: None. Enemies: None...enemies, alive.*

Don't think that the gringos have the monopoly on philosophy. The bandit Calvera is one of the most likable, folksy, garrulous cutthroats to ever bushwack a trail (though he is the racist archetype of the smiling, wolfish bandito), at one point even offering to let the seven ride off unharmed after a particularly embarrassing encounter. Do they? *The Magnificent Seven* may be a thoughtful yarn, but it is also a rip-roarin' action fest. Four of the seven die, one stays, and two leave together (ironically, the very two actors who didn't get along during the filming).

He's a tall drink of poison—and one of the creepiest heavies you'll ever meet. Say hello to Hank Wilson (Jack Palance), the rancher's hired gun in George Stevens' Shane (1953).

> *I'm one of those who feels everything. Everything that goes into a picture affects the viewer, although he doesn't realize the impact of tiny, minor things that are built up for him. This working upon the subconscious has a great effect, greater than most moviemakers or moviegoers realize.*
>
> **—George Stevens, director**

THE GOOD BAD-MAN

Good guys don't get any "gooder" than *Shane* (1953), and neither do westerns. George Stevens' $3 million masterpiece seems, at first viewing, such a simple thing, until you realize that 1) a seamless series of steps builds to its incredible climax, 2) tremendous care has been taken to ensure the simple reality of the West that it presents, and 3) rarely before have archetypal characters like the gunfighter, farmer, cowboy, and rancher been so flesh-and-blood.

Reality and myth ride together on this trail, in what critics called the centerpiece of Stevens' American Trilogy (*A Place in the Sun,* 1951; *Shane,* 1953; and *Giant,* 1956). A buckskinned, soft-spoken, golden-haired (OK, let's say it, Christlike) Shane (Alan Ladd, in the performance of his career) rides into a nameless valley in search of a new start and finds it with the Staretts, a struggling farm family, (played by Van Heflin, Jean Arthur, and little Brandon de Wilde). Though he's reluctant to talk about it, it's clear Shane was a gunfighter: when little Joey playfully cocks his toy gun behind Shane's back, the man whirls around, drawn: "You had me snortin', son."

Shane puts away his gun, and trades in his buckskins for farm duds, only to find that local rancher Ryker (Emile Meyer) is escalating a campaign of violence to drive out the farmers. He's even hired a Cheyenne gunny, Hank Wilson (an equally soft-spoken but almost demonic Jack Palance, in a role that would cement him as king of the heavies) to do his dirty work (Ryker: "I like Starett, too, but I'll kill him if I have to." Wilson: "You mean I'll kill him if you have to."). It's only a matter of time before Shane will have to put those guns back on.

Although the story by Jack Schaefer, discovered by Stevens' son one summer at college and finally scripted by the veteran

Puttin' the pistol away is easy—it's keepin' it away that's so darn hard. So Shane (Alan Ladd at left) explains it to the hero-worshiping Joey Starrett (Brandon De Wilde at right) in Shane *(1953).*

the West. The massive saloon brawl that begins with Shane and Chris (a ruggedly complex Ben Johnson) was devoid of pyrotechnics, and though they whip their weight in wildcats, both Shane and Starett need medical attention when it's all over.

Likewise, in later gunplay—like the confrontation between Wilson and the bantam southern farmer Torrey (Elisha Cook, Jr.)—death was far from glamorous. Wilson sadistically lets Torrey draw and waver a moment in terror before shooting him down on the muddy street. For the first time in a western gunfight, the impact of a bullet hitting the human body was visible (hidden wires yanked Cook off his feet and backward into the mud).

The vivid realism was a good idea: most real gunmen favored a large-caliber bullet because, once winged by a ricochet, their adversary was usually knocked down by the impact (of course, fighting recoil as you shot was the tradeoff). The U.S. Army tested the gun that won the West, the Colt Peacemaker, by shooting cattle in the Chicago stockyards. A .45-caliber slug could easily bowl over a half-ton (0.4t) steer even if no vital spot was hit. Torrey was a pushover.

Though Stevens' first picks were Montgomery Clift (with whom he'd just wrapped *A Place in the Sun,* 1951) and William Holden for Shane and Starett, respectively, he had no complaints about Alan Ladd and Van Heflin. Stevens shot and reshot scene after scene, driving his cast crazy (and leading young Brandon de Wilde to forswear all but pirate movies in the future), but getting enough coverage to have a field day in the projection room. And that he did, running dual projectors like a Moviola editing system. By the time the weary Shane tells the impressionable Joey, "I gotta be goin' on. A man has to be what he is, Joey. Can't break the mold. I tried and it didn't work for me....There's no living with the killing, but there's no going back. Right, wrong, it's a brand and a brand sticks....Now run on home to your mother and father and tell them everything's alright. There aren't anymore guns in the valley...." and rides his own gun up into the cold mountains and out of their lives, with Joey calling after him...well, if you're a real man, you'll be crying your eyes out. (And if you were a real director, like Clint Eastwood, you'll be doing a grittier, yet more supernatural remake set in the mining camps of Carbon Canyon, called *Pale Rider,* in 1985.)

western wordsmith A.B. Guthrie, Jr., was simple, there was nothing simple about the making of the film. Stevens studied paintings by Charles Russell and Henry Jackson to get a mindset on the real look and feel of the people of the West. "Homespun clothing" would be just that: "My father had a fetish against calling what people wore costumes. They were clothes," remembers Stevens' son. The director then toured the West with sketch artist Joe De Young, looking for a perfect setting for his realistic town. They settled on Jackson Hole, Wyoming, where the jagged, Grand Tetons rise from earth tones to an almost ethereal icy blue. It was a grandly beautiful setting for one of the most drably realistic western towns ever built—realistic enough for the Secretary of the Interior and the Rockefellers to request the whole shebang for their Ferry Museum as an example of nineteenth-century authenticity.

To add realism, Stevens ditched the gloss of Technicolor stock for regular film stock and decided to shoot in all kinds of western weather (the cloudy scenes are among the most moody and beautiful). He also brought a new reality to the violence of

THE SURREAL THING

Before we leave the good guys, it's worth noting a special breed that went beyond good into the realm of downright wholesome: the singing cowboys. "B" cowpokes may have put tunes into their action-packed oaters, but two hombres perfected the crooning buckaroo to a fare-thee-well and opened the door to countless others. Sneer not, brothers and sisters! When westerns were wobbly, these overdressed dudes kept their studios afloat.

Gene Autry was the king. Brought in by Republic pictures in 1935 as an almost unknown, he sang up a storm in Ken Maynard's *In Old Santa Fe*. Singing, riding, and fighting his way through everything from the classic *Tumbling Tumbleweeds* (1935), with its classic ballad, "That Silver-Haired Daddy of Mine," to the sci-fi/western serial *The Phantom Empire* (1935), to the star-studded *Melody Ranch* (1940), which featured Jimmy Durante and Ann Miller, to the unreleased *The Silent Treatment* (with Jerry Lewis, Milton Berle, George Raft, and Jackie Coogan), for twenty years Autry brought film, television, and records together into an institution as American and lucrative as (mass-marketed) apple pie. Even the most hard-core western fan has tapped his feet to tunes like "Back in the Saddle Again," "Home on the Range," or "El Rancho Grande." And anyone who's ever visited Autry's Western Heritage Museum in Los Angeles' Griffith Park knows the debt of gratitude all western fans owe him.

Roy Rogers was Autry's heir apparent. Originally a Cincinnati farmboy who made good as a professional guitarist, square-dance caller, and expert yodeler, the former Leonard Slye moved from being a member of the incomparable singing group the Sons of the Pioneers (immortalizers of "Wagon Wheels," "Whoopie-Ti-Yi-Yo," "Cool Water," "Twilight on the Trail," and, of course, "Tumbling Tumbleweeds") to a contract with Republic when Gene was gettin' uppity about his salary. He had a little more sex appeal than Autry (Roy was advertised as "a cowboy who looks like a wrangler, is a looker, an actor, and a singer," and as one hostess said behind his back at a party, "There goes the purtiest behind in Hollywood"), and his films were a little more action-packed. Soon Rogers was the western's number one box-office star (thanks in part to Autry's call to military service for World War II). With his own television show premiering in 1952, various product endorsements, and his leading lady of twenty-eight films, Dale Evans, Roy lived long and prospered. Happy trails, Roy.

Good guys don't get much more "good" than this. That blinding smile, those chiseled features, those duds, that yodel...it can only be the cowboy crooner himself (minus Dale and Trigger), Mr. Roy Rogers.

The Rugged Code of the West

The following are Gene Autry's official rules of cowboy conduct for all his buckarooos. Grab a glass of milk for this one.

A cowboy...

1. *Must not take unfair advantage of an enemy.*
2. *Must never go back on his word.*
3. *Must always tell the truth.*
4. *Must be gentle with children, elderly people, and animals.*
5. *Must not possess racially or religiously intolerant ideas.*
6. *Must help people in distress.*
7. *Must be a good worker.*
8. *Must respect women, his parents, and the nation's laws.*

Chapter Three

THE GOOD, THE BAD, THE FAMILY

Trouble? You're lookin' at it, from left to right. A consumptive Doc Holliday (Dennis Quaid), Morgan Earp (Linden Ashby), Wyatt Earp (Kevin Costner), and Virgil Earp (Michael Madsen) go to carve out a little destiny with the Clantons at the OK Corral in Wyatt Earp (1994).

NOW, LET'S SEE WHAT YOU'RE MADE OF, PART II

> *I like you, Vic. I've always liked you. But Dave's my blood. Him I love. And likin' ain't lovin'.*
>
> —From Anthony Mann's *The Man from Laramie*

Here's the situation, hoss. It's taken blood, sweat, and tears (someone else's, of course), but you've raised a family and built a small empire of your own. Still, somewhere along the way you became a man "as hard as the land around you." Your tyrannical ways have put your wife half-way into her grave. One son lives an embittered milquetoast, trying to but never measuring up to your long shadow. The other son you spoil because he's as wild as you once were, until he becomes a lawless sociopath whose answer for everything is a bullet. Do you...

A) Encourage him to find a creative or artistic outlet for his aggression, after turning him over to a sidearm-abuse program?

B) Send your wife and other son Back East to live with relatives?

C) Reassess your lifestyle and sell off some of your land to make your golden years more stress-free?

D) Trek to Dodge once a week with the whole clan for family therapy? Or...

E) Stick it out for better or worse—much worse?

If your answer is E, continue.

Morality and family values are nowhere more hallowed, nor at times more dysfunctional, than in westerns. It's a mean old world out there. Who else do you have, hold, and occasionally kill other than your kith and kin?

As Nicholas Earp (Gene Hackman) tells his sons around a midwestern dining table early on in Lawrence Kasdan's *Wyatt Earp* (1994), "Remember this, all of you. Nothing counts so much as blood. The rest are just strangers." Lawyer though he is, papa Earp proves it some years later by riding all the way to some southwestern hellhole to bail out and abet his drunken, reprobate son (Wyatt) in his escape from the law. Wyatt learns the lesson well (as well as Michael Corleone did in another genre) as he changes from a fair-minded young man into a remorselessly judgmental xenophobe and harsh imposer of law and punishment. In this case, the family that fights together, dies together as one of the West's most celebrated events, the Gunfight at the OK Corral, and its retribution takes their toll. Unfortunately for Wyatt and his brothers, the Clanton family (the other party in the altercation) has similar feelings of kinship...and revenge.

LEFT: He ain't a heavy...he's my brother. Wyatt (Kevin Costner) hovers protectively over his plugged brother, Morgan (Linden Ashby), moments after the famed shootout at the OK Corral, in Wyatt Earp *(1994). OPPOSITE: Martin Pawley (Jeffrey Hunter) could be protecting the abducted Debbie Edwards (Natalie Wood) from renegades or her uncle, Ethan (John Wayne), in John Ford's bittersweet* The Searchers *(1956).*

Stickin' Together

Things don't always work out so badly. It may not all be *Little House on the Prairie* (television series, 1974–1982) or *Seven Brides for Seven Brothers* (1954), but in John Huston's grim and gripping *The Unforgiven* (1959), Ben Zachary (Burt Lancaster, in his thirty-second film role in fourteen years) keeps the home fires—as well as, eventually, the home itself—burning. When the truth comes out that his adopted sister Rachel (Audrey Hepburn) is a full-blooded Kiowa, Zachary risks the hatred of friends, neighbors, and business partner, as well as the full-scale attack of the Kiowas, to hold his clan together. Luckily for Rachel, she wants to stay with her adopted people. Ben might have something to say about it if she didn't.

Natalie Wood isn't quite so lucky, even though her film is based on the same Alan LeMay novel as *The Unforgiven*. Straying beyond the family is strictly taboo in John Ford's thorny visual masterpiece *The Searchers* (1956). Wood plays Debbie Edwards, a white girl on the Texas frontier of 1868 who has been abducted by Comanches after they rub out her parents, brother, and sister. Along comes Uncle Ethan Edwards (John Wayne, in his first anti-heroic role) back from the Civil War. He dedicates himself to the search for her long after posses and parties have given up. For five years he hunts her, and hunt is the word, for as Debbie is old enough to marry within the tribe, Ethan feels he must kill her for her inevitable impurity. He finds her, and (you guessed it) she wants to stay with her new people. In LeMay's novel, Wayne's character pulls the trigger. Let's just say that John Ford is a kinder, gentler auteur. As Max Steiner's score swells to a close, our hearts and tear ducts swell right along with it.

Duke got more lighthearted practice in family defense in 1965 with Henry Hathaway's rough-and-tumble *The Sons of Katie Elder*, in the role of John Elder, the no-good, gunslinging son-of-a-good-woman. Returning to Clearwater, Texas, for his ma's funeral, John meets his reconvened brothers, Tom (Dean Martin, as a gambler with a wonderful trick for scrounging up bar money), Matt (Earl Holliman, as a cut-and-dried merchant), and Bud (Michael Anderson, Jr.), the spunky kid who stayed at home.

The late and saintly Katie wanted Bud to make something of himself in college, and his guilty siblings aim to make sure he does (even if it means roughing him up). But first they have to find out who killed their old man and cheated their ma out of the family ranch. As if fighting among themselves isn't enough to contend with, they soon become the targets for a cover-up foisted by a businessman (James Gregory), his hired gun (the hulking George Kennedy), and the businessman's weakling son (an innocent-looking Dennis Hopper). Gregory brings home the darker side of parental fealty in the film's violent climax.

Though Wayne is the only Elder (and the elder Elder at that) who emerges unscathed, he hardly felt it. Only a few days before shooting was to start, Wayne called all involved together to inform them that he had been diagnosed with lung cancer. Though he offered to withdraw from the project, Hathaway opted to wait the

sixteen weeks for the Duke's recovery from surgery. True to form, once out of bed and back in the saddle, Duke insisted on doing all his own riding, shooting, and fighting.

Parent Problems

Special as the parent-child relationship is, not all mas were Katie, nor were all pas cut from the same cloth as, say, the rugged patriarch (Jimmy Stewart) struggling to keep his eight kids together through the Civil War in *Shenandoah* (1965). Some parents were blind: the great silent-film star Donald Crisp played cattle baron Alec Waggoman, who was literally blind (by way of his failing eyesight) to his sadistic son Dave's (Alex Nicol) treachery, cruelty, and weakness in director Anthony Mann's final and perhaps finest collaboration with James Stewart (seven of his last eight pictures had starred Jimmy), *The Man from Laramie* (1955).

Will Lockhart (Stewart), on his fanatical search for the man who sold the Apaches the rifles that were used to wipe out his brother's army unit, finds himself embroiled in a battle between foster brothers and a father who is convinced that Lockhart is the man from a recurring nightmare who will kill his son. The truth seems to be quite the opposite.

"No bitin', or gougin' and no kickin', either!"
–Reverend Samual Clayton, in John Fords' The Searchers

In the old days, movie cowboys just hit one another (mostly in the shoulders). With the advent of the "pass system," tightly choreographed swings a hair away from a man's face was the safer way to go. It did look stagey at times. If you're tired of heroes who take it on the chin without even wincing, and more realistic fisticuffs are what you're after, here are a few of the best fights the West(ern) has ever seen:

✳ *Frenchy (Marlene Dietrich) and Mrs. Callahan's (Una Merkel) ferocious fisticuffs, chair smashing, hair pulling, and bottle throwing, until Jimmy Stewart pours scrub water over them in* Destry Rides Again *(1939)*

✳ *Montgomery Clift (a newcomer to celluloid combat) trying to keep John Wayne from bouncing him back to Broadway in* Red River *(1948)*

✳ *Jimmy Stewart and Arthur Kennedy tussling in the dust among the cattle in* The Man from Laramie *(1955)*

✳ *Ben Johnson and Alan Ladd's almost slo-mo saloon slugfest in* Shane *(1953). Ladd's later fight with Van Heflin isn't bad, either.*

✳ *The Duke in a multistory fistfight with Randolph Scott in* The Spoilers *(1942)*

✳ *Steve McQueen against everybody at the Prescott Bar in* Junior Bonner *(1972)*

✳ *Gregory Peck's dawn-to-dusk match with Charlton Heston in* The Big Country *(1958)*

✳ *Paul Newman playin' dirty with the giant (Ted "Lurch" Cassidy) in* Butch Cassidy and the Sundance Kid *(1969)*

So was Stewart's slow-burn performance, which could be as soft and folksy as all get-out one second and explode into the kind of passion that took a fistfight (with Arthur Kennedy) sprawling all over the center of town and smashing into a cattle pen the next. Stewart insisted on doing all his own stunts. But what could he lose? He was, after all, wearing his lucky hat, which he kept in a fireproof vault between pictures.

In King Vidor's 1946 David O. Selznick megaproduced epic symphony of dysfunction, *Duel in the Sun* (which we'll dish later), Senator McCanles (Lionel Barrymore) was just as blinded by the son. Two brothers, the soft-spoken lawyer Jesse (Joseph Cotten) and the spoiled, horse- and gun-savvy Lewt (Gregory Peck, showing what a surprisingly good bastard he could be), battle it out for the soul of Pearl Chavez (Jennifer Jones), a reckless girl of Anglo/Indian parentage.

Some parents were hell on wheels, and about the same on their children. A gray and grizzled (though by no means old) Duke was no exception in Howard Hawks' first western, *Red River* (1948), loosely based on the seagoing story *Mutiny on the Bounty*. As cattleman Tom Dunson, the Duke's heart is hardened early by the

ABOVE: The odds may not have been quite as stacked against James Stewart as this publicity shot suggests, but they weren't much better in the action-packed The Man from Laramie *(1955). OPPOSITE: Father (John Wayne at left) and son (Montgomery Clift at right) are in for one bumpy trail as they drive their cattle to Missouri Territory and each other to violence in Howard Hawks'* Red River *(1948).*

This film is an unrivaled feast for the eye. There's no one like Mann for gracing nature with a camera. Unfortunately, the cast paid dearly for it. Shot in the area around Santa Fe, New Mexico, on a compressed, twenty-eight-day schedule, Mann expanded his separate shooting locations from six to eighteen, with a 104-mile (166.4km) trek between the two main sites. The Winnebagos had logged 2,954 miles (4,726.4km) by the end of the month. The results were worth it.

Indian attack (blame it on the Indians) on a wagon train that has killed his fiancée. With seemingly the last drop of tenderness left in him, Dunson adopts the sole young survivor of the slaughter, Matt (who later grows up to become Montgomery Clift), whom he rears as only the no-frills Duke could.

Matt, not welded to the West's hard-bitten codes of behavior, explodes into conflict with his fierce foster father in the chaos of a cattle drive along the Chisholm Trail. The dictatorial Dunson wants to do it the hard way (isn't that just like a father?) on a treacherous route to Abilene. Matt knows that taking the trail to Kansas City will exact less of a toll on both drivers and dogies. When Dunson executes one of the cowhands, that tears it—Matt and crew commandeer the steers and head for K.C., with the mutinized Duke in pursuit. He catches up with Matt in Kansas City, ready to kill him, which he almost does, until Matt's new love, Tess (Joanne Dru), intercedes as an armed family counselor.

Duke and Monty had rough-and-tumble company. Hawks had put his own kind of closure on his relationship with MGM by shoving studio chief Louis B. Mayer and walking off the set of *Viva Villa* (1934). He had later wrangled with eccentric billionaire Howard Hughes during Jane Russell's steamy assault on the West in *The Outlaw* (1940), and was canned for his troubles. He just couldn't seem to finish a western.

The tough guys were a little nervous. Hawks had wanted Gary Cooper for Dunson but it was too negative a character for him. Cary Grant had turned down the role of gunfighter Cherry Valance (John Ireland) because it was too small. It was Clift's first film, though he had long been courted by Hollywood, and he couldn't even ride a horse. Wayne was leery about Clift and Hawks, and wanted to help steer the production. Walter Brennan (as trail cook Nadine Groot) was leery about playing someone who lost his false teeth at a poker game and could only borrow them at mealtimes. (He shouldn't have been—his three-day role was expanded to six weeks and won him an Oscar for Best Supporting Actor.)

Shooting along the San Pedro River in the Whetstone Mountain area of Arizona (approximating the Texas and Kansas badlands) had its pitfalls. Rainstorms (like the one filmed while Dunson reads the Bible over the grave of the cowboy he has just killed) gave the Duke a cold and Dru the flu. A poisonous centipede put Hawks in the hospital. Locusts plagued the crew but sounded just fine on tape. The stampede scene (with a record-breaking nine thousand out-of-control cattle) took ten days to shoot and injured seven wranglers. Howard Hughes even threatened to sue for the similarity of the fight scene to that of his film *The Outlaw*.

Despite all the obstacles, after two months on location (where Hawks would entertain the locals by screening rushes as well as full-length features for them), doubling the original $1.5 million budget, and Wayne calling on his friendship with Hughes to drop the lawsuit, *Red River* was released to accolades. Clift was a sensation. Hawks was a westerner after all. And John Wayne had tackled the most complex character of his career. (It would send him on his way to *Rooster Cogburn* [1975] and an Oscar).

Of course, kids can be hell on parents, too. If Clift was subbing for Oedipus in *Red River*, then Barbara Stanwyck was on deck as Elektra in *The Furies* (1950), written by Niven Busch and darkly directed by Anthony Mann. T.C. Jeffords (Walter Huston, the expensive, expansive actor at forty thousand dollars a picture) was the kind of father you could either try to live up to or destroy. Barbara Stanwyck tried to do both.

She had her reasons. To run the great ranch where they lived was all she wanted for her future. As thick as thieves with her father, she assumed she'd get the place. But after T.C. estranges her brother, bribes her gambler boyfriend (Wendell Corey) to cancel his engagement plans, and hangs her only other male friend (a Mexican neighbor, Gilbert Roland), her father whimsically decides in his will not to make her a cattle baroness, but rather to leave it all to his gold-grubbing socialite of a new wife (Judith Anderson). What's a daughter to do? Why, stab her stepmother in the face with a pair of scissors. And perhaps buy up enough of her free-spending father's IOUs to bankrupt him. Families don't get any more mythic.

Riders in Rehab

Occasionally, Dr. Freud was paged directly to the cutting room for a family drama. One of his earliest visits paid off with one of the best noir westerns ever shot, thanks to writer Niven Busch; originator of the sound western, Raoul Walsh; and black-and-white cinematographic genius James Wong Howe. *Pursued* (1947) was a

It's no use, padre—this hombre has vengeance on his mind. Father Zaccardi (Italian star Raf Vallone at right) tries to soften the hardened heart of Sam Sand (Steve McQueen at left) in Nevada Smith *(1966).*

Freudian field day. Jeb Rand (Robert Mitchum) waits in the ruins of his ancestral home for the men who are bent on killing him. With him waits his adoptive sister, Thorley (Theresa Wright), who has married him in order to kill him on their wedding night for his murder of her brother (even though it was self-defense).

Something that happened when Jeb was too young to remember (or something simply too traumatic to remember) is the key to his savage dilemma. Yet all he recalls is hiding under a trap door as a gunfight raged overhead...a pair of spurred boots...flashes of light...and the memory of a fallen woman. What is the root of the curse he seems to be living under? Why is his adoptive mother, Medora (Judith Anderson), so full of twisted love, guilt, shame, and hatred for him? Why does his one-armed uncle, Grant (Dean Jagger), seem to live to see him dead?

It's a hell of a revelation come the final moments. And the brooding buildup (complete with more mood music from Max Steiner) is incredible—almost as incredible as Howe's shadowy, deep-focus photographic treatment of the Monument Valley location. Mitchum (who had drifted to extra work in westerns because it was easier than prizefighting, ditch digging, sheet-metal working, or being a longshoreman) may have crabbed about his early days doing Hopalong Cassidy westerns, saying, "I got a hundred bucks a week and all the manure I could take home," but he had no reason to beef here.

Mitchum got more psychological family work done seven years later in a film produced by his old *El Dorado* buddy, John Wayne. *The Track of the Cat* (1954), directed by William A. Wellman, took family turmoil to a snow-choked farm in northern California, where, in claustrophobic confrontations worthy of Eugene O'Neill, the matriarch (Beulah Bondi) reigns while brothers (Tab Hunter and Robert Mitchum) go for each other's throats and track a mysterious mountain lion, which seems to symbolize the whole family's pent-up aggression. cinematographer William H. Clothier's color photography drenched in stark, black-and-white imagery gives the gloom even more room.

One final contender for the family analyst's couch was Anthony Mann's *Man of the West* (1958), in which Gary Cooper, as a former outlaw living on the straight and narrow, is pitted against Lee J. Cobb (his murderous uncle) and his ruthless gang while trying to deny his past. Not easy to do. As Cobb (Doc Tobin) says, "Do you remember Uvalde...eleven thousand dollars...you held him, I took off the top of his head." Not only does Coop have to kill his extended family to purge the bad blood that rages within him, and not only does Tobin finally compel him to shoot him by raping his traveling companion, but the traditionally whole-some, now demented Coop also forces cousin Jack Lord to strip at gunpoint (in revenge for Lord making his lady companion do the same). It's not surprising that Mann's last project (left unpro-duced) was a western version of King Lear.

VENGEANCE IS SWEET, BUT IT SURE MAKES YOU THIRSTY: NOW, LET'S SEE WHAT YOU'RE MADE OF, PART III

> S'wounds, I should take it for it cannot be but I am pigeon-liver'd, and lack gall to make oppression bitter, or ere this I should have fatted all the region kites with this slave's offal. Bloody, bawdy, villain! Remorseless, treacherous, lecher-ous, kindless villain! O! Vengeance!
>
> —Hamlet,
> talking the talk

Here's the situation, hoss. You come home one day and find your family gunned down by strangers, scalped by angry Indians, incinerated by vigilantes, or abducted by who knows who. Do you...

  A) Call the authorities?
  B) Retain a defense lawyer?
  C) Sign up for long-term psy-choanalysis?
  D) Start putting out feelers for a book deal? Or...
  E) Settle the score?

If you answered E, continue.

Ah, sweet revenge. There's nothing like it. A person can dedicate his life to vengeance. The Jacobeans may have invented it, the Sicilians may have perfected it, but westerns have truly immortalized it.

Steve McQueen downright mythologizes it in Henry Hathaway's 1966 film, *Nevada Smith* (named for a character in Harold Robbins' novel *The Carpetbaggers*). As the young Sam Sand, McQueen returns home to find that his folks (a Kiowa Indian woman and an Anglo miner) have been brutally butchered by three men—Jesse Coe (a particularly sleazy Martin Landau), Tom

Kind of a Drag

Being dragged by your horse might just be the worst thing that could happen to a man who rides tall in the saddle. It's also one of the most dangerous stunts in filmmaking. The stuntman wears a tight-fitting, tough-hided jacket, from which a wire runs down his leg and attaches to his saddle's stirrup (less twisting and tearing on foot and hip that way). The second-unit director tries to find a nice level piece of ground. But you just never know what's going to come along and smack the old cabeza. If you want to see this trick in action, here are a few hombres (or their stunt doubles) who were tough enough to take the wild ride.

* *Lionel Barrymore in* **Duel in the Sun** *(1946)*
* *Jimmy Stewart (through a campfire) in* **The Man from Laramie** *(1955)*
* *Richard Rust in* **Comanche Station** *(1959)*
* *Paul Newman (getting hanged in a unique way) in* **The Life and Times of Judge Roy Bean** *(1972)*
* *Richard Boone in* **Rio Conchos** *(1964)*
* *Steve McQueen (through a river) in* **Nevada Smith** *(1966)*
* *Jaime Sanchez as Angel (from a car, yet) in* **The Wild Bunch** *(1969)*
* *Jason Robards (getting what he deserves) in* **Comes a Horseman** *(1978) (Stuntman Jim Shepherd was killed while doubling for him when his head slammed into a fence post.)*
* *An unfortunate cowboy (an extra) in* **Pale Rider** *(1985)*

Bowdrey (a particularly tough Arthur Kennedy), and Bill Fitch (a particularly paranoid Karl Malden)—who had asked him direc-tions to his homestead that morning. "They don't even look like people anymore," says the disbelieving Sam of his parents as he squats outside the family cabin, letting the view of the carnage burn into his brain.

He soon does a little burning of his own: his parents, the home-stead, and everything around it, waiting until the last ember dies before ceasing his vigil. Then, still in his buckskin and moccasins and ignoring the entreaties of friendly neighbors to live with them, he takes rifle and horse and sets off on an odyssey of revenge.

Misfortune rolls in right behind him. The first men he mistak-enly tracks as his parents' butchers prove to be innocent, but not so innocent that they don't steal his horse and rifle after feeding him and watching him fall asleep. Stranded in the desert, Sam wanders, thirsts, hungers, and finds a rusted old pistol. When he uses it to try to buffalo a passing stranger into parting with his horse, he finds that the stranger is a gunsmith named McCord (Brian Keith) who knows the boy's hundred-year-old model won't shoot. Luckily, McCord takes a shine to Sam and teaches the very apt pupil the fine art of shooting. He also teaches him how to play cards and how to drink (if Sam is looking for cutthroats, he'll probably find them in a saloon). Though McCord offers the young man a normal life and an apprenticeship, Sam opts for taking the loan of horse and gun and continuing his bloody quest.

McCord doesn't let him go before giving a few choice words of fatherly advice. As for Sam's gun skill and odds of success: "You get so you can do that with either hand: when you're half drunk, or

half awake, in a dark room, or off the back of a running horse, and you might stand a chance—a small chance." And as for how to settle the score: "Plan your moves. Always pick your place to fight. Don't make any threats and never walk away from any." Girded, Sam continues his murderous journey, sacrificing more than he'd ever imagined and covering more ground than most humans could. Vicious knife fights, thankful prostitutes, a compassionate Kiowa maid, prison time in the depths of the Louisiana Bayou, a self-sacrificing Cajun queen, an Italian padre who once sought vengeance himself, and life as an outlaw in the California gold country all await the Ulysseslike vigilante. And it's a torturous moment when he's finally had his bellyful of vengeance. The therapy is over.

The Brando Brand

Karl Malden, the final target of McQueen's revenge in *Nevada Smith*, got himself in another tight spot with Marlon Brando's directorial debut (and directorial finale), one of the best, most romantic, most infamous revenge westerns ever made: *One-Eyed Jacks* (1961). One-eyed Jacks are, of course, wild cards in poker, and according to some aficionados of the game, also an affectionate name for the, ahem, male member. Karl certainly fits that description as the treacherous, two-faced Dad Longworth—friend, father figure, and nemesis to Brando's Rio the Kid.

Rio is a rascal. Shortly after the film begins, he almost cons his way around a virtuous maid's virginity by ceremoniously offering her a ring that "belonged to [his] mother." When the consummation is interrupted by the law riding in after him and his compadre, he just as unceremoniously strips his intended of her bauble (for future use) and vamooses. Soon it is he and Longworth who are pinned together under crossfire on a Mexican hilltop with one horse between them. Dad offers to risk the ride for help while Rio holds the fort. Rio ends up holding the bag—and it isn't the one with the money.

Released from prison years later, Rio and two compadres (one of whom is played by Ben Johnson) make for the California coastal town of Monterey, where a reformed Dad just happens to be sheriff. Rio visits him at his homestead, and the now very paternal Longworth braces for a shoot-out. Instead, Rio plays cat-

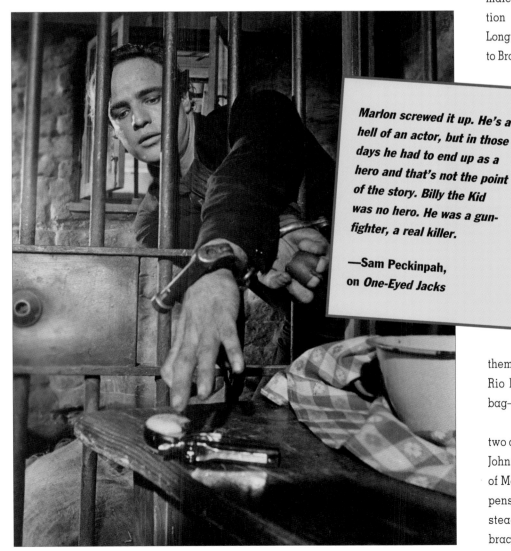

and-mouse mind games with him, pretending to be naive to his former friend's betrayal. He also meets Dad's stepdaughter (Pina Pellicer), an unconventional and uncommonly believable beauty, and works his magic with her. But she works hers with him, too.

Rio decides to rob the bank and spare her stepfather, but glad-handing Dad savagely heads him off at the pass. With the help of his swinish deputy (Slim Pickens), he brutalizes Rio in public as an example of what happens to outlaws in his town. Then—making damn sure that Rio won't be holding a gun for a while—he damns himself in the process.

Crushed and humiliated, the rebellious Rio heads north to nurse his wounds, regret his mercy, and brood (as only Marlon can). His brooding explodes in one tremendous scene where Ben Johnson says something he oughtn't about Rio's new love. (Brando is one of the few actors who can go from zero to ninety in a nanosecond.) Brooding leads to planning. Dad should have finished the job; his bank, deputy, stepdaughter, and life are all forfeit. It's just a question of time.

You might not immediately recognize Billy the Kid and Pat Garrett amid the mood of sadomasochism and Charles Lang's sensational photography of the lush Big Sur coast, but they're in there. Brando's young Pennebaker production company had been looking to do a discrimination western called *A Burst of Vermilion*. After five years of hemming and hawing, they melded their idea with a dark script written by director Sam Peckinpah, based on both Charles Neider's 1956 novel *The Authentic Death of Hendry Jones* and Peckinpah's own delvings into the complex relationship between William Bonney (Billy the Kid) and his friend and eventual executioner, Pat Garrett. Once the permutation was in production, Brando went through six directors (one of whom was Stanley Kubrick) before he himself took over direction. His director's cut ran five hours, but he trimmed it down to two and a half so that Paramount would distribute it. Despite the convolutions and a bit of Brando indulgence, it's one of the best of the West.

Virtuoso Avengers

Some don't start out looking for revenge. They get pushed to it. In Arthur Penn's field day for antiheros, *The Missouri Breaks* (1976), good-natured cattle rustler Tom Logan (Jack Nicholson) bides his time to pay back regulator (manhunter) Robert E. Lee Clayton (Marlon Brando) for killing three of his closest compadres. Logan cuts Clayton's throat while he's sleeping and wakes him up to tell him about it. In Anthony Mann's *Winchester '73* (1950), it's only when Len McAddam (Jimmy Stewart) has his one-in-a-thousand rifle (which only President Ulysses S. Grant and Buffalo Bill Cody possess companions to) stolen from him that he goes after Dutch Henry Brown (Stephen McNally), a.k.a. his brother Matthew, for murdering their father. (Sorry, Jimmy, but Dan Duryea steals this one with his portrayal of truly wacko gunslick Waco Johnny Dean.)

OPPOSITE: Marlon Brando gives a masterful variation of the Billy the Kid myth as Rio in the only western he ever directed, One-Eyed Jacks *(1961). ABOVE: Here's Raquel Welch getting some shooting lessons in* Hannie Caulder *(1971). Some publicity shots had her wearing nothing under that poncho.*

From the opening credits, avengers are in it for blood. Raquel Welch goes after the three depraved gunmen (you can't get more depraved than Ernest Borgnine, Jack Elam, and Strother Martin) who killed her husband and gang-raped her in *Hannie Caulder* (1971). She may be dressed in only a poncho and a gun belt, but that doesn't stop bounty hunter Robert Culp from teaching her how to get the job done (and femininely, too—she kills one in a brothel and another in a perfume shop).

Sometimes avenging angels help each other. Clint Eastwood made a western career of vengeance, culminating with directing and starring as the bad-man-gone-good-gone-bad-again William Money in *Unforgiven* (1992). Eastwood's directorial debut came twenty-five years earlier in a vengeance film that cost his own Malpaso production company $1.6 million to make, brought that money back at the box office within the first ten weeks of its opening, and netted Clint a neat $400,000 plus 25 percent of the take. You figure the profits.

What didn't take much figuring was that American audiences who had sunk their forks into Clint's spaghetti westerns with director Sergio Leone were hungry to see a homegrown product. They got it in *Hang 'em High* (1967). This time, nine evil men fail to finish a job they started (the job of hanging Clint). Inger Stevens nurses

Bad Deeds for Bad Men

Just ask the Marquis de Sade: writers are always thinking of new ways to torture folks. The phobic minds of nineteenth-century novelists credited "bloodthirsty Indians" with everything from nailing captives to trees to be consumed by animals, to skinning them alive, to burying them alive in the arms of a dead friend, to eating pieces of them while they themselves watched, to plucking their eyes out and inserting hot coals in their place, and, of course, to pouring molten gold into miners' mouths. Hollywood writers were just as imaginative when it came to bad deeds committed by bad men, white and red. Here are some examples, if you're sick enough to look for them.

* *Smearin' sticky mescal juice on the face of a helpless pioneer, trussin' him up, and dumpin' him in a pit for the ants to eat his eyes out*—Broken Arrow (1950)

* *eavin' a cowboy saddled on a skittish horse with his hands tied, a noose around his neck roped to a nearby tree, and an open bag of angry rattlesnakes at the horse's feet*—Maverick (1994)

* *Slow roastin' your prisoner over a fire to get him to talk*—The Plainsman (1936)

* *Bullwhippin' your buddy in public and then shatterin' his gun hand with a rifle butt*—One-Eyed Jacks (1961)

* *Blastin' an unarmed man with a long-range hunting rifle while he's sitting in an outhouse; blastin' another in the throws of connubial ecstasy; burnin' another one out of* a shack only to skewer him to a tree with a cruciform throwing-knife; and ropin' a cowboy who can't swim off his horse in midstream and drowning him—**The Missouri Breaks (1976)**

* *Skinnin' a woman while her husband watches*—Nevada Smith (1966)

* *Shootin' bullets around a young'un who's cryin' and crawlin' in the dirt*—Rawhide (1950)

* *Buryin' a fella up to his mouth in the burnin' desert sand*—Jeremiah Johnson (1972)

* *Makin' a bridegroom kneel by blowin' his kneecap off, slicin' a fella's face open with the spur of your boot, and offerin' your pistol barrel as a pipe to an opium-stoned cowboy...and then givin' him a shot he'll never forget*—Tombstone (1993)

* *Shootin' a settler's dog full of arrows, tyin' the settler to a tree with his legs spread sittin' on the ground, stuffin' the dead dog's tail in his mouth, and settin' a campfire on the ground between his legs*—Ulzana's Raid (1972)

* *Stabbin' a fella, burnin' him with a flaming stick, strippin' him and coverin' him with water, then leavin' him for the winter wind to finish off*—Will Penny (1967)

* *Meetin' a nice kid on a rickety rope bridge, askin' to look at his gun so maybe you can give him some pointers on shootin', and then drawin' on him when he takes it out of the holster to show you*—McCabe and Mrs. Miller (1971)

ABOVE, LEFT: If Jed Cooper (Clint Eastwood) were to lower that bandana, you'd see a nasty noose scar around his neck, but he has more murderous things on his mind in Hang 'em High (1967).

the victim back to health and deputization by hanging judge Isaac Charles Parker. Soon, the murderous nine are being hunted by the stoic marshal with the scar around his neck (which he likes to reveal just prior to retribution).

Eastwood brought revenge to new murderous heights five years later in his *High Plains Drifter* (1972). This time it's an entire town that is worthy of metaphysical wrath. The populace of Lago (sounds kinda evil, don't it?) hire Clint's bearded drifter to rid their stinking desert town of the desperados who are terrorizing it.

Clint's "Man with No Name" (and man with no compunction about killing anyone) compels the locals to paint their entire town red and post a WELCOME TO HELL sign for the benefit of the returning bad men. And hell it is, because under that beard, Clint is the sheriff who the whole town lets get bullwhipped to death by those very same men. Everybody gets buried in *High Plains Drifter*. And in a wry nod of thanks to his mentors Sergio Leone and Don Siegel, Clint gives each a tombstone all his own in the film's opening minutes.

BLOOD FOR THE SMART SET, OR, LAYING AN AMBUSH FOR GODOT WHILE MACKIE PUTS AWAY HIS KNIFE AND PICKS UP A SIX-GUN

Sometimes western revenge has literary overtones. One of the most celebrated B westerns of all time, Joseph H. Lewis' *Terror in a Texas Town* (1958)—in which Sterling Hayden's seafaring son of a Swedish farmer harpoons his father's murderer—vibrates with a certain Melvillian allusion. Roger Corman fostered two of the most artful revenge westerns when he gave director-producer Monte Hellman and writer-producer-actor Jack Nicholson $150,000 and round-trip tickets for the Utah desert. They came back seven weeks later with the footage for both *The Shooting* (1966) and *Ride the Whirlwind* (1966).

Nicholson based his script for the latter on the poetic cadences and the sense of agrarian futility from old western frontier diaries he had dug up at the Los Angeles Public Library: two innocent cowhands (Nicholson and Cameron Mitchell) make the fatal mistake of giving sanctuary to a band of outlaws on the run from a vigilante mob. The chase is on, and their pursuit is a juggernaut, as endless as the plight of sodbusters hacking at a monumental tree stump. Even as the picture ends—with the death of one of them—you can hear the hoofbeats of the sole survivor pound out on his infinite flight from vengeance.

The rest of the footage took vengeance to places doubly strange. *The Shooting* is a masterpiece of existential isolation. Characters speak dialogue so cryptic and clipped that it never quite communicates what they desperately need to get across. Even the camera depicts characters by isolating parts of their bodies, like the vengeful protagonist (Millie Perkins, introduced by a close-up of her hand shooting a horse) who hires and accompanies a bounty hunter (Warren Oates) on a mission to find a nameless man. The bounty hunter doesn't know that the man has murdered the woman's child and husband. Nor does he know that she has left a trail for another killer (Nicholson) to follow and eventually gun down the quarry they've cornered. And he sure doesn't know that that quarry will turn out to be his twin brother. Dizzy yet? If Samuel Beckett had written westerns, this would have been the best of them.

If Beckett could inspire a revenge western, why not Bertolt Brecht? Why should it be verboten for the brilliant German director of *M* (1931) and the silent classic *Metropolis* (1926) to don western duds? Who could do a western better service than Marlene Dietrich? Revenge didn't get much lyrically stranger than Fritz Lang's *Rancho*

Notorious (1952), in which the hero searches for a sinister place he knows nothing about, a beefy-sounding baritone continuously strums and croons a ballad, and flashbacks ride the range.

The film opens with the rape ("she wasn't spared anything") and murder of rancher Vern Haskell's fiancée during a holdup. Though the posse peters out, Vern (Arthur Kennedy) manages to snag Whitey, the dying albino accomplice of the savage he seeks. But the only word he can get from him on his partner's whereabouts is the cryptic last gasp, "Chuck...a...luck."

Armed with that crumb (and an unquenchable hatred), Vern sets out on a mission to find Chuck-a-luck and his man. After years of searching, he discovers that Chuck-a-luck is not a person but a safe house for outlaws run by someone named Altar. He later finds out through other folks' flashbacks of an ex-chanteuse and fabled beauty named Altar Keene (Dietrich). She has vanished. She is legend.

Ready to ride the high plains of your mind? If so, tag along with Millie Perkins and Jack Nicholson as they do a little tripping out in **The Shooting** *(1966).*

From encounter to encounter (flashback to flashback), an increasingly intriguing and, yes, arousing picture of the teutonic temptress is put together ("I like a woman who's cold like ice or burning like the sun"). After more searching, Vern discovers that her longtime lover, the legendary gunman Frenchy Fairmont (Mel Ferrer), is in a nearby hoosegow (nabbed while buying perfume for Altar). Getting himself thrown in the tank with the amiable but deadly Frenchy, Vern helps the gunman escape and is at last taken to Chuck-a-luck.

What Vern finds is a ranch hideaway where a fading but still formidable Keene takes 10 percent of her guests' latest loot in return for sanctuary. Hold on to your hats, pard, because here is where the goin' gets rough: Lang turns his western into a sexually laden thriller. For though Vern sees on Altar's Bavarian bosom the brooch that was ripped from his intended's bodice, he can't come out and ask her which killer gave her the bauble (the killers include a very young Jack Elam and George "Superman" Reeves). She has laid down the sultry law: "There are no questions here." It's up to Vern to defrost the ice goddess he now wants, risking Frenchy's heat in the process, to uncover the man he's wanted for so long. But all his work just blackens his soul in the end. As the singing cowboy sings...

> Two men rode away from Chuck-a-luck.
> And death rode beside them on the trail.
> For they died that day so the legends tell.
> With empty guns they fought and fell.
> And so ends the tale of hate, murder and revenge.

Bad Karma on the Trail

Just ask a hangin' judge like Roy Bean. Law was personal west of the Pecos. It was the kind of thing you wanted to take into your own hands, and sometimes you realized too late that the blood there wouldn't wash off. William Wellman's *The Ox-Bow Incident* (1943), one of the first antiwesterns to emerge from World War II's grim consciousness, brought that home with a vengeance.

When Gil Carter (Henry Fonda) and Art Croft (Harry Morgan) ride into Bridger Wells, Nevada, in 1885, they find themselves in Vigilanteville, U.S.A. A cattleman named Kincaid has reportedly been murdered. With the sheriff out of town, a former Confederate major (Frank Conroy) raises the rabble—plus a few solid citizens—

Tell Becky I Love...Her...

When your number's up and you know it, words can be pearls, even if they're cast in a pigsty. Movie cowboys like Crazy Lee in Sam Peckinpah's The Wild Bunch *(1969) might have had the wherewithal to utter such quips as, "Well now, how'd you just like to kiss my sister's black cat's ass," but most mortals let off simpler stuff. Let's take a look at some famous last gasps of the real West:*

"We are friends. We are friends." —Captain John W. Gunnison, killed by Paiute Indians, 1853

"I will throw up my hands for no gringo dog!" —Three-Fingered Jack Garcia, California bandito, 1853

"It is enough. Shoot no more. The job is finished. I am dead." —Joaquin Murieta, California bandito, 1853

"Gentlemen, I am not used to this business. Shall I jump or slide off?" —George Shears, hanged from a stepladder in Hell Gate, Montana, 1864

"Take good care of my horse." —General Winfield Scott, 1866

"Texas. Texas. Margaret." —Sam Houston, 1863

"Adiós, compadre." —Kit Carson, 1868

"Hasta el inferno." —Tiburcio Vasquez, California bandito, 1875

"I feel better." —Brigham Young, 1877

"Let me go. The world is bobbing around." —Bad-man Sam Bass, shot by Texas posse, 1878

"Hanging is my favorite way of dying." —Bill Longley, Texas gallows, 1878

"Good-bye boys, go away and let me die." —Billy Clanton after the gunfight at the OK Corral, 1881

"This is the last game of pool I'll ever play." —Virgil Earp, Tombstone Saloon, 1882

"Damned if I'll die with my boots on." —Lafayette Grime, about to be lynched, Arizona, 1882

"I have nothing to say and guess it would not do any good anyway. I forgive you all and hope you forgive me." —Thomas Halderman, hanged in Tombstone, 1900

"Bury me next to Bill [Wild Bill Hickock]." —Calamity Jane, 1903

"Things break about even for us.... we all get about the same amount of ice. The rich get it in the summer and the poor get it in the winter." —Bat Masterson, from a paper on his desk where he died of a heart attack as a New York City sports editor, 1921

"Cowboys. There are no more cowboys." —Frederic Remington, 1909

"Hurry it up. I'm due in Hell for dinner." —Black Jack Ketchum to the hangman, 1901 ("Bad Luck" Ketchum may have been more like it—he had once publicly flogged himself with his own saddle rope upon learning of his sweetheart's betrayal, got caught after holding up the same train four times in almost the same spot, and, because of a previously stretched hanging rope, had his head torn off at his execution.)

to go after the culprits. Carter and Croft tag along to avoid the wrath of the angry mob. What they find in the dead of night are three men sleeping under the trees: Donald Martin (Dana Andrews), a Mexican (Anthony Quinn), and a dotty old man (Francis Ford, John's older brother). Kincaid's cattle are nearby. The three say they bought them, yet the hangin' ropes are thrown.

In this creepily subdued film, the violence is more in word, thought, and expectation than in action. Through that long, dark night as the three plead for their lives, arguments beget counter-arguments, division begets mob rule, and eloquence begets three bodies swinging as the sun rises. The sheriff finally shows, only to tell them (you guessed it) that Kincaid is alive and well and all the richer for the sale of his cattle.

Director "Wild Bill" Wellman was no stranger to westerns with a message. He had made the unique *Robin Hood of El Dorado* in 1936, a gangster western about political corruption. In 1940, he bought the rights to Walter Van Tilburg Clark's novel *The Ox-Bow Incident* for $6,500 from a producer who had intended to make the movie as a vehicle for Mae West. Clark's story was a hard sell to the studios, as it didn't exactly promise to perk up a wartime audience.

In fact, the only interested party was Twentieth Century Fox vice president Darryl F. Zanuck, with whom Wellman had the kind of rough-and-tumble relationship that included throwing bricks through Zanuck's office window. Zanuck gave the project the green light—as long as Wellman made another picture for Fox along with it, and behaved himself.

As so much of the story was set at night, it was decided to shoot indoors where light and depth were more controllable. Sets were made as nightmarish as possible. Wellman, who was not used to the constraints of set work, was also under pressure to live up to his reputation as a director who never wavered for one moment. To facilitate this well-tended mystique, he hired (as he usually did) character actor George Chandler: whenever Wellman felt he needed time to think his way around the set, he'd cue Chandler, and the actor would deliberately flub a line or knock something over. Wellman would fly into a towering rage, call a break to cool down, and secretly go off to work out his problem.

Wellman was a handful, as likely to grant Dana Andrews a sleeping scene one morning (after the actor had been up all night witnessing the birth of his daughter) as he was to slug one of his other stars in the face in a restaurant one night when the actor complained of the indignity of shooting with the second-unit director. Rowdy though Wellman was, he got the job done his way, which was fine with just about everybody.

Of *The Ox-Bow Incident, New York Times* film critic Bosley Crowther claimed, "Wellman has directed the picture with realism that is as sharp and cold as a knife." Yet the review ranking the film below any of the then-current B westerns was the one the

Gil Carter (Henry Fonda at center) doesn't like the vigilante twinkle he sees in that old geezer's eye as he gets the lowdown on a little frontier justice in The Ox-Bow Incident *(1943).*

director kept in a bank vault for safekeeping. Reviews aside, Fonda and Andrews both said that Carter and Martin were two of the best roles of their respective careers. Andrews' opinion may have had something to do with his character's (or screenwriter Lamar Trotti's) last words to his wife. Carter reads them to a stunned and shamed barful of men in the final scene:

My Dear Wife,

Mr. Dees will tell you what happened here tonight. He's a good man and has done everything he can for me. I suppose there's some other good men here, too, only they don't seem to realize what they're doing. They're the ones I feel sorry for, 'cause it'll be over for me in a little while but they'll have to go on remembering it for the rest of their lives. Man just naturally can't take the law into his own hands and hang people without hurting everybody in the world. Then, he's not just breaking one law but all laws. The law isn't just words you put in a book or judges or lawyers or sheriffs you hire to carry it out. It's everything that people have found out about justice and what's right and what's wrong. It's the very conscience of humanity. There can't be any such thing as civilization unless people have a conscience. If people touch God anywhere where is it but through their conscience? And what is anybody's conscience except a little piece of the conscience of all men that ever lived. I guess that's all I've got to say except kiss the babies for me and God bless you.

Your Husband, Donald

Words to live by. Words to die by.

Chapter Four

HOW THE WEST WAS WON (AND OTHER HISTORICAL EMBELLISHMENTS)

The endless beauty and bounty of the Great Plains is about to yield itself up to Lieutenant John Dunbar (Kevin Costner), Kicking Bird (Graham Greene), Wind in His Hair (Rodney Grant), and another Lakota friend in the tatanka (buffalo)-filled Dances with Wolves (1990).

Like Strother Martin said as he squirted his chaw into the dust of the South American West during *Butch Cassidy and the Sundance Kid* (1969), "'Course you probably think I'm crazy, but I'm not. (patooiee!!!) I'm colorful. That's what happens to you when you live ten years alone in Bolivia—you get colorful. (patooiee!!!)"

Then he was shot to death by bandits.

It took sand (a.k.a. guts) to survive in the colorful land of sand, sage, and mountains. Some—like Texans—even managed to make a mystique out of it. As General Philip Sheridan said in 1855, "If I owned Texas and Hell, I would rent out Texas and live in Hell." Personal notoriety in a hard land meant doing hard things, often killing or not being killed in situations where odds were that you should have ended up pushin' up daisies. Word of mouth made tales of individual triumphs taller. Books and dime novels jacked them up even taller, and Wild West shows, taller still. But movies lifted mortal lives to almost Olympian heights.

Some of the best westerns ever made were about the exploits of these riding, roping, shooting, and scouting heroes, villains, wild women, madmen, and general giants of the plains. Of course, when the dust cleared from the collision of life and legend, historical accuracy was often the first casualty. But accuracy never sold popcorn. As John Huston said in the first frames of

The Life and Times of Judge Roy Bean (1972), "Maybe this isn't the way it was. It's the way it should have been."

Forging new territory for the melting pot was a team effort: great trappers and scouts were needed to penetrate it, great soldiers to seize it, great Indians to defend it, great lawmen to tame it, and great entrepreneurs to make the most of it. Let's take a look at the marks that some of these living legends have left on celluloid...and where life left off and legend began.

ROUGHIN' IT

Mountain men! Many would have killed for their experience in the untouched American frontier; many more would have been killed by it. The trappers who truly pioneered the western wilderness were often more uncivilized than any "savage" they traded with or fought. (Sleeping uncovered in the snow and eating anything that comes along will do that to you.)

Meriwether Lewis and William Clark started things rolling when they took their historic 8,000-mile (12,800km) ramble (with a party of thirty, losing only one man in the process) up the Missouri River, across the Rockies, and on to the Pacific mouth of the Columbia River and back again between 1804 and 1806. It took nearly 150 years, but their exploits were immortalized in true Hollywood fashion: Fred MacMurray and Charlton Heston filled their respective well-worn boots in *Far Horizons* (1954), and Clark Gable did a little fictitious swaggering along the same vein in *Across the Wide Missouri* as Flint Mitchell in William Wellman's passionate but savagely cut 1950 tribute.

The Colorado Rocky Mountain adventures of trapper John Colter got him in trouble in 1808 with the Blackfoot Indians, who sportingly offered him a chance to run for his life. He did—with five hundred warriors in pursuit, evading all but one, whom he killed with the brave's own weapon. Charlton Heston and Brian Keith followed those hasty footsteps in *The Mountain Men* (1979).

Fur trapper Hugh Glass had just as much grit. In 1823, while up the wide Missouri, he was mauled so badly by a bear that after five days his companions (one being the famed scout Jim Bridger) gave him up as a goner. Relieving Glass of his knife and rifle, the men rejoined the main party and claimed they had buried their buddy. But after ten days, the unburied Hugh came 'round. Surviving on nuts and berries and dragging himself halfway across South Dakota, he gave them a little surprise back at Fort Kiowa. King of pain Richard Harris (almost wordlessly) crawled that path in *Man in the Wilderness* (1971).

But there were perks to make up for the hardship. In 1824, Jedediah Smith was the first white man to go through the South

ABOVE: Last thoughts before a last stand. Things could be better in Bolivia for Paul Newman (left) and Robert Redford (right) in Butch Cassidy and the Sundance Kid **(1969). OPPOSITE: Redford as a legendary mountain man in the exquisitely photographed Sydney Pollack film** Jeremiah Johnson **(1972).**

Pass of the Rockies. Two years later, he traveled from the Great Salt Lake along the Colorado River, across the Mojave Desert, and into what would become L.A. rush hour in 170 years. On the way back, he was the first of his kind to cross the magnificent mountains of the Sierra Nevada.

Smith's pal James Pierson Beckwourth—legendary guide, friend to the Crow (the tribe he lived with for six years), enemy to the Cheyenne (the tribe he helped Custer eradicate at the Sand Creek Massacre), and son of a slave—was the first African-American to gain fame on the frontier (thanks to Thomas D. Bonner's 1854 interview, "The Life and Adventures of James P. Beckwourth, Mountaineer, Scout, Pioneer and Chief of the Crow Nation"). Unfortunately, the only film incarnation Beckwourth garnered was distinctly "whitewashed" by caucasian actor Jack Oakie in *Tomahawk* (1950).

Famed western explorer Joseph Reddeford Walker may have gotten the "white man's" premier peek at the wonders of Yosemite in 1833 (long before the tour buses chugged in), but actor Robert Redford and director Sydney Pollack gave themselves and audiences an eyeful of the Rockies in one of the most visually stunning and moody westerns ever to hit the snow country (and giving the 1970s wilderness craze a jumpstart in the process) in *Jeremiah Johnson* (1972). A veteran of the Spanish-American War, Johnson has had his bellyful of civilization and heads up into the Rockies with just a rifle and a horse to trap for furs "for a while"—meaning forever. The film is his transformation from man into myth, and his education at the hands of the elements and wild animals (weathering everything from winter storms to wolf attacks), more experienced mountain men (some wise, some crazed), and the Crow Indian population. Johnson is a searcher who learns self-reliance through experience, the power of family through the unexpected gift of an Indian bride and the responsibility of a mute boy, pain through their murder in his absence, soul-searing hardness through his revenge of that murder, and uncanny vigilance against the Crow avengers who then seek his life.

As beautiful as a mountain spring; as crusty as his teacher, grizzly-bear-claw-

necklace-wearing Chris Lapp (Will Geer: "You're the same dumb pilgrim I've been hearin' for twenty days and smellin' for three"); as haunting as his fateful ride through a winter-shrouded Crow burial ground; as aching as his final greeting of an old enemy—this is a film that gets under your skin. That's because the Rockies had gotten under the skin of longtime friends Redford and Pollack, who had homes up in the Colorado resort area of Sundance (which Redford happens to own).

Tackling the problems of mountain filming was a challenge. Twelve- to fifteen-foot-deep (3.6 to 4.5m) snow cover made reshoots impossible—no "Take Two" with footprints everywhere. Floundering cast members, horses, and equipment-carrying mules necessitated a submerged track of six-foot-wide (1.8m) chain-link fence (like a huge snowshoe) to move anywhere. The script proved to be on just as tricky footing: Vardis Fisher's book *Mountain Man* and Raymond U. Thorp and Robert Bunker's *Crow Killer* were a little too unheroic. John "Red Dawn" Milius' script was gorier still. Pollack's friend David Rafael provided a ten-page short story on family life. By this time, Redford was willing to improvise.

Though the footage took eight months to edit and though the director had scrapped an ending where Johnson freezes to death

> *I'm that same David Crockett, fresh from the backwoods, half-horse, half-alligator, a little touched with the snapping-turtle; can wade the Mississippi, leap the Ohio, ride upon a streak of lightning, and slip without a scratch down a honey locust; can whip my weight in wild cats,—and if any gentleman pleases, for a ten dollar bill, he may throw in a panther, hug a bear too close for comfort, and eat any man opposed to Jackson.*
>
> **—Sketches and Eccentricities of Col. David Crockett, of West Tennessee, 1833**

> *I told my pap and mam I was comin' to the mountains to be a mountain man. They acted like they was gut shot. They said, "Son, make your life go here. Here is where the peoples is. Them mountains is for animals and savages." I said, "Mother Gue, the Rocky Mountains is the marrow of the world!" and by God, I was right!*
>
> **—Del Gue (Stefan Gierasch), Jeremiah Johnson**

on a remote mountaintop, Pollack's end product, a minimally narrative film which, as its director admits, "sustains itself on characters and moods, and therefore rhythms" brought its message home. In Pollack's words: "If I had to say in words what Jeremiah Johnson was about, for me it was about a man who wanted to find some place in the world where he and only he was in total control of his destiny, and found that no such place exists."

THE PRINCE OF PISTOLEERS

Quite a few mountain men (and desert rats) hired themselves out as guides and scouts when they returned to civilization. Some made their fame that way, like Kit Carson, who became so celebrated during his lifetime that he was a hero of boys' comic books. Some died that way, like Davy Crockett and Jim Bowie (creator of the bowie knife), who defended a little mission fortress in San Antonio, Texas, against General Antonio Lopez de Santa Anna's five thousand Mexican soldiers after a thirteen-day siege in 1836. Remember *The Alamo* (1960)? John Wayne and Richard Widmark did.

One of the West's most famous scouts, stage drivers, gamblers, shootists, and marshals (of Hays City, Kansas) was James Butler Hickock, known to his friends as Wild Bill. Unlike other boasters, Bill was truly a dead shot and had killed at least seven men (though in interviews he tended to up the number). With his long hair, immense mustache, buckskin outfits, unique way of wearing his ivory-han-

dled pistols (butts forward, ready for a flashy cross-draw), notorious recklessness (Buffalo Bill Cody sacked Hickock from his Wild West show for shooting so close to the actors that he gave them powder burns), and alleged relationship with Calamity Jane, he was just right for movies. William S. Hart (who apologized to audiences for not looking like Wild Bill), Yakima Canutt, Richard Dix, Forrest Tucker, Howard Keel, Robert Culp, Don Murray, Jeff Corey, Charles Bronson, and Richard Farnsworth are only a handful of the many who took a shot, so to speak, at portraying Bill. In the early forties, actor Bill Elliot made a career of it, playing Wild Bill in seven films.

Gary Cooper did Wild Bill proud, romancing a plucky Jean Arthur as the tomboyish Calamity Jane, in Cecil B. De Mille's lavish spectacle *The Plainsman* (1936). (You know it's got to be a De Mille picture when a solid wall of opening credits rises up into the clouds.) The film was a big, breathtaking adventure with Abraham Lincoln inspiring Bill Hickock and Bill Cody to help a heroic General George Armstrong Custer fight the renegade Cheyenne, with Jane following for love. Not a film for the history buff, but what fluff!

De Mille was game for this adventure: all sixty-four pistols in the film came from his private collection. He proved even gamer when he allowed Arthur to practice flicking a pistol from his hand with her twelve-foot (3.6m) bullwhip. (The actor De Mille was standing in for was a little nervous about it.) Eventually, she got it right...and the welts on De Mille's arm went down.

Wild Bill Hickock (Gary Cooper at right) has his hands full in a fight for his life in Cecil B. De Mille's paean to frontier romance (if not reality) **The Plainsman (1936).**

NOT LONG HAIR FOR LONG

George Armstrong Custer was undoubtedly the most famous—and infamous—American soldier who ever lived. At age twenty-three, he was the youngest brevet brigadier general in the Union Army and a Civil War hero. By age twenty-eight, he had been courtmartialed and suspended from a year of duty for harshness to his troops. At twenty-nine, he was reinstated and later charged the 7th Cavalry through heavy snow to his favorite tune, "Garry Owen," on the way to slaughtering a sleeping village of one hundred Cheyenne men, women, and children. At thirty-three, the dandy was posing for hunting pictures with the visiting Grand Duke Alexis of Russia. By age thirty-five, Custer had published an autobiography, *My Life on the Plains*, and at thirty-six, he was violating America's treaty with the Sioux and scouring their sacred Black Hills (Pah Sapa) for gold. A year later, he was one of three generals chasing the renegade Sioux and Cheyenne in Montana. Anxious for a first strike, victory, and perhaps even a shot at the presidency (against Ulysses S. Grant, who hated him), Custer surged 250 members of the 7th Cavalry ahead from the rest of the army's forces, thundering into the Little Bighorn River Valley, and found himself face-to-face with twenty-five hundred warriors. He didn't get any older, but he became one hell of a hero.

From 1909 onward, a lot of movies have shown Custer in a lot of lights: Francis Ford was heroic in *Custer's Last Raid* (1912). Richard Mulligan was a narcissistic psychopath in Arthur Penn's lusty adaptation of Thomas Berger's sprawling novel *Little Big Man* (1970). Henry Fonda approximated Custer as a cold but noble martinet in *Fort Apache* (1948). Ronald Reagan fraternized with Reb Jeb Stuart (Errol Flynn) in *The Santa Fe Trail* (1940). Leslie Nielsen, Robert Shaw, Bruce Dern, Robert Lansing, and Keir Dullea all turned in stands as Custer. And even Marcello Mastroianni had his chance in *Touche Pas la Femme Blanche* (1973).

Errol Flynn immortalized a splendid, if slightly swashbuckling, rendition in Raoul Walsh's *They Died with Their Boots On* (1941). His Custer is rootless, arrogant, defensive of his masculinity, and impatient for personal gain (in the manner of some current opinions), but his Custer is also (sit down for this one) an Indian advocate. Here, it's Custer's old West Point nemesis, Ned Sharpe, Jr. (a pinch-faced Arthur Kennedy), who plans to run a railroad through the Black Hills. Custer pledges to protect the Sioux's sacred domain and is ultimately forced into his Last Stand, where he is cut down— albeit with respect—by Crazy Horse (Anthony Quinn).

Walsh's film was the eighth time that Flynn had been teamed up with Olivia de Havilland (Libby Custer). Their goodbye before Custer leaves for the Little Bighorn is one of the most touching partings in western film history. The film had its less graceful goodbyes as well: director Michael Curtiz, originally slated for the project, was fired before filming ever started because the sensitive Tasmanian Flynn could no longer stomach working with the bullying Hungarian.

The Screen Actors Guild's poor selection of mounted extras led to more tragic partings. So many extras were falling off horses that Warner Brothers sent doctors, nurses, hospital tents, and an ambulance to the location, forty miles (64km) north of Hollywood; Anthony Quinn added to the merriment by hiring a hearse to follow along behind. The hearse was not uncalled for, as three extras died during the filming: one broke his neck, one had a heart attack, and the sword of a third lodged (hilt down) into an exploding bridge he was riding over, and he landed on it. Truly, they died with their boots on.

Reality Check: Just Because You're Paranoid Doesn't Mean They're Not Out to Get You

It wasn't easy being the Prince of Pistoleers, not when you were broke, your reputation preceded you, and your eyesight was failing. Wild Bill Hickock was so jumpy that he shot and killed his friend Mike Williams, who was rushing to help him in a gunfight with a gambler in Abilene. Sliding into any saloon, Hickock watched the crowd like a hawk. As one observer noted, he "looked like a man who lived in expectation of getting killed." Usually insisting on sitting with his back to the wall, he was finally teased by his friends into relaxing his habit.

As it turned out, he relaxed a little too much. On August 2, 1876, Hickock was shot in the back of the head in Deadwood saloon number 10 by a cross-eyed drunk named Jack McCall, who said he didn't face Bill directly because "I didn't want to commit suicide." Bill's last poker hand—a full house, aces over eights—became known as the "dead man's hand." The bullet itself went through Hickock's skull and lodged in the hand of Captain Frank Massey, who never had it removed and was fond of saying, "Gents, the bullet which killed Wild Bill has come to town."

LADIES AND GENTLEMEN, IN THE CENTER RING...WITH HIS PANTS DOWN

A legend in his own time, Buffalo Bill Cody's life has long been romanticized on celluloid. Wild Bill Wellman's debt to Darryl Zanuck for *The Ox-Bow Incident* put a 1944 Buffalo Bill bio pic on his plate whether he wanted it or not. His screenwriter, Gene Fowler, had originally wanted to do a film about "the fakiest guy who ever lived." But after three months of digging up dirt together, Fowler blurted out, "Bill, you know, you can't stab Babe Ruth, you couldn't kill Dempsey, you can't kill any of these wonderful heroes that our kids, my kids, your kids, my grandchildren, your grandchildren, everyone else worships and likes. Buffalo Bill is a great figure, and we cannot do it. What do you say? What do we do?" What they did was get drunk and burn the original script, page by page.

Buffalo Bill Cody (Paul Newman) made up in wardrobe what he lacked in morals in Robert Altman's icon-bashing **Buffalo Bill and the Indians: or Sitting Bull's History Lesson (1976).**

> I looked on Buffalo Bill [Cody] as being the first movie star and went from there.
>
> —Paul Newman

Reality Check: Just Plains Jane

Jean Arthur was pert. Doris Day was more so. Yvonne De Carlo was lovely. Frances Farmer was fine. Jane Russell was more full-figured. Abby Dalton was beautiful. Stephanie Powers, Kim Darby, and Jane Alexander were all attractive tomboys. Ms. Martha Jane Canary, however, was no looker, though she was a hooker for the army. She could shoot, swear, and booze with the best of them. She could spit pretty well, too. One night after lobbing a gob of tobacco juice at an actress she didn't particularly like, Jane tossed a dollar onto the stage, yelling, "That's for your damn dress!"

By 1976, someone else had worked up the nerve to take Bill down a peg or ten: "When you give someone a hero you are lying to them," Robert Altman stated simply. That attitude made him the perfect debunker to show the seamy underside of one of America's greatest bunco artists. Scalpel set to separate tarnish from tinsel (a theme Altman had explored in *Nashville*, 1975, and would return to later in *The Player*, 1992), the director served up a Buffalo Bill who, as critic Jack Kroll of *Newsweek* said, "couldn't track an Indian across a sandbox."

Altman's *Buffalo Bill and the Indians: or Sitting Bull's History Lesson* (1976) may have been iconoclastic, but it was a spectacle almost as grand as Cody's original show (ready?), "Buffalo Bill's Wild West, or Life Among the Red Men and Road Agents of the Plains and Prairies, an Equine Dramatic Exposition on Grass and Under Canvass of the Advantages of Frontiersmen and Cowboys." Having assembled a cast that included Paul Newman, Burt Lancaster, Geraldine Chaplin, Harvey Keitel, Kevin McCarthy, and Joel Grey (and an eight-track system for recording his Altmanesque overlapping dialogue— this time cowritten with Alan Rudolph), the director then called on production designer Tony Masters *(2001: A Space Odyssey)* to build an entire tent town (what Bill's troupe had actually lived in) for his ensemble to frolic in and get the feel of for two weeks before shooting began at the Stoney Indian Reserve in Alberta, Canada. Bill's (Newman's) tent alone boasted $500,000 worth of antiques.

Altman also roped in performers who Cody himself would have been pleased to snag: Tom Bews, Canada's primo saddle bronc rider; Fred Larson, the six-foot-six-inch (198.1cm) former FBI agent who was the seventh-ranked steer wrestler in the world; Jim Dodds, a three-time Canadian bull-riding champ; Canadian wagon-driving champ Tommy Class, who was at the reins for the Deadwood Stage attack; and Joy and Jerry Duce, sisters who taught themselves to ride at ages seven and nine, respectively, with the help of a trick saddle and a book called *140 Ways to Break Your Neck*, and performed the "Hippodrome Stand" (standing on the back of a galloping horse) and the "Suicide Drag" (hanging upside down between a galloping horse's legs).

Joel Grey, whom Altman had recruited because of his work in *Cabaret* (1972), was back in the emcee saddle again, devising florid speech patterns based on the original publicity material created by Major John Burke. Grey also helped Geraldine Chaplin (Annie Oakley) with her "Bullet Ballet." Altman even went Cody one better and staged the first-ever exhibition of buffalo wrestling.

Before he was "Branded" or "The Rifleman," Chuck Connors (center) was none other than Geronimo in the 1942 film of the same name.

DOING A GOOD TURN FOR THE RED MAN

> *I don't go as far as to think that the only good Indians are dead Indians, but I believe nine out of every ten are, and I shouldn't like to inquire too closely into the case of the tenth.*
>
> —**Theodore Roosevelt, from a lecture in 1886**

Why in the movies did so many Plains Indians make suicidal charges on fortified army positions, when their historical counterparts usually rode just out of rifle range, committing to full-scale attack only if they were assured of a win? Why was "How" so often the western Indian greeting, when there are about two hundred distinct Indian dialects in North America alone? Why did so many Indian extras slap on a generic war bonnet, breastplate, fringed buckskin shirt, moccasins, tomahawk, shield, bow, arrows, and rifle to look authentic, when there are nearly five hundred Indian nations that could have been represented—all in strikingly different dress—on screen?

What can we say about the Indians in westerns? For starters, they usually weren't Indians. In Cecil B. De Mille's *They Died with Their Boots On* (1941), actual Native Americans were so scarce on the set (the authentic cast consisted of sixteen braves from North Dakota) that some of the warriors filmed for Custer's Last Stand had to be kept far enough from the camera to hide their blond handlebar mustaches and full beards. And in the much idealized *Geronimo* (1962), star Chuck Connors was told to ditch his brown contact lenses because they dulled his sparkling blue eyes.

Over the years, there have been a few Indian stars, their careers almost always limited to westerns: William Eagle Shirt, John War Eagle, Chief Thundercloud, Chief Yowlachie, Jay (Tonto) Silverheels, Iron-Eyes Cody, Chief Big Tree, Chief Dan George, Will Sampson, and Graham Greene. But more commonly, lead Indian characters were the realm of paler players like Frank De Kova *(F Troop)* and a whole tribe of others.

Let's not mince words. Movie Indians were usually the bad guys, one of the natural hazards of western migration (like rattlesnakes, deserts, mountains...), with an added zest for fire water, roast dog, and torture. According to Ralph and Natasha Friar's book *The Only Good Indian*, from the years 1909 to 1964, Indians swarmed over the hills to attack peaceful settlers in 112 films, plundered wagon trains in 72, fell on forts in 45, sacked stagecoaches in 32, and rushed the railroad in 14. Ironically, of the 170 ethnic groups that make up Native Americans today, the vast majority of westerns focused on the Sioux and Apache tribes, those most famous for their ferocity in fighting white encroachment.

Even when filmmakers woke up and smelled the sage tea, the outcome could still be a little incomplete. John Ford, though he did occasionally use Indian actors, saw the error of his ways (in gleefully killing them off like flies in most of his movies). His last picture, *Cheyenne Autumn* (1964), though a fine apology, is still a melodramatic account of the Cheyenne's flight from the arid wastes of Oklahoma reservations to their homeland in Montana, with non-Indians starring in major Indian roles and the character of a reliable schoolmarm thrown in to vouch for their good conduct.

Richard Brooks' uncompromising and powerful *The Last Hunt* (1955) showed the wholesale slaughter of buffalo on the Great Plains (and the planned starvation of the Indians there), but its focus was still white. In Samuel Fuller's wonderful 1957 film *Run of the Arrow* (which brought Colonel Tim McCoy back to the screen after a fifteen-year absence), Confederate soldier Private O'Meara

(Rod Steiger) joins a cultured group of Sioux rather than accept defeat at the hands of the North, only to turn away from them in the end to become a "true American."

The Vietnam War in turn brought a 1960s sensibility about ethnic genocide to films like *Soldier Blue* (1970), whose prerelease ads called it "the most honest American film ever made." The film depicted the 1864 Sand Creek Massacre of five hundred Cheyenne and Arapaho men, women, and children. (One of the massacre's leaders, John Chivington, managed to coin these immortal words: "Kill and scalp all, big and little, nits make lice.") Its heart was in the right place, but it was a white heart.

Similarly, Robert Redford was originally offered the title role of a Paiute Indian in *Tell Them Willie Boy Is Here* (1969). When

Redford declined the role and suggested that the filmmakers cast a real Indian, Universal told Redford they couldn't find one. Robert Blake did it full of admirably cool fire, but he weren't no Paiute.

We can't quite seem to let go of ourselves, can we? Will Rogers (who was part Cherokee) may have campaigned for Indian equality. And Marlon Brando may have sent Sacheen Little Feather to refuse Brando's Oscar for *The Godfather* (1973) and to chastise Hollywood. But films that have treated Indians as regular human beings with worthwhile cultures, as opposed to victims or aggressors, are few and far between.

Two movies released in 1950 made an early moral stab at doing so. Anthony Mann's *Devil's Doorway* shows a Shoshone chief, Lance Poole (Robert Taylor), coming back from white school and highly decorated white service as a sergeant in the Union Army, only to find that the the Homestead Act has taken away his ranch. In a breathtaking Medicine Bow, Wyoming, setting, Poole gets a big dose of white prejudice. Though he enlists the legal help of Orrie Masters (Paula Raymond) and falls in love with her in the legal process (though, sadly, it is a love that can never be), corruption wins out. Finding no other way to protect his land and his Shoshone people (from, among other things, an invasion of the white man's grazing sheep), he organizes his braves into a tactical fighting unit. The final battle scene is tremendous (and tremendously strange with its incessant bleatings of sheep), but as usual, the odds make for a tragic ending.

MGM, playing a waiting game, didn't release *Devil's Doorway* until the ethnocentric ice had been broken that same year by a film called *Broken Arrow* (itself held by Twentieth Century Fox for more than a year until its star, Jimmy Stewart, proved himself bankable in the saddle with *Winchester '73* (1950). The fact-based story of *Broken Arrow* reverses the color scheme: Stewart plays Civil War veteran Tom Jeffords, who, sick of killing, saves the life of a wounded Apache boy. Jeffords ruminates: "'My mother is crying,' he said. Funny, it never struck me that an Apache would cry over her child like any other woman. Apache's a wild animal, we always said."

Jeffords' narration sets the tone for tolerance for the rest of director Delmer Daves' beautiful film. With his newfound insights, Jeffords tries to mediate a peace between Chiricahua chief Cochise (Jeff Chandler) and the Arizona army (and Indian-hating locals). Along the way to forging this fragile truce, he falls for the young Apache Sonseeahray (Debra Paget). After a courtship as fragile as the truce that Jeffords, the Apache, and the one-armed "Christian General" Howard (Basil Ruysdael) are trying to hold to, the couple marries (in one of a number of beautiful and realistic Native American ceremonies shown in this film). But with renegades on both sides brewing hatred, their love is short-lived. In the end, it is the bereaved white man who must listen to the red man for words of tolerance.

Ironically enough, Delmer Daves wanted to cast a Native American as Cochise, but when Cochise's real grandson, Nino Cochise, tried out for the role, the studio told him he just wasn't the

What's in a Name!

Wild Bill wasn't the only dude to get a fancy moniker hung on him. Here are a few other nom-de-shoots—the real McCoy, courtesy of quote collector Richard Dillon.

Screen Name	Real Name	Screen Name	Real Name
Annie Oakley (Little Sure Shot)	Phoebe Anne Mozee	Jay Silverheels	Harold Smith, actor
Apache Kid	Sergeant Kid, U.S. Army Apache scout turned renegade	Johnny-Behind-the-Deuce	John O'Rourke, Tombstone gambler
Baron of Arizona	Jim Addison Reavis, frontier conman	Kid Curry	Harvey Logan, member of Butch Cassidy's Wild Bunch
Bat Masterson	Bartholomew Masterson	The Law West of the Pecos	Judge Roy Bean, Texas politico
Big Foot Wallace	William Wallace, Texas Ranger and gunman	Long Hair	General George Armstrong Custer
Black Bart	Charles E. Bolton, bandit poet of California	Lost Dutchman	Jacob Walz, Arizona prospector
Buckskin Frank Leslie	Tombstone gunman	Mysterious Dave	David Mather, Dodge City gunman
Bullmoose	Theodore Roosevelt, U.S. president and western devotee	Ned Buntline	Edward Zane Carroll, dime-novel author
Cattle Annie and Little Britches	Oklahoma girl bandits	Old Fuss-and-Feathers	Winfield Scott, Mexican War general
Cattle Kate	Ella Watson, accused of rustling and lynched in Wyoming	Old Rough-and-Ready	Zachary Taylor, U.S. president and Mexican War general
Cherokee Bill	Crawford Goldsby, half-breed and outlaw	Pancho Villa	Doroteo Arango, Mexican revolutionary
Deadwood Dick	Nat Love, African-American cowboy	Pathfinder	John C. Fremont, western explorer
Deaf Charley	O.C. Hanks, member of Butch Cassidy's Wild Bunch	Poker Alice	Alice Tubbs, mining-town gambler
Dynamite Dick	Dan Clifton, Oklahoma outlaw with Bill Doolin gang	Pegleg Annie	Annie Morrow, western prostitute
El Patrio	Joaquin Murieta, California rebel leader	Rattlesnake Jake	Charles Fallon, possible outlaw
		Robin Hood of Texas	Sam Bass, outlaw
Grizzly Adams	James Capen Adams	Soapy Smith	Jefferson Smith, saloon owner lynched in Alaska
Hurricane Bill	William Martin, Texas gang member	Three-Finger Jack	Manuel Garcia, California bandit

Red Like Me

The question is, who hasn't gotten gussied up in buckskin and body makeup to go on the warpath or nobly pass the peace pipe? See if you can guess which white-eyes go where by the subtle hints about their other gigs.

Film	Role	Hint	Actor
1. Behold My Wife *(1935)*	Tonita Stormcloud	Sabotage *star*	A. Adam West
2. Ramona *(1936)*	Allesandro	Cocoon *comeback kid*	B. George C. Scott
3. Desert Gold *(1936)*	Moya	Me Tarzan, Buck Rogers, Flash Gordon	C. Rock Hudson
			D. Leonard Nimoy
4. Northwest Mounted Police *(1940)*	Louvette Corbeau	Mrs. Chaplin	E. Sam Waterston
5. Buffalo Bill *(1944)*	Yellow Hand	Zorba the Greek	F. Sylvia Sidney
6. Marshall of Cripple Creek *(1947)*	Little Beaver	Our Gang kid, without cockatoo	G. Buster Crabbe
7. Unconquered *(1947)*	Chief Guyasito	Frank-ly, a monster	H. Buster Keaton
8. Winchester '73 *(1950)*	Young Bull	A Giant of a picture	I. Elvis Presley
9. Across the Wide Missouri (1951)	Yellow Shirt	Fantasy Islander	J. Dennis Weaver
10. The Battles of Chief Pontiac *(1952)*	Chief Pontiac	The Old Wolf	K. Don Ameche
			L. Yul Brynner
11. Arrowhead *(1953)*	Torriano	Billy Crystal's Curly	M. Boris Karloff
12. Column South *(1953)*	Menquito	McCloud riding bareback	N. Raquel Welch
13. Old Overland Trail *(1953)*	Black Hawk	Vulcanized	O. Robert Wagner
14. Broken Lance *(1954)*	Joe	He's only half a Hart	P. Paulette Goddard
15. Drum Beat *(1954)*	Captain Jack	Dirty Harry's Polish rival	Q. Desi Arnaz, Jr.
16. Walk the Proud Land *(1956)*	Tainay	"Oh, Mrs. Robinson"	R. Robbie Benson
17. The Light in the Forest *(1958)*	Young True Son	"Book 'em, Danno"	S. Ricardo Montalban
18. Geronimo *(1962)*	Delahay	"To the Bat Cave!"	T. Martin Landau
19. Kings of the Sun *(1963)*	Black Eagle	"Etcetera, etcetera, etcetera"	U. Anthony Quinn
20. Pajama Party *(1964)*	Chief Rotten Eagle	The great stone face	V. Paul Lynde
21. The Hallelujah Trail *(1965)*	Chief Walks Stooped Over	I.M.F. makeup master	W. Charles Bronson
			X. Lon Chaney, Jr.
22. Texas Across the River Kronk *(1966)*	Oceans Eleven	Ecclesiast	Y. Joey Bishop
			Z. Robert Blake
23. Navajo Joe *(1967)*	Navajo Joe	What would Loni say?	AA. Anne Bancroft
24. Stay Away, Joe *(1968)*	Joe Lightcloud	The King of any nation	BB. Julie Newmar
25. Mackenna's Gold *(1969)*	Heshke	Catwoman the second	CC. David Carradine
26. 100 Rifles *(1969)*	Sarita	A.D. 1969	DD. Jack Palance
27. The McMasters *(1970)*	White Feather	Grasshopper	EE. Burt Reynolds
28. Billy Two Hats *(1973)*	Billy	"Son of Lucy..."	FF. James MacArthur
29. Rancho Deluxe *(1975)*	Cecil Coison	He'll fly away	
30. The Villain *(1979)*	Nervous Elk	Hollywod Squares center square	
31. Running Brave *(1983)*	Bobby Mills	Voice of Beauty's Beast	
32. Firestarter *(1984)*	John Rainbird	Patton's Hollywood stand-in	

Answers: 1=F, 2=K, 3=G, 4=P, 5=U, 6=Z, 7=M, 8=C, 9=S, 10=X, 11=DD, 12=J, 13=D, 14=O, 15=W, 16=AA, 17=FF, 18=A, 19=L, 20=H, 21=T, 22=Y, 23=EE, 24=I, 25=BB, 26=N, 27=CC, 28=Q, 29=E, 30=V, 31=R, 32=B

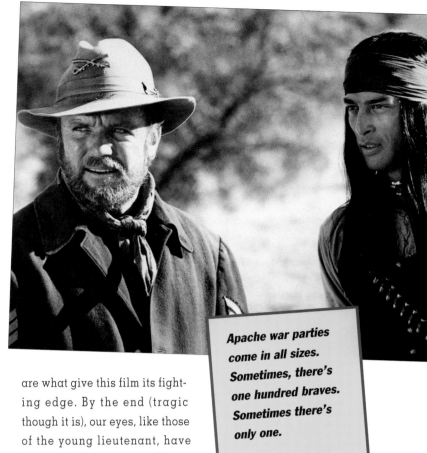

Crusty cavalry corporal (Richard Jaeckel at left) and Ke-Ni-Tay (Jorge Luke at right) may be wondering if following scout MacIntosh (a great and grizzled Burt Lancaster) will get their throats cut Apache-style in Robert Aldrich's brutal Ulzana's Raid *(1972).*

right type. Perhaps this was because Jeff Chandler's agent had bought the script and sold the actor along with it (though not fully accurate, Chandler's performance was genuine: he came only three votes shy of getting a Best Supporting Actor Oscar for his work in the film). Four hundred other Apaches were used, however; one of them, Jim Red Finger, had to wear the uncharacteristic covering of a buckskin shirt to cover up the REMEMBER PEARL HARBOR tattoo on his chest.

Stewart, though hesitant to commit to a multipicture deal with Fox (he was one of the few stars who didn't hitch up with any one studio for security), dived into his role. The seventeen-year-old Paget jumped into the deep end herself: one of her brown contact lenses went weird under the spotlights (and the 110°F [43.3°C] Arizona summer heat), she was bitten by a tarantula, and she was rescued from drowning at a local swimming hole. She must have loved location work.

Showing the Apache in an equally honest (comparatively speaking) but distinctly more brutal light was Robert Aldrich's *Ulzana's Raid* (1972), which replaced sticky sentiment with large doses of respect and fear. When MacIntosh, an aging scout (a fifty-seven-year-old battered and buckskinned Burt Lancaster), agrees to lead an army detachment after a renegade named Ulzana, who has fled Arizona's San Carlos Indian Reservation with stolen horses and a handful of men, he knows how harrowing his pursuit will be. But the young eastern officer with him, Lieutenant Garnet DeBuin (Bruce Davison), hasn't a clue.

The mayhem that their quarry leaves in his wake is mind-bending: a woman shot in the head by a soldier who then killed himself to spare them both inevitable torture; a rape victim trussed in a wagon; homes and bodies burned—all fodder for past stereo-types, but this time, just real. For in the Apache way, Ulzana is out to reclaim his stripped power via the deaths of others. As Apache army scout Ke-Ni-Tay (Jorge Luke, in a marvelously taciturn perfor-mance) explains to the uncomprehending DeBuin: "Ulzana is long time in the agency. His power is very thin. The smell in his nose are all smells of the agency; old smell, smell of woman, smell of dog, smell of children. Man with old smell in the nose is old man. Ulzana looking for new smell: smell of pony running, smell of burn-ing, smell of bullet, power."

The journey becomes a highly strategic game of cat-and-mouse with Ulzana's alternately mounted and (through a slick trick) dismounted band of warriors. The examination of ethnic identity, the unflinching specifics of Apache war strategy (gutting one of your horses into a water hole to poison it for a pursuing ene-my, for example), and MacIntosh's appreciation of their harsh life

are what give this film its fight-ing edge. By the end (tragic though it is), our eyes, like those of the young lieutenant, have been opened in respect and fear.

A more historic film on the Apache that tries to tell it like it was (for the most part) is Walter

> *Apache war parties come in all sizes. Sometimes, there's one hundred braves. Sometimes there's only one.*
>
> *—Burt Lancaster,* Ulzana's Raid

Hill's *Geronimo* (1993). Geronimo—as he was named by the Mexicans; his Indian name was Goyathlay—succeeded Cochise in the spiritual-military leadership of the Chiricahua Apache. Already embittered by the murder of his mother, wife, and three small chil-dren by Mexican troops (who were then trying to stamp the Chiricahua out of Arizona), Geronimo was eventually herded by the newly empowered whites onto the San Carlos reservation in 1877.

But Geronimo wasn't the stay-at-home type. By 1886, he and his band had broken out three times. During his raids, he forced the resignation of famed Indian fighter General George Crook (Nan-Tan-Lupan, or "Grey Wolf Chief," played here by Gene Hackman); incurred the wrath of Buffalo Bill's nemesis, General Nelson Miles; eluded forty-two formidably outfitted companies of U.S. troops, not to mention four thousand Mexican soldiers; and became the last Indian leader to surrender to the U.S. government.

Hill's beautifully landscaped, historically framed tribute to this drama follows an impressionable West Point graduate, Britton Davis (Matt Damon), as he assists a sympathetic young southern officer, Charles Gatewood (the sensitive Jason Patric), in his mis-sion to bring in the vengeful war chief (the forbidding Wes Studi, who chilled audiences as the heartless Magua in *Last of the Mohicans*, 1992). The focus here is on principles (embodied by Gatewood) versus pragmatics (embodied by Crook), and personal honor (embodied by Geronimo) versus deceit (embodied by

ABOVE: Richard Harris prepares for the trial of his life as he is about to be hung from eagle claws inserted through slits in his chest in a sacred ceremony from A Man Called Horse *(1970). OPPOSITE: Kicking Bird (Graham Greene) passes something to ex-lieutenant John Dunbar (Kevin Costner) for his journey away from the Lakota people at the heartfelt ending of* Dances with Wolves *(1990).*

to become a chief. The film was unique: what other Hollywood production could boast 80 percent of its dialogue in unsubtitled Lakota, and with so many Indians playing Indians?

Though shot with what the *New York Daily News* praised as "unflinching realism" in Durango, Mexico, and on the Rosebud Indian Reservation, some viewers flinched at the sight of Dame Judith Anderson playing an old Lakota crone. Credibility was further dented by the fact that the film's torturously famous test of manhood—the "Sioux Sun Vow"—turned out to be much closer to an O-ki-pa ceremony of the Mandan tribe used to attract buffalo to their hunting grounds. In the ceremony, Harris (under stuntmeister Enos Yakima Canutt's supervision, and falling only once, when the cords suddenly snapped), was hanged and twirled 7 feet (2.1m) off the ground by spikes lanced through his pectoral muscles (really a camouflaged belt around his chest). Apart from that scene's artistic license, it was quite a movie.

And now the envelope please....It wasn't until 1990's *Dances with Wolves* that Indian life got the kind of popular spotlight to enthrall audiences (without the distractions of ritual sacrifice). Kevin Costner's adventures as Civil War veteran John Dunbar, whose one-man frontier posting brings him into intimate contact with a group of Lakota people (and the dangers the tribe faces from an encroaching white military presence), swept a saddlebag full of Oscars and brought the western back onto its feet (with a little extra help from the televised version of Larry McMurtry's *Lonesome Dove*). How can you not relate to a film that shows a tired Indian father lying down to rest in his wickiup (tipi), only to dislodge a child's toy from under his back and fling it to the side with a grunt, just like any other father would?

This time around Indians played Indians as people. Graham Greene (Kicking Bird), who would soon be costarring in *Thunderheart* (1992); Rodney A. Grant (Wind in His Hair), who would costar in *Geronimo* (1993); and Tantoo Cardinal (Black Shawl), who would costar in *Silent Tongue* (1994), all turned in fully fleshed performances.

The actors certainly weren't rushed. Even at a generous 181 minutes (what most of us saw in the theaters), the film had been considerably consolidated from the 330 minutes of Costner's first whack at editing and the 240 minutes of the "director's cut," which

General Miles, who lured in Geronimo only to literally railroad him, his followers, and even the Apache scouts who helped Miles catch him, to banishment in Florida).

Screenwriter John Milius' (*Jeremiah Johnson*) violence-laden story is right on the money. With excellently underplayed performances from all, including Rodney A. Grant's renegade, Mangas; Steve Revis's conflicted scout, Chato; Studi's hard-bitten warrior, played without sentiment or resentment; and Robert Duvall (whose penchant for reality in death scenes is unnerving) as grizzled scout leader Al Sieber, who supposedly sustained twenty-nine bullet and arrow wounds in his time, *Geronimo* is worthy of the man whose name paratroopers yell as they jump into the abyss.

Occasionally—very occasionally—westerns focus on Indian culture. In *A Man Called Horse* (1970), Richard Harris predated the white-Indian wars with his portrayal of an 1820s English aristocrat captured by the Lakota (Sioux) during a hunting party. Harris' character is at first made a virtual slave, but through courage and appreciation of the Lakota way of life, he rises through their ranks played in London and found its way to video release. (The director's version includes Dunbar and Kicking Bird hunting in a forest ruined by white hunters; a scene in which the Lakota attack a band of white buffalo hunters, which motivates Dunbar's tragic return to white society; more courtship with Stands with a Fist [Mary McDonnell]; Kicking Bird's report of his original sighting of the naked Dunbar; and more madness at Fort Sedgewick.)

The script was by Michael Blake, who had written Costner's screen debut, *Stacy's Knights* (1981), a gambling film. Costner began filming near Pierre, South Dakota, on July 18, 1989, and was finished by November 23. In the process, 150 locals were hired on as extras, 200 period costumes were crafted (by costume designer Elsa Zamperelli, whose budget came in at $400,000), 625 deerskins were tailored, 18 world-class Indian riders (who hailed from ten different tribes) were hired, and 2,300 buffalo were rented from the largest privately owned herd in the world, housed full-time at Roy Houck's Triple U Ranch. (Later, Houck made a few extra dollars supplying Al's Oasis in Oacama, South Dakota, with 100 percent pure *Dances with Wolves* burgers made from some of his four-footed celebrities. Fame has its price.)

The ceremony of the Lakota buffalo hunt (all 60,000 filmed feet [18,288m] of it) is perhaps the most spectacular scene. It was tough enough to muster the needed beasts, but keeping the unpredictable creatures running in the right direction was no joyride, either. At 1,600 pounds (726.4kg) each, it took wranglers six hours to round up all 2,300 critters (along with Cody and Mammoth, two buffs lent by musician Neil Young). Add to that 24 "buffaloids" (fiberglass phonies equipped with pneumatic breathing and kicking devices), horses, and actors, and you have controlled chaos at its best. Oddly, the chaos was quiet (as is a real buffalo hunt) and the requisite snorting, screaming, and neighing had to be dubbed in later.

Also of note is the fact that Two Socks (the movie's lupine hero) was played by two timberwolves, Buck and Teddy, and though trained by the same folks who brought us Benji (that wonderful canine hero of the 1970s), they weren't quite as cuddly. In fact, during the filming of the wolf scenes, kids were removed from the set because wolves tend to turn nasty when they're stared at too long (it's a good thing the drama wasn't a play). Kevin avoided the attack hazard in his nine days of playing with them by separating himself from the pair with a thin wire that Buck and Teddy were trained not to cross. Good wolves.

> This movie is certainly not a history lesson or an attempt to set the record straight. But I do hope that our efforts to authenticate the people and places we're dealing with will finally show a side of their legacy that has been forgotten— their honor.
>
> **—Kevin Costner, on Dances with Wolves**

Arrows for Their Quivers

If you were lucky enough to be a critic seeing Dances with Wolves, *you may have received a little extra ammo in your press kit: a five-page glossary of Lakota words (just in case you wanted to tone up your review). Here are some of the words they learned, minus the hard-to-explain markings. See what kind of phrases (critical and otherwise) you can patch together. We'll give you a few examples of pidgin Lakota, Hollywood-style, to start off with.*

English Phrase	Lakota Equivalent	English Phrase	Lakota Equivalent
Attack friend	Takpe kola	Like book better	Wastelake wowapi isom waste
Write wrong word	Wowa ipayeh wicoiye	Challenge morning paper	Anike hihanni hci mni hwoha
Hot air	Kate wiconi	Hate bad language	Walitelasni sica woglaka
Need happy end	Taku cin iyuskin ihanke	No taste	Hiya yuta iyute
Summer hit	Bloket'u ape	Invite revenge	Kico tokicun
Shoot star	Kute wicahpi		

English Word	Lakota Equivalent	English Word	Lakota Equivalent	English Word	Lakota Equivalent	English Word	Lakota Equivalent
air	wiconi	dream	ihanbla	hunt	wokilepi	ride	akan yanke
ancestor	unki tokaptu	drink	yatke	hurt	yazan	see	iyokisice
arrow	wahinkpe	eat	wote	ill	kuje	scare	yusinyeye
attack	takpe	end	ihanke	invite	kico	shoot	kute
bad	sica	enemy	toka	knife	mila	sleep	istinma
believe	wicala	evil	sice	know	slolye	small	cikala
better	isom waste	face	ite	language	woglaka	smoke	sota
best	lila waste	fall	pt'anyetu	like	wastelake	spring	wetu
blood	we	fight	kiza	love	tehila	star	wicahpi
bone	huku	find	iyeya	luck	oglu	strong	wasake
book	wowapi	fly	kinyan	man	wicasa	summer	bloket'u
breathe	oniyan	friend (male)	kola	many	ota	talk	iye
buffalo	tatanka	gift	waku	marriage	kiciyuzapi	taste	yuta iyute
burn	span	girl	wicincala	medicine	pejuta	thank you	pila maya ye
bury	ha	give	ku	morning	hihanni hci	tired	yugo
carve	bago	good	waste	mother	ina	ugly	owanyank sice
challenge	anike	hair	pehin	name	caje	vegetable	watotola
chicken	koke yahùnla	hand	nape	need	taku cin	war	okicize
climb	ali	happy	iyuskin	new	teca	water	mni
cold	osni	hatchet	nazunspe cikala	night	hanhepi	winter	waniyetu
cook	spankiyan	hate	walitelasni	no	hiya	wolf	sungmanitu tanka
corn	wagmiza	head	nata	one	wanji	woman	winyan
courage	woohitika	heart	cante	pain	tawa	word	wicoiye
cry	ceya	hero	wohiye najin	paper	mni hwoha	work	wowasi
dark	oiyakpaza	hide	taha	peace	wowahwa	write	wowa
day	anpetu	hit	ape	pretty	owayang waste	wrong	ipayeh
dead	te	hot	kate	read	wayawa		
doctor	pejuta wicasa	hunger	ocin	revenge	tokicun		

LEGENDARY GUNS

Some say that the right to bear arms is the root of ensuring individual freedom. Some say that same cherished habit (with its canonization in the West and in the western) is the root of a deadly "gun culture" and the soaring crime rate that plagues America today. Eli Whitney (inventor of the cotton gin) gave gun totin' its first big boost at the end of the eighteenth century when he began to mass-produce interchangeable musket parts. Samuel Colt took it further when he patented the first practical revolver in 1836 and then cranked out 300,000 of them during the Civil War. By 1873, Colt's .45-caliber "Peacemaker" revolver got the benefit of a metallic cartridge in place of the traditional powder and ball. Eventually, the Colt .45 would take the same ammo as the most famous gun in the West, Oliver Winchester's .44-caliber "Frontier Model" repeating rifle, with its fifteen-bullet capacity.

With Colts, Winchesters ("the rifle that won the West"), Henrys, Sharps (favored by buffalo hunters for their long range and heavy bullet), Springfields (the economical single-shot favorite of the Civil War and the Indian wars of the 1870s and 1880s), Smith & Wessons, Remingtons, shotguns (considered unfair in combat), Gatling guns (the seven-barreled precursor to the machine gun), and Derringer's "Little Darlin'" (the gun used to assassinate Abraham Lincoln), the West was armed and dangerous.

If you could use it well, a gun could make you rich, famous, dead...or any combination of the three. Preacher's son John Wesley Hardin (whom Rock Hudson portrayed in *The Lawless Breed*, 1953) killed forty-four men (even with the respite of a seventeen-year jail term), and was eventually shot in the back of the head in an El Paso saloon by a lawman whose life he had previously threatened. (The outlaw's infamy was secured with the title of Bob Dylan's 1968 album,

John Wesley Harding.) Rock's Hardin died remorseful. The real John Wesley did not.

True, gunslingers often filed off the sights on their pistols for a faster draw, but a gun didn't even have to be loaded to make you famous. In California between 1875 and 1882, Black Bart (Dan Duryea in 1948's *Black Bart*), whose calling cards read the "Po-8", managed to rob twenty-eight Wells Fargo stages with an empty shotgun. He left a little poem at each holdup, such as:

> I've labored long and hard for bread,
> For honor and for riches,
> But on my corns too long you've tread,
> You fine-haired sons of bitches.

Just a Couple of Nice Guys

In the gentler mode of Black Bart were a couple of gunslicks who made a killing at the box office: George Leroy Parker and Harry Longbaugh. George Roy Hill's good-natured *Butch Cassidy and the Sundance Kid* (1969) was one of the most popular (and highest-grossing) westerns ever made. Hollywood may have whitewashed outlaws in the forties and psychoanalyzed them in the fifies, but with the success of Arthur Penn's *Bonnie and Clyde* (1967), the late 1960s could serve them up just as they were.

Following this duo of turn-of-the-century bank and train robbers and their "Wild Bunch" (a.k.a. the Hole in the Wall Gang), Hill's movie hightails it to South America with Butch (Paul Newman) and Sundance (Robert Redford), after a Pinkerton Detective Agency manhunt has put an end to their stateside activities. Once in Bolivia, Butch and Sundance eventually revert to their old outlaw ways—with tragic results. Hunted down in a small mining camp by the Bolivian army, the two go out in a blaze of glory and friendship.

And friendship is the real appeal here. They're a great team: with Butch's fast brain and Sundance's fast gun, they don't have to kill anybody. "Just keep thinkin', Butch. That's what you're good at," says the taciturn Kid. They share the same love interest in Etta Place (Katherine Ross). They share the same bewilderment at the Pinkerton posse, which seems to be able to track them anywhere ("Who are those guys?!"). They even share an ironic laugh (because Sundance can't swim) before tandem jumping into a watery chasm to escape their pursuers.

Ironically, the "friendship thing" was just the problem for writer William Goldman (*Marathon Man*), as he tried to peddle the script he had worked on for six years. These movie bad guys just weren't bad enough for most studios. Luckily, Richard Zanuck (visionary Darryl's visionary son) of Twentieth Century-Fox was

> [The Jersey Kid] was on the brag about how good he was with a gun, but no one paid any attention to him. One day in the Long Branch [a Dodge City saloon named after Long Branch, New Jersey] he started to pick on a young Texan who was drifting through—just a saddle tramp. The Texan didn't answer the Kid and moved away. Finally the Kid said something you don't say unless you want to back it up with your hardware. They stepped out onto the street, and the Kid started fanning. The bullets flew everywhere. The Texan drew also, but just calmly aimed and fired. Someone sent the Kid's folks a telegram, and the local undertaker arranged for the body to be shipped Back East. That was the only fanning I ever saw in my life.
>
> —Plainsman George "Cimarron" Bolds

> God created men. Colonel Colt made them equal.
>
> —Unknown

enough for the role of Butch, finally agreed.

Once the cameras were rolling, Hill gave celebrity (Newman) and relative unknown (Redford) equal focus—unheard-of even-handedness in Hollywood. The director was also equally at ease with Redford's more spontaneous style and Newman's studied thoroughness. The actors grew to trust him implicitly. Newman even subjected himself to take after take of falling backward into a pool of (freezing) water during a sweltering scene in the script (though it was a frigid day on the set) without much complaint.

A sixties attitude of playfulness permeates this nostalgic, if historically inaccurate, character study. When Butch's real sister, Lula Parker Betenson, visited the set, Newman saucily introduced himself, saying, "Hi, I'm Butch." She came back with, "Hi, I'm your sister." In order to flesh out Etta Place's character, Hill inserted the famous, wordlessly frolicsome bicycle scene. Believe it or not, he cut it to Simon and Garfunkel's "Mrs. Robinson" because the song had the right feel, later hiring songwriter Burt Bacharach and singer B.J. Thomas to record the soon-to-be smash "Raindrops Keep Fallin' on My Head."

Rather than opt for a bullet-riddled death a la *Bonnie and Clyde* for the film's climax, Hill ran two cameras—one fast, the other slow-motion—to create a freeze, blur, and sepia-toned focus on the eternal image of two compadres meeting their fates together. See this film with a friend, but don't rob a convenience store afterward. (Remember, this was Hollywood's version of a "happy ending"—researchers have recently determined that Butch and Sundance were found dead inside that mining shack. Rather than be caught, Butch had plugged the Kid through the forehead and then shot himself in the temple.)

> *Fair play is a jewel, but I don't care for jewelry.*
>
> —John King Fisher, gunfighter

Believe it or not, this famous gorge jump was filmed in one state and the splashdown in another, but it looked just fine in the romanticized and irreverent Butch Cassidy and the Sundance Kid **(1969).**

broad-minded enough not only to say yes, but to offer Goldman a record $400,000 for his script. (The writer would later get an Oscar to go with his cash.) Then the real team playing began. Goldman wanted Newman for Sundance and (can you imagine) Jack Lemmon for Butch. Zanuck said no to Lemmon, but yes to Steve McQueen. Newman demanded billing over McQueen, and McQueen quit over the issue. George Roy Hill wanted Redford, but Zanuck didn't think much of Redford's track record. Hill used his clout to get a script to Redford, but the actor preferred the role of Sundance over Butch. Newman, though worried about being comic

Blood Is Slicker than Water

In 1948, eighty-five-year-old Al Jennings, former small-time bank robber and self-made authentic-western moviemaker, weepingly embraced J. Frank Dalton, who, at 101 years old, was claiming to be the unslain Jesse James. Jennings chokingly told reporters, "Boys, there isn't a bit of doubt on earth." When Al was later asked by Jesse James' biographer, Homer Croy, why he had said that when he'd never met Jesse (added to the fact that unlike Dalton, the tip of one of Jesse's left-hand fingers had been blown off), Jennings gave Croy a doughnut.

Jesse and Frank James were no cream puffs—they were killers. The brothers had learned their lessons well, riding and raiding (along with their compatriots, the Youngers) with Confederate guerrilla leader "Bloody Bill" Quantrill in the savage Kansas-Missouri border wars (the 1863 raid on Lawrence, Kansas, resulted in the deaths of nearly 150 men and boys and the burning of the town to the ground). The South's defeat left the boys bitter toward Yankee carpetbaggers, but also provided Frank and Jesse with the tools for extracting vengeance...and cash. The duo (along with various cohorts) is credited with robbing twelve banks, seven trains (several of which they wrecked), two stagecoaches, and the Kansas City State Fair (where they shot a young girl in the leg) between 1866 and 1882, hauling in $250,000 and killing sixteen people along the way.

Legends about the boys abounded. Jesse was said to have given a poor widow money to stave off a foreclosing banker, only to relieve the banker of the same cash a few miles up the road. Though hailed as Robin Hoods by southerly-leaning newspapers (the boys had actually sent in a note to one paper that said, "We rob the rich and give to the poor"), some of their victims hired the Pinkertons to break the James gang—and these law enforcers were no cream puffs, either. In January 1875, the Pinkertons tossed a flare bomb into the boys' mother's home, blowing off her right arm and killing the boys' nine-year-old brother.

Sympathy for the James boys increased, but not in Northfield, Minnesota. In 1876, the whole town turned on the gang during a botched bank job, killing three and capturing three more (the wounded Jim, Cole, and Bob Younger, whom Jesse and Frank had deserted). By 1879, Jesse (now alias J.B. Howard) had put together a new gang. But on April 3, 1882, one of its members, Bob Ford, shot Jesse in the back of the head while Jesse was standing on a chair to straighten a "God Bless Our Home" needlepoint sampler. The price on that head was ten thousand dollars.

Bob Ford was pardoned for murder and went on to reenact his "showdown with Jesse" onstage (before being shotgunned to death himself). Jesse's one-armed ma sold pebbles from his grave (scooped up from a neighboring creek) for two bits apiece as well as horseshoes that the boys' mounts had worn. And though Frank eventually turned himself in, public sympathy thwarted a conviction. He lived to run a Wild West show with none other than Cole Younger (one of the three men he'd abandoned in Minnesota). In

The brothers James (Tyrone Power as Jesse at left and Henry Fonda as Frank at right) weren't born bad but driven to being that way in the horse- and stunt-filled fable Jesse James *(1938). Jesse's real-life son, Jesse Jr., took a turn at advising the two actors.*

Cole Younger (Cliff Robertson at left) and his band case out Northfield, Minnesota, a town where they're about to do a little bank business, in **The Great Northfield Minnesota Raid** *(1972).*

caught up in the fun and frenzy of criminality.

The harsh light of truth didn't shine on the James boys until later. *The Great Northfield Minnesota Raid* (1972) was Philip Kaufman's *(Invasion of the Body Snatchers)* first big-budget feature, and he sure teed off a lot of Jesse James admirers. This believably dank and dirty piece of backwoods iconoclasm swung the pendulum so far as to make Jesse (the incomparable Robert Duvall) a conniving, cross-dressing, trigger-happy Yankee-phobe, while Frank was no more than a Bible-quoting cut-throat. The brains and heart of this operation was Cole Younger, portrayed by a hairy Cliff Robertson (before he started specializing in playing corporate heavies), whose performance—like the newfangled things the gang kept running into: baseball games, calliopes, time locks, Swedish whorehouses—is, in his own words, "a wonderment."

The second great James film was a family affair. Acting brothers Jim and Stacy Keach were having so much fun filming a PBS special on the Wright Brothers that they got an idea. Jim wrote a country musical about the James boys, mentioning a possible film adaptation to the young Bob Carradine (son of John) while the two were shooting a picture on the feuding Hatfields and McCoys. Both Bob and Jim pestered other Carradines (David and Keith) to sign on as the rest of the rough-and-tumble Younger clan. After Beau and Jeff Bridges balked at playing faithful Clell and faithless Ed Miller (other members of the James gang), those parts went to Dennis and Randy Quaid. The creepy Bob and Charlie Ford roles went to Nicholas and Christopher *(Spinal Tap)* Guest.

In 1980, eight years after inception, Walter Hill brought the Keach boys' story of the James boys to the screen in *The Long Riders* (the title refers to the bank robbers' trade secret of relaying through a hidden series of fresh mounts during their escapes). The brothers (all four sets of them) have an incredible naturalness together onscreen. And while likeable to a point, they're mostly rotten. James Keach is righteously icy as the humorless, autocratic Jesse. David Carradine is wry and dangerous as the cool cutthroat Cole Younger (especially in a bowie knife fight at opposite ends of a teeth-clenched banana—fought over his sweetheart, Belle Starr, played by tough cookie Pamela Reed). Despite Ry Cooder's folksy score, Hill's direction is relentlessly brutal, with enough slow-motion bloodshed to make Sam Peckinpah blush.

condemning the 1902 stage production *The James Boys in Missouri*, Frank once said, "The dad-binged play glorifies these outlaws and makes heroes of them. That's the main thing I object to. It's injurious to the youth of the country. It's positively harmful."

Hollywood didn't heed his words in most of the more than thirty films made since 1908 that featured the boys (two of which starred Jesse's own son, Jesse Jr.). Henry King's *Jesse James* (1938), with Tyrone Power and Henry Fonda (which gave grown-up A westerns a tremendous boost in popularity), pits Jesse against an evil railroad empire, which has blown up his ma when she refused to sell the family homestead for a pittance. A stretch from the truth? King said, "But what we were trying to do was create a Jesse James who would be worthy of the legend."

In 1940, Fritz Lang lensed a wholesome follow-up: *The Return of Frank James* has Henry Fonda (repeating his previous role) going after the baby-faced Bob Ford (played again by the rat-faced John Carradine) and his brother. Fonda didn't even have to get his hands dirty, as vengeance was not approved of by those enforcers of the Production Code, the Hays Office. In place of murder, one Ford falls off a cliff, and the other is shot by someone else.

John Carradine bounced back to marry Jesse (Robert Wagner) to his bride (Hope Lange) in noir master Nicholas Ray's *The True Story of Jesse James* (1957). This time, Jesse and Frank (Jeffrey Hunter) are troubled youths (with six-guns instead of switchblades)

Such Good Compadres

What do (singin') Roy Rogers, (squintin') Michael J. Pollard, (football star) Johnny Mack Brown, (war hero) Audie Murphy, (Greek god) Paul Newman, (pretty boy) Robert Taylor, (songwriter) Kris Kristofferson, (teenage werewolf) Dean Stockwell, (Truffaut enfant) Jean-Pierre Léaud, and (Flash Gordon) Buster Crabbe all have in common? Or put it this way: what New Yorker, though dead at twenty-one, lived on to riff with Bob Dylan, battle Dracula, grope Jane Russell, and inspire a ballet by Aaron Copland, a top-ten hit by Billy Joel, and a noogie by the Three Stooges? William Bonney, Henry Antrim, Henry McCarty, and Billy the Kid are all acceptable answers.

The real Kid (in brief) was born in New York around 1859; nabbed for stealing clothes from a Chinese laundry in Silver City, New Mexico, in 1875; shot a blacksmith who was bullying him in Fort Grant, Arizona, in 1877; fled jail into New Mexico, where he signed on as a cowboy with English cattleman John Tunstall, and found himself embroiled in the "Lincoln County War" for cattle and control; avenged Tunstall's ambush and murder by killing two of the killers' leaders and a corrupt sheriff; escaped the arsonized house of a friend; accepted Governor Lew Wallace's (author of *Ben Hur*) offer of amnesty in exchange for his eyewitness testimony concerning the death of a lawyer; was thrown in jail anyway after squealing; escaped, rustled, and killed a man named Joe Grant; fled from former friend Pat Garrett, who had been elected sheriff of Lincoln County; was ambushed by Garrett at Old Fort Sumner; pushed pal Charlie Bowdre out a door as a human shield; was taken to jail as "rope meat" for the old sheriff's murder; killed two guards and escaped; and was shot dead without warning by Garrett in a friend's darkened bedroom on July 14, 1881.

Many have cinematically sculpted the life of this crowned prince of outlawdom, perhaps the most depicted gunfighter in history (though no one has chosen to sport the "squirrelish" buck teeth the Kid was cursed with). Bob Steele and Buster Crabbe almost made careers of playing the Kid in serials that had no bearing on history at all. A less sanitized, illiterate, and distinctly more psychologically

For a nice guy, he sure kills a lot of people. Billy the Kid (Kris Kristofferson) has just turned the tables at the Lincoln County Jail in Sam Peckinpah's dreamy and deadly **Pat Garrett and Billy the Kid** *(1973).*

All who ever knew Billy will testify that his polite, cordial, and gentlemanly bearing invited confidence and promised protection....He [ate] and laughed, drank and laughed, rode and laughed, talked and laughed, fought and laughed, and killed and laughed.

—Pat F. Garrett, *The Authentic Life of Billy the Kid*

tortured performance was turned in by Paul Newman in Arthur Penn's *The Left-Handed Gun* (1958).

When Tunstall hires on the horseless Kid at a dollar-a-day salary (and gives him a copy of *Through a Glass, Darkly*), it seems like the first time anyone's ever taken an interest in the young man. The Kid's devotion to the old man is touching, but when the gunless Tunstall gets bushwhacked (having just refused the Kid's protection), Billy gets touched in the head. The rest of the film is a tour-de-force degeneration of an alienated, angry young man who tries to play by the rules but can't grasp the hurtful world around him—including his own celebrity. Pat Garrett stays on the sidelines here—it's only after the Kid wrecks Garrett's wedding (by killing a man) that the lawman comes after him.

There's a lot to love about this besides Newman's performance (which includes one of the fastest draws on film). Slow, moody fades, plans drawn on steamed windowpanes, pistol-shooting the moon's reflection, the origin of the best-known (and perhaps only) photograph of Billy, disillusioned dime novelists, and the Kid's final, empty-holstered, childlike stagger to Pat all make this movie a work of intelligence and art. You would expect no less from Arthur Penn.

Pat got his turn to share the spotlight in Sam Peckinpah's bloody but beautiful farewell to the western: *Pat Garrett and Billy the Kid* (1973). Peckinpah's 1957 script for this film may have been mangled by Marlon Brando (in *One-Eyed Jacks*), but that was nothing compared to the problems he would face on his own: MGM gave Peckinpah thirty-six days to shoot; he needed fifty-eight. He wanted to shoot in New Mexico; they said Durango, Mexico (where it was cheaper, but any film for dailies had to be shipped to Los Angeles for developing and back again for viewing). He, like many of the cast and crew, came down with "Las Turistas" (a.k.a. "Montezuma's Revenge"). He had a powerful rock star (Bob Dylan, who plays Alias) to contend with on and off the set. Kris Kristofferson was replicating the Kid's legendary (and historically untrue) whiskey consumption, bottle for bottle. The filmmaker had a studio chief who lived to undermine him. The studio itself, in debt because of its suffering Las Vegas hotels, wanted a rushed release in order to show a profit at the annual stockholders' meeting. It was quite a row to hoe, but Peckinpah did it.

Life imitated the piece of art it was bent on destroying. Ironically, Peckinpah's film is about selling out (as Pat Garrett did when he accepted his sheriff's job; it was a way to ensure a loan for land he wanted) versus stayin' free, like Billy did. In covering the final three months between Billy (easygoing, Christlike killer Kris Kristofferson) and Pat (a suavely macho but self-loathing James Coburn), the film is a leisurely feast of telling images (Billy shooting the heads off half-buried live chickens for sport; Pat shooting his own reflection in a mirror), almost nonstop Dylan music (after Dylan drove composer Jerry Fielding off the project), fascinating personal interplay (perhaps the best scene is Pat managing to hold hostage a poker game full of armed enemies), realistic violence (the ubiquitous Slim Pickens' life literally seems to pass before his eyes after he is shot in the gut), and strikingly honest dialogue (like Pat's line: "It's a job. There's an age in a man's life when you don't want to have to figure out what comes next").

The film's final version is, sadly, in less than its original glory. Peckinpah's first cut came in at 165 minutes. The studio, hiring other editors on the sly, slashed it down to 96. Gone were the framing scenes of Pat's karmic comeuppance (gunned down in his dotage while peeing near his buggy). Gone were the scenes between Pat and his wife, and those with Chisholm, which explained why he was turning on his own. Gone was Billy's tender courtship of Maria (singer Rita Coolidge), which was intended to counter a now seemingly gratuitous scene with Garrett and three hookers. Instead, dubbed over a slaughtered shepherd's final babble, was pop psychoanalysis of

Billy: "You say you go back because of what they did to me, but it is really because you are afraid to change."

As Peckinpah owned up in a 1960 *Film-world* interview, "Men who have lived out of their times, et cetera, I've played that out." He has here, beautifully. The film's release in video may restore more of it. But as lyrical, slightly existential westerns about the end of the good old days go, *Pat Garrett and Billy the Kid* is a masterpiece.

Fear, Loathing, and Capitalism in Tombstone

OK, OK, so it wasn't exactly at the OK Corral. So it only lasted about thirty seconds (in *Gunfight at the OK Corral*, it took six minutes to run and forty-four hours to film). So Wyatt's brother Virgil only got to be a lawman in the first place because the Tombstone marshal went on permanent vacation. So, Wyatt (who made a lot of his money gambling, with a reputation for cheating), as a deputy, got to wear a gun in a gunless town (a handy thing for quelling potential card disputes). So the fight with the Clantons and McLaurys may have only been a snuff job so that they wouldn't squeal on Wyatt and his brothers for organizing a stage ambush that had left two dead. So the Earp boys (now lawmen) spent days trying to goad the men into a fight. So the Clantons may have been trying to leave town when the Earps found them. So the Earps had been told by the sheriff that half the opposition were unarmed. So witnesses say that several of their quarry had their hands up when the shooting began. So Doc Holliday didn't die (as he did in John Ford's *My Darling Clementine*, 1946). So Wyatt was in so thick with the justice of the peace that the Earps didn't even stand trial. So they may have gotten away with murder. It was still the greatest blaze of glory in the American West!

Though Wyatt wasn't made into an all-American hero until two books—Walter Noble Burns' *Tombstone* and Stuart Lake's *Wyatt Earp: Frontier Marshal*—were published around the time of his death (c. 1930), since then the shoot-out of that famous day of October 26, 1881, has been re-created in many a movie. Henry Fonda was gentle and sensible in John Ford's poetic *My Darling Clementine*, a film supposedly made according to Earp's own descriptions to Ford of the day's events. (Wyatt's version didn't include the hauntingly beautiful but fabricated moonlit murder of James Earp while the young man guarded his brothers' cattle.)

Walter Huston, Randolph Scott, Errol Flynn, Ronald Reagan, Joel McCrea, Barry Sullivan, Will Geer, James Stewart, Hugh O'Brien, and Kevin Costner have all taken their turn with Wyatt. Burt Lancaster (though Wyatt's relationship with Doc Holliday came

> The most important lesson I learned from those proficient gun-fighters was that the winner of a gunplay was usually the man who took his time.
>
> —Wyatt Earp, from Stuart Lake's *Wyatt Earp: Frontier Marshal*

OPPOSITE: Billy the Kid (Paul Newman) and friend (Lita Milan) take a little siesta in the hay in Arthur Penn's psychosexually charged The Left-Handed Gun *(1958).* **ABOVE: You tell 'em Hell's a-comin'. Wyatt Earp (a flinty Kurt Russell) wades through gore almost as deep as this water as he quests for vengeance in perhaps the best Earp flick of them all,** Tombstone *(1993).*

uncomfortably close to being a love affair) was otherwise stalwart and true in John Sturges' *Gunfight at the OK Corral* (1956). Its $4.7 million North American box-office success opened doors to the big-budget A westerns of the 1960s. Sturges got to revamp the story on a darker note with his 1967 sequel, *Hour of the Gun*, in which Earp (James Garner) goes after vengeance for subsequent attacks on his brothers—Virgil had been crippled by an anonymous shot-gun blast, and Morgan had been killed within months of the infamous shoot-out by a bullet through a poolroom window.

In Lawrence Kasdan's *Wyatt Earp* (1994), Dennis Quaid (who lost 40 pounds [18.1kg] for the role of the tuberculosis-afflicted Doc Holliday, who had lost 60

> I can't imagine why anyone called it the gunfight at the OK Corral. It could more accurately be called the gunfight west of Fly's house. The OK Corral was several doors up the street.
>
> —Josephine Marcus (Mrs. Wyatt Earp)

percent of his lung tissue to the disease) gave a knockout performance as the foghorn-voiced, dissipated dentist. Victor Mature's Doc, a demonic and despairing intellectual, also stole the show in *My Darling Clementine*. Cesar Romero may have played Holliday as an obstetrician in *Frontier Marshall* (1939). But Val Kilmer turns in a virtuoso Doc of his own in the best Earper, bar none, a remorseless film called *Tombstone* (1993).

Director George P. Cosmatos had set his sights high and wide. He wanted to direct a western version of *The Godfather* and he pretty much did—the gunfight was, after all, the Old West's version of the Saint Valentine's Day Massacre. His film pits a money-hungry Wyatt *et al.* against the real red-sashed organized criminals of the Arizona range, who called themselves "The Cowboys." As the battle unfolds, friendship is central (Johnny Ringo: "Doc, why you doin' this for?" Doc: "Wyatt Earp is my friend." Ringo: "Hell, I got lots of friends." Doc: "I don't."), but ugly pragmatics are just as important (Wyatt keeps a shotgun wired under the table he deals cards from), as is bloodlust. As Wyatt says, "You can tell them I'm comin' and hell's comin' with me!" There is plenty of hell ahead.

Kurt Russell (as Wyatt) and Val Kilmer turn in nuanced performances as the hardest-assed lawman and the sickest, slickest, southernest Doc you ever saw. Character details are etched everywhere in Kevin Jarre's gritty script. The perpetually perspiring yet cold-blooded Doc answers the murderous challenge of a gunslinger's pistol pyrotechnics with the same flashy handling of his silver whiskey cup. Wyatt intimidates the hell out of a saloon bully as a prelude to buying an interest in the place: "Skin that smoke wagon and see what happens!...I'm gettin' tired of your gassin', now jerk that pistol and go to work! I said throw down, boy! You gonna do somethin', or just stand there and bleed?"

The famous gunfight (which left three dead) may have been infinitely shorter than most of its replications, but authenticity was adhered to in other ways. Western neophyte (as was almost everyone else in the cast) Russell had counseling from Glen Wyatt Earp, the real McCoy's cousin. Seventy-three-year-old western veteran Harry Carey, Jr. (whose father, Harry Carey, had known Earp), played an aging lawman. Cosmatos insisted on interior details, too: almost every woman (even while in childhood) was corseted in those days; some had ribs removed to achieve the proper cinch-waisted shape. Actress Dana Delany (Josie Earp, who in reality didn't meet Wyatt until after Tombstone) said, after squeezing into her costume, "I'm convinced it's the reason why so many women died at a young age."

Shooting in and around Tombstone ("The town too tough to die," with a local paper called *The Epitaph*) found things wonderfully unglamorized from bygone days. The population—seven thousand at the time of the shootout—had shrunk to one thousand.

A gentler, kinder Wyatt Earp (Henry Fonda) surveys his not-so-quiet town of Tombstone in John Ford's stylish if sanitized **My Darling Clementine** *(1946).*

Rest in Peace

Before we head out from the old historic West, let's take a gander at a few epitaphs that weren't quite so famous (again, courtesy of Richard Dillon's Western Quotations).

A fearless hero of Frontier days
Who in Cowboy chaos
Established the supremacy of law.
—Thomas J. Smith (?–1870), marshal of Abilene

Hung by mistake
—Unknown Chinaman in Florence, Idaho

Murdered by a Traitor and coward
Whose Name is not worthy to Appear Here.
—Jesse James (1847–1882)

Shed not for her the bitter tear
Nor give the heart vain regret
Tis but the casket that lies here
The gem that filled it sparkles yet.
—Belle Starr (1848–1889), bandit queen

He knew the horse.
—Frederic Remington (1861–1909)

Murdered on the streets of Tombstone.
—Frank and Tom McLaury and Billie Clanton,
*   Boot Hill Cemetery, killed by the Earp brothers*
*   and Doc Holliday, 1881*

A brave man reposes in death here.
Why was he not true?
—Sam Bass (1851–1878), Texas outlaw

Paso por aquí.
—Eugene Manlove Rhodes (1869–1934),
*   cowboy and author*

Though the OK Corral itself had burnt down the year after the gun battle, the town's simple grid of ten 75-foot-wide (22.8m) streets had been preserved. The gods must have smiled on some sacrifice they all made (perhaps that they endured stifling 115°F [46.1°C] Arizona summer heat during filming), for as the cameras rolled on the fateful fight, distant thunder cracked; it cracked once more when Cosmatos yelled, "Cut!" Now that's better muscle than even Don Corleone could have hoped for.

Chapter Five

OUT ON THE TRAIL AND BACK AT THE RANCH

The U.S. Cavalry of the Wyoming National Guard storms through Johnson County in Michael Cimino's maligned megamovie, Heaven's Gate (1980).

EPIC JOURNEYS

Like any good studio vice president, Jesse Lasky was on the phone one perfect, sunny southern California day in 1922, getting chewed out by his boss, studio president Adolph Zucker, for spending too much money. It seems Jesse had turned in a budget to "the suits" Back East for the upcoming Paramount Studies production of an adaptation of Emerson Hough's novel *The Covered Wagon*, to be directed by James Cruze. The total: a staggering $500,000.

In the boom years of the twenties, lots of movies—good, bad, and indifferent—were needed to fill the theaters springing up across America. Nevertheless, public enthusiasm for western melodrama was on the wane. There was nothing little about Lasky's figure, however, which was easily five times that of any other "hoss opera" in production. Zucker tersely asked him if perhaps the young man had put a decimal in the wrong place.

Lasky had to scramble. The genre was in trouble, but this picture would be big—the first to show westward migration on a massive scale. With any luck, this sweeping celebration of the American spirit would sweep western audiences back into the movies, and their cash right along with them. Scrambling for a pitch, Lasky finally blurted, "But this is more than a western! It's an epic... [and for emphasis he spelled it out in big, epic-sized letters for his boss] E-P-I-C!" After a moment of excruciating silence, the voice on the other end of the line rumbled, "An epic, eh? Well. That's different. Go ahead."

> There is more poetry in the rush of a single railroad train across the continent than in all the gory story of burning Troy.
>
> —Joaquin Miller, western writer

When *The Covered Wagon* (1923) finally rolled into movietown, it had cost $300,000 more than anticipated to make, using 200,000 acres (80,000ha) of Nevada's Snake Valley, 1,000 extras, 750 Indians, a herd of buffalo, hundreds of technicians, a tent city for the cast and crew, 8 trucks for food, and a line of 500 covered wagons stretching 3 miles (4.8km). Production had triumphed over every element, even a blizzard, which was hastily written into the script. There was something for everyone: a buffalo hunt, Indian attacks, prairie fires, fording flooded rivers, campfire singing (silently, of course), even birth and death on the trail. D.W. Griffith would have been jealous, especially since his old cameraman, Carl Brown, had lensed it.

The film proved so popular that it had extensive runs at both Grauman's Egyptian Theater in Hollywood and the Criterion in New York City. Despite cowboy actor William S. Hart's attacks on its inaccuracies (no wagon train in its right mind would camp in a box canyon in Indian territory!), the film grossed more than $4 million and boosted western production from 50 films in 1923 to 125 the next year. One of those progeny was to be directed by an Irish-American hothead from Portland, Maine, who at age twenty-nine had already made fifty pictures, thirty-nine of which were westerns.

The Iron Horse (1924) and its director, Sean O'Feeney (a.k.a. John Ford), gave the western epic the extra steam it needed. Like Cruze's *The Covered Wagon*, Ford's story of the historic 1869 linking of the Union Pacific and Central Pacific railroads was gargantuan (1,280 scenes, 275 subtitles, 12 reels of film) and shot entirely on location—even the cabin interiors were real. The production employed 5,000 extras; 800 Pawnee, Sioux, and Cheyenne; 1,000 Chinese; 100 cooks; 3,000 workmen; a regiment of U.S. Cavalry; 2,000 horses; 10,000 cattle; 13,000 buffalo; and a train with 56 coaches for transport. Original locomotives were borrowed, as was Wild Bill Hickock's derringer revolver and a stagecoach used by Horace Greeley (westbound, no doubt).

But unlike Cruze's epic, Ford's had a personal story line as important as historical events surrounding it: in this case, the hero (played by George O'Brien, who had been Tom Mix's assistant camera-

George O'Brien has a little track to lay, but he means business in John Ford's early railroad epic The Iron Horse (1924).

man) sought his father's digit-deprived murderer (played by actor Fred Kohler, who really was missing three fingers). Nor did Ford shoot big scenes from one static position, as did Cruze. Risking being labeled as "arty," as most of Hollywood thought mobile camera work was for Europeans, Ford caught each action sequence from multiple angles—mounting his cameras on moving trucks and trains, and even under horses' flying hooves—and intercut action footage with other scenes to build excitement to a fever pitch.

In this movie, which revolved around but never quite adhered to historical detail, the track-laying race (10 miles [16km] in a single day, spurred by a ten-thousand-dollar bet from Union Pacific's vice president) was the only real fictional concession, but it was a myth-over-truth preference that would become a hallmark for Ford and a trend for the genre. Who needed technicalities when the film's signature shots (like Indians silhouetted against a towering sky, riders riding into a dusky sunset, or a mournful dog resting its head on a fallen warrior) burned so brightly in the popular imagination? The film was sold ten ways to Sunday: separate ad campaigns designed to appeal to women, men, and Americans in general proved so persuasive that the film ran a solid year at New York City's Lyric Theater. Its success spawned similar films all over the world, such as Russia's *Turksib* (1929) and England's *The Great Barrier* (1937).

Ridin' High, Wide, and Out in Front

In 1939, after a thirteen-year, thirty-two-film leave of absence from the western, John Ford burst upon the scene once again with an E-P-I-C that breathed new life into a genre dominated by B pictures with narratives about as deep as the average comic book and characters as complex as a Saturday matinee idol, more likely than not, crooning from the saddle. *Stagecoach* (1939) welded spectacle and compelling narrative forever in the hearts and minds of fans and filmmakers, becoming known as the most influential western ever made.

The story is a simple one: thrown together by fate, nine diverse specimens of humanity make a desperate stagecoach journey from Tonto to Lordsburg,

Arizona, during an Apache uprising. There is Dallas (Claire Trevor), the whore with a heart of gold who's being railroaded out of Tonto by the ladies of the Law and Order League; Doc Boone (Thomas Mitchell), the loquacious, alcoholic physician suffering similar banishment; Hatfield (John Carradine), the gentlemanly but dangerous southern gambler; Mrs. Mallory (Louise Platt), the doughty but very pregnant wife of a cavalry officer; Peacock (Donald Meek), the mild-mannered whiskey-drummer with a case full of tempting samples; Gatewood (Berton Churchill), the blustering, embezzling banker hiding fifty thousand dollars in his valise; Curley (George Bancroft), the dedicated Tonto sheriff who's riding shotgun; Buck (Andy Devine), the perpetually hungry and whiny driver; and Ringo (John Wayne), a cowboy jailed for avenging his brother's murder, who's just busted out to settle things with the Plummer brothers in Lordsburg once and for all.

Ford masterfully mixes external hurdles (rugged majestic country, Indian attacks, rivers to ford, thirst, runaway horses) with internal ones (sexual and social prejudice, childbirth, alcoholism, greed, shame) the same way he mixes sweeping panoramas of Monument Valley's mesas (passed at least three times in the long journey) with intimate close-ups of each of the characters huddled together in the confines of the coach. His night shots don't look like slightly filtered daytime skies, but as night shots should—moody and mysterious. His characters are at once achingly human in their dialogue yet mythic in the power of their actions. Will they survive the trip? Will the sheriff send Ringo back to prison? Will Dallas get the second chance she prays for? Will Ringo survive all three Plummer brothers (in one of the shortest and most stunning gunfights ever)? All western fans owe it to themselves to find out firsthand.

In the spring of 1937, Ford, having read Ernest Haycox's short story "Stage to Lordsburg" in the April issue of *Collier's* magazine, bought the film rights for less than $7,500. With writer Dudley Nichols, he wove in colorful characters from Bret Harte's "The Outcasts of Poker Flat" (Ford had directed a film version of the story in 1919) and borrowed the prostitute who crosses war-torn France with a coachful of scandalized bourgeoisie in Guy de Maupassant's "Boule de Suif" (Tub of Lard). Nichols thought of their end product as a mixture of *Grand Hotel* (1932), *The Covered Wagon* (1923), and *The Iron Horse* (1924), jokingly dubbing the project "The Grand Covered Iron Stagecoach."

With David O. Selznick as the film's original producer, Ford cast Wayne and Claire Trevor in the good bad-man and good bad-woman parts, but as Selznick wanted stars—specifically Gary Cooper and Marlene Dietrich—Ford walked, and took the film with

Giants of the Plains, Part III: Man of Contradictions

John Carradine called John Ford a sadist who loved to terri-fy actors. Katharine Hepburn said she and Ford were "great friends" while filming. Henry Fonda found him "egomania-cal": he loved getting his print on the first take, right or not. Anne Bancroft said he was "marvelous but loony": he often reacted to actors' questions about their scenes by tearing the pages from his script. Walter Brennan couldn't tolerate him after My Darling Clementine, *and vowed never to work with him again. Jimmy Stewart didn't like the way Ford made acting competitive, by whispering direction to each player. He was a director who could bring John Wayne and Victor McLaglen to tears, a man who made 137 movies in close to sixty years of work and emerged with a record four Oscars for best director. Many consider him the great-est American filmmaker; to say he was a man of contrasts is the understatement of the century. Here are some scat-tered scenes from the kind of life possessed by those behind the camera, rather than in front of it.*

★ *Ford, who had followed his big brother Francis to Hollywood, got one break while working at Universal as a prop man. Studio president Carl Laemmle saw the younger Ford in action and said, "He hollers the loudest. Make him the director."*

★ *As an assistant director (along with George Marshall) in 1914, Ford got another break when a Hollywood party left the directors too hung over to work, leaving the assistants to fill the breach.*

★ *He lived and drank with former cowboy Hoot Gibson during the silent years. Gibson relates: "He was worse Irish than me. He wanted to play 'My Wild Irish Rose' on the piano and I wanted something else. He picked up the piano stool and broke it on my head. And it was my piano."*

★ *Ford composed everything in his head and shot such min-imal footage that studio executives had little influence on how his films were made. He also whittled scripts down to the bone, saying once to Fred "Wagonmaster" Nugent, "I liked your script. In fact, I actually shot a few pages of it."*

★ *Ford believed in economy with actors, too. He once told future director Robert Parrish to go off in a dark (screening) room and count the number of speeches Ford had given John Wayne in* Stagecoach *(1939) and* The Long Voyage Home *(1940). Parrish reported four-teen for each film. Ford said, "That's how you make 'em good actors. Don't let any of them talk."*

★ *Ford constantly badmouthed his own films and claimed not to have seen them. Of his documentary* Sex Hygiene, *he said, "I looked at it and threw up."*

★ *Ford didn't talk to Andy Devine for a full six years after the character actor once talked back to him. For Henry Fonda the silence lasted ten years, following a fistfight during* Mister Roberts *(1955).*

★ *Once Ford had achieved mogul status, he shunned using veteran actor Harry Carey, who had helped forge Ford's reputation in the silents for twenty-five years. Yet at Carey's death, he wept in his widow's arms so much that she reported, "The whole front of my sweater was sopping wet." Ford then immediately hired his son, Harry Carey, Jr., as an actor, employing him for the next sixteen years.*

★ *During a Red Scare witch-hunt meeting of the Screen Directors Guild, Ford interceded in Cecil B. De Mille's attempt to oust President Joseph L. Mankiewicz by say-ing, "My name's John Ford. I make westerns. I don't think there's anyone in this room who knows more about what the American public wants than Cecil B. De Mille—and he certainly knows how to give it to them. But I don't like what you stand for, C.B., and I don't like what you've been saying here tonight. Joe has been vilified, and I think he needs an apology." Ford then proposed removing De Mille and the entire board of directors, adding, "And then let's all go home and get some sleep. We've got some pictures to make tomorrow." They did.*

★ *Near his death, Ford was visited by the equally renowned western director Howard Hawks.*

HAWKS: Just came back to say good-bye, Jack.
FORD: Good-bye, Howard….Howard?
HAWKS: Yes, Jack?
FORD: I mean really good-bye, Howard.
HAWKS: Really good-bye, Jack?
FORD: Really good-bye.

As his son Pat said of his famous father, "He'll be making westerns a couple of years after he's dead."

him. After trying unsuccessfully to sell it to his ol' Irish pal Joe Kennedy (John F. Kennedy's father) at RKO, Ford wooed United Artist independent producer Walter Wanger with the promise of quality on the cheap ($546,000 for a film without color and without stars) side. Stars they may not have been, but every principal player except Louise Platt was an old Ford actor and was used to "Pappy's" autocratic ways: during one of Wayne's early tests in the picture, Ford grabbed him by the chin and said, "Why are you moving your mouth so much? Don't you know, you don't act with your mouth in pictures, you act with your eyes?"

Wayne was, for better or worse, used to the director's harsh style. On another picture, Ford screamed at a sauntering Wayne, "Chrissakes! Can't you even walk? Not skip, just walk! Goddamn fairy, put your feet down like you were a man!"

The Ringo Kid (John Wayne) and Dallas (Claire Trevor) share a rather rare moment of near domesticity in the immortal Stagecoach *(1939).*

Wayne may have been riled, but he maintained, "[Ford] knew he couldn't get a good job...out of me unless he shook me up so damn hard I'd forget to worry about whether I was fit to be in the same picture with Thomas Mitchell." (He might well have worried—Mitchell won the Best Supporting Actor Oscar for his Stagecoach ride.)

Speaking of shook up, the cast's journey was just as bumpy as the real thing—for a true sense of authenticity, Ford employed a 2,500-pound (1,135kg) maroon Concord coach from Abbot, Downing & Co. Used on an El Paso–San Diego run for eighty-five years, the stage had an ash frame, poplar body, and almost no metal parts, bouncing through filming on shock absorbers fashioned of layered steerhide straps.

If Pappy was tough, "Yak" was tougher. Duke brought his old stunt mentor Enos Yakima Canutt along to make the ride wilder during the Indian attack. Dressed in Apache garb, Yak leapt from his mount alongside the moving stage onto the lead horses (a stagecoach is pulled by three pairs of horses: the lead, the swing, and the wheel teams), where Duke's character shot him. Then all Yak had to do was fall down among six sets of thundering hooves, hang on to the stage's tongue (the projection the bottom front of a wagon that connects the vehicle to the horses) while dragging along the ground, and, when Ringo shot him again, let the stage

roll right over him. To complete the scene, Yak, now dressed as Ringo, had to jump from the driver's seat to the wheel team, to the swing team, and straddle the lead team to stop the runaway stage. The successful roll-over stunt was so dangerous that after Canutt's performance, it wasn't attempted again for forty-two years, until Terry Leonard tried it in *The Legend of the Lone Ranger* (1980)—and got run over for his troubles.

It's easy to forget that Ford had a softer side, giving special attention to his actors' comfort level. He often quietly rehearsed scenes before shooting and provided live music on the set to get his cast in the proper mood (a holdover from his silent days). More often than not, these set tunes usually worked their way into the score—in the case of *Stagecoach*, it was the music of Danny Borzage on accordion.

After *Stagecoach* was "in the can," Ford said to Duke, "You may get some real good parts from this one. If this picture is half as good as I think it is, you're actually going to have to go out and buy some clothes."

Wry asides aside, the film's significance can perhaps be best summed up with an example: when boy genius Orson Welles came to Hollywood to make *Citizen Kane* (1941), believed by many to be the finest film ever made, he reportedly screened *Stagecoach* every night for a month in preparation. When asked which American directors he admired, Wells replied, "The old masters, by which I mean John Ford, John Ford and John Ford." 'Nuff said?

The Rest of the Herd

John Ford didn't corner the market on great epic westerns, nor was Monument Valley the only available location. Cecil B. De Mille took the epic onto tracks remarkably similar to those in Ford's *The Iron Horse* with his *Union Pacific* (1939). Fritz Lang commemorated the telegraph in *Western Union* (1942). Singing-cowboy director Joseph Kane switched horses in midstream (from Roy Rogers to John Wayne) on his way to the casinos of San Francisco in *Flame of the Barbary Coast* (1945). Elia Kazan brought Tracy and Hepburn back to the ranch in *Sea of Grass* (1947).

Howard Hawks took a black-and-white ("Dirt looks more like dirt in black and white") river journey up the wide Missouri with Kirk Douglas, the incredible Arthur Hunnicutt, and a bunch of Cajun boatmen to Jackson Hole, Wyoming, at the foot of the Grand Tetons (40 miles [64km] from where George Stevens was shooting *Shane* in color) to make the beautiful *The Big Sky* (1952). He also got to make the drunken finger-amputation scene he was unable to persuade the Duke to do in his other esteemed epic, *Red River* (1947). That same year saw Anthony Mann and James Stewart (as a former Kansas guerrilla raider from the Civil War) together again, shepherding a wagon train of pioneers' provisions up the Snake River, over Mount Hood, and into the providence of Oregon country—fighting off corrupt merchants, hungry gold prospectors, the man he saved from hanging (Arthur Kennedy), and the stigma of his own past—in the classic *Bend of the River* (1952).

George Stevens oiled things up down Texas way with *Giant* (1956). *How the West Was Won* (1962) tried to become the last word in episodic epics with three directors taking part: Henry Hathaway in the saddle for its sections titled "The Rivers," "The Plains," and

Stuntgods

He made more than 140 films. From rodeo to silents, Republic's B serials to the big leagues, to an honorary Oscar in 1966, to his last film involvement in 1976's Equus, *Enos Yakima Canutt was the king of stunts. He staged the grueling chariot races in* Ben Hur *(1959). As Clark Gable, he drove a careening wagon through Atlanta as burning buildings collapsed around him in* Gone With the Wind *(1939) (in which you can also see his mug as the bearded brigand who tries to waylay Miss Scarlett's buggy on the bridge). He's directed snake wrestling in* The Swiss Family Robinson *(1964), jousting knights in* Ivanhoe *(1953) and gorillas in* Mogambo *(1953), and broken more bones than ten clumsy humans put together. Let's take a look at some of Yak's (and those of a few others) more memorable "gags" from western stuntdom.*

* *Yak, doubling for Harry Carey, hangs by his feet from the neck of* The Devil Horse *(1932) as it bucks, gallops, and rolls in the dust.*

* *Horse falls, in transition: in the early days, horses ran over tripwires or into a pit. Later, for a "Running W," piano wire was attached from hobbles on the horses' hooves to a fixed post 80 to 100 yards (73.1 to 91.4m) away. Following the extensive horse injuries in 1936's*

Charge of the Light Brigade, *the American Humane Association cracked down—it was the riders' turn to be wired and yanked out of the saddle. Finally, stuntmen got wiser and kinder and trained their horses to fall down on command (freshly plowed earth made the falls softer).*

* *In* The Trail Beyond *(1934) Yak sets another standard: he jumps from his horse to the side of a rolling wagon, then clambers to the front, fights, falls between the wheel team's legs, hangs dragging on his back, slides to the back axle behind the wagon, flips over, pulls himself up the back of wagon, and finishes his fight.*

* *Yak, doubling for John Wayne, drives a wagon and its team of horses off a high cliff into a lake in* Dark Command *(1940): a greased chute had to be used, as horses won't willingly run into space.*

* *William S. Hart rides through a plateglass window in* Truthful Tulliver *(1916).*

* *The most dangerous of all western stunts was tried only once: jumping horses from a moving train and galloping down a hill in* When the Daltons Rode *(1940).*

Male bonding amid the Blackfoot Indians. From left, Zeb (Arthur Hunnicutt), Boone (Dewey Martin), and Jim Deakins (Kirk Douglas) do a little deal making in Howard Hawks' The Big Sky **(1952).**

"The Outlaws"; John Ford tackling "The Civil War"; and George Marshall running "The Railroad." And the cast list reads like a Hollywood "Who's Who": Debbie Reynolds, Carroll Baker, Lee J. Cobb, Henry Fonda, Karl Malden, Gregory Peck, George Peppard, Robert Preston, James Stewart, Eli Wallach, John Wayne, Richard Widmark, Walter Brennan, Andy Devine, and the voice of Spencer Tracy were all on board for this one.

Ridin' High, Wide, and Meddlesome

Sometimes, epics didn't start out as epics. It's ironic that one of the biggest and most successful megawesterns ever made began conventionally. Niven Busch wanted to write and produce a vehicle for his wife, actress Theresa Wright, set against the backdrop of the conflict between a cattle baron and the railroad. His work resulted in *Duel in the Sun* (1946) (affectionately called *Lust in the Dust* by many): the story of the dysfunctional McCandles family and a wild girl named Pearl.

When Wright became pregnant prior to filming, a search went out for another Pearl. Independent movie mogul David O. Selznick (*Gone With the Wind*) got wind of Busch's script and bought it from

RKO as a vehicle for his wife, actress Jennifer Jones. Selznick promised the American public the best western of all time; what he didn't add was that it would also be the longest (1,490,000 feet [454,152m] of film), the most sexual (count 'em, two lascivious dances), and the most expensive ($7 million, as opposed to the paltry $3 million spent on *Gone With the Wind*) film of its time. Selznick was notorious for getting personally involved with his pictures, but his big bank account and track record with Rhett and Miss Scarlett made Busch willing to yield the producer's reins and hope for the best. He lived to regret it.

The first thing that Selznick did was hire Oliver H.P. Garret to inflate Busch's lean, mean script to epic proportions. Then he brought director King Vidor, with whom he had a twenty-year friendship, on board and recast the film to include Butterfly McQueen, Lillian Gish, Lionel Barrymore, Joseph Cotten, and Gregory Peck (who replaced John Wayne). Land struggle quickly took a backseat to the tussle of a wanton good girl's sexual and emotional subjugation to a boy so bad he sings "I've Been Workin' on the Railroad" after derailing a train.

Selznick was into everything: he had composer Dimitri Tiomkin compose no fewer than eleven leitmotifs, including an "orgasm theme." He hired a Beverly Hills bartender to ensure that the fake liquor was the right color. Jones' Mexican makeover, as a measure of reality suggested by Selznick, became so detailed that it took two hours to achieve every day. He constantly rewrote dialogue for entire scenes.

Selznick wanted to take over the direction himself, but Vidor hung in. To get his way, the producer asked for whole scenes to be reshot simply because he didn't like the way Peck was wearing his hat. He sent memos so lengthy about how much time was wasted on the set that it took Vidor forever to read them. The director would often find his crew missing for scheduled shots because Selznick had already sent them somewhere else. A bevy of other directors, among them Sydney Franklin, William Cameron Menzies, William Dieterle, and even Joseph Von Sternberg were brought in to "consult." (After Sternberg started imposing camera set-ups that took four to five hours, he was pulled as well.) Vidor quit two days before the film was finished. According to Hollywood lore, his parting words were, "You can take this picture and shove it."

...And Starring Monument Valley

It was there 160 million years before John Ford made it famous, again and again—just ask the Navajo people. Straddling an area measuring roughly 100 by 400 miles (160 by 640km) in southern Utah and northern Arizona, Monument Valley sits 4,000 feet (6,400km) above sea level, yet is itself a rugged sea of earth with huge monuments rising up from it like islands.

As a location, it was a trek in the early days. Farther from a railroad than any other place in the United States (175 miles [280km] from the Flagstaff, Arizona, train station), the area could be penetrated only by unpaved roads whose rough terrain could snap an axle like a matchstick. Still, the valley's unmistakable grandeur made it a western setting rivaled in popularity only by the stunning areas (such as Arches National Park, Canyonlands National Park, and Dead Horse Point State Park) surrounding a little town called Moab, Utah, less than a hundred miles (160km) to the northeast. Here are some of the movies shot in these locations that might have a certain look in common, though not all of them wear boots and spurs.

Filmed in the Monument Valley Area

The Vanishing American (1925)
Stagecoach* (1939)
Kit Carson (1940)
Billy the Kid (1941)
The Harvey Girls (1946)
My Darling Clementine* (1946)
Fort Apache* (1948)
She Wore a Yellow Ribbon* (1949)
The Searchers* (1956)
Sergeant Rutledge* (1960)
How the West Was Won* (1962)
Cheyenne Autumn* (1964)
2001: A Space Odyssey (1968)
Again a Love Story (1969)
Easy Rider (1969)
MacKenna's Gold (1969)
Joshua (1970)
Wild Rovers (1971)
Electra Glide in Blue (1973)
The Trial of Billy Jack (1974)
The Eiger Sanction (1975)
The Villain (1979)
The Legend of the Lone Ranger (1981)
National Lampoon's Vacation (1983)
Thunder Warrior II (1983)
Back to the Future III (1990)

Tall Tales (1993)
The Ride (1993)
Forrest Gump (1994)

Filmed in the Moab Area

Rio Grande* (1950)
Wagonmaster* (1950)
Battle at Apache Pass (1952)
Border River (1953)
Siege at Red River (1953)
Taza, Son of Cochise (1953)
Canyon Crossroads (1954)
Smoke Signal (1954)
Fort Dobbs (1956)
Warlock (1958)
Ten Who Dared (1959)
Gold of the Seven Saints (1960)
The Comancheros (1961)
The Greatest Story Ever Told (1963)
Rio Conchos (1964)
Wild Rovers (1966)
Blue (1967)
Fade In (1967)
Run, Cougar, Run (1970)
Vanishing Point (1971)
Alias Smith and Jones (1972)
Birds of Prey (1972)
Against a Crooked Sky (1975)
Savage Waters (1978)
Jupiter Menace (1981)
The Returning (1981)
Spacehunter: Adventures in the Forbidden Zone (1982)
Choke Canyon (1984)
The Survivalist (1986)
Nightmare at Noon (1987)
Indiana Jones and the Last Crusade (1988)
Sundown: Vampires in Retreat (1988)
Thelma and Louise (1990)
Equinox (1991)
Rubin and Ed (1991)
This Boy's Life (1992)
Double Jeopardy (1992)
Josh and S.A.M. (1992)
Knights (1992)
Slaughter of the Innocents (1992)
Dark Blood (1993)
Geronimo: An American Legend (1993)
Lightning Jack (1993)
Pontiac Moon (1993)
City Slickers II (1994)

(* indicates a film directed by John Ford)

Fifteen thousand dollars a day was the tab. Cast and crew traveled 200,000 miles (320,000km) among six locations before the year of filming was over. There were fifty speaking parts, 6,526 extras, a ranch that took five weeks to construct, moveable trees, and a forty-man crew that spent two months altering the very landscape. Selznick spared no expense in his steamy, dusty star vehicle for his wife. But his obsessive vision for the picture had gone beyond even her.

For the film's powerful finale, Jones spent fifteen-hour days crawling over hot rocks, dirt, and sand for a lover's showdown with Peck (where they gun each other down at Squaw's Head Rock and die in each other's arms) and had the cuts, burns, and scrapes to prove it. She also slaved away to learn three tough dances, one of which was scrapped at the last minute because when it finally came time to film it, Peck was needed elsewhere. Another dance died in the censor's clutches: "It tends to throw audiences on the side of sin," reported *Tidings*, the official journal of the Los Angeles Catholic Archdiocese. Additional wholesome revisions cost another $200,000. By the time it was all over, Selznick had garnered a cowriting credit (Garret had quit), tried for a codirecting credit (but was stopped by the Directors Guild), and had shot enough film for 137 two-hour movies.

What could be more "touching" than a mother's love? Here, Mrs. Pendrake (Faye Dunaway) spares no effort in abluting her strapping (but short) foster son (an abashed Dustin Hoffman) in one of the West's best comedies, **Little Big Man** *(1970).*

Ridin' High, Wide, and Jaundiced

Another sprawling tale from the Old West came courtesy of the pen of Thomas Berger, the script of Calder (*The Graduate*) Willingham, the vision of Arthur Penn, and the eternally questing soul of Dustin Hoffman. *Little Big Man* (1970) is simply one of the funniest, truest, meanest, and most epic westerns ever lensed.

It tells a good part of the life story of 121-year-old nursing-home inmate Jack Crabbe, who (prepare yourself) has been: plucked by the Cheyenne at the age of ten after they rub out most of his family; raised by Grandfather, a.k.a. Old Lodge Skins (Chief Dan George), as one of the tribe's own; reclaimed as an adolescent by the Reverend Pendrake and his nymphomaniac wife (Faye Dunaway); lured into life as a shill for mutilated conman Allardyce T. Merriweather (Martin Balsam); rescued by his surviving Calamity Jane–esque sister and taught to shoot; made notorious as the Sodapop Kid while befriending a paranoiac Wild Bill Hickock (Jeff Corey); redeemed after becoming a storekeeper and marrying a goodhearted Swedish girl, who later gets abducted by Indians; taken back by the Cheyenne to become the great warrior Little Big Man, take another beautiful wife, Sunshine (Amy

> *Jack Crabbe is a sort of pilgrim who takes us through the convulsions of the West, when two cultures came to know each other and eventually loathe each other.*
>
> —Arthur Penn, on *Little Big Man*

Lawman James Averill (Kris Kristofferson) pays an unwelcome visit to the Johnson County Cattlemen's Club as Billy Irvine (John Hurt) looks on spinelessly from the background in a scene from Heaven's Gate.

Eccles), and "service" her three widowed sisters; condemned to watch the whole clan, except Grandfather, get wiped out by a psychotic Custer (Richard Mulligan) at the Battle of the Washita River; reduced to a drunken bum in his grief; soothed in isolation as a hermit; signed on as a scout for Custer; asked to lead the 7th Cavalry into the valley of the Little Bighorn; and finally left to help Grandfather prepare to die (who then doesn't). Tom Mix, eat your heart out!

Adverse and amusing obstacles permeated this funny film, which also shows more detail about Indian life than any film until 1990's *Dances with Wolves*. Taking his cast and crew to Calgary, Alberta, Canada, in search of snow in October 1968, Penn found 55°F (12.7°C) temperatures and had to pay George Kaquitts, a medicine man of the Stoney tribe, one hundred dollars to call down snow. He was successful—4 inches (10cm) of snow fell, but melted in the heat.

By the following January, heat was no longer a problem. There was plenty of snow and -40°F (-40°C) temperatures to go around. All the eastern city boys were meeting their respective challenges. "I literally broke my butt learning to ride," confessed the diminutive Penn. Mulligan, who had suffered 112°F (44.4°C) Montana heat while covered in buckskin, only got skimpy cottons during the deep freeze. Still he waxed, "It was every nine-year-old Bronx boy's dream to lead 250 men in a Cavalry charge." Dustin Hoffman, the Little Big Man himself, had this to say: "I never realized it could be so cold that you lose the feeling in your fingers when you have your gloves off for thirty seconds....The cold was murder. Learning to do a fast draw for the picture, I shot myself. When you draw very rapidly, sometimes you're pulling on the trigger, and it fired while coming out of the holster. I burned my leg with the powder from blank cartridges. The worst thing was learning to ride a horse. I'm short in the legs, short in the hamstrings. Every night I sat in Epsom salts."

That was the least of Hoffman's agonies in searching for the many facets of his character—a task he has never shied away from. Dick Smith's amazingly transformative makeup was challenge enough, demanding five hours for each application. But it was the narrator's 121-year-old voice that eluded the master actor. These are some of the lengths he went to get it, in the maestro's own nasal words. "....One day I got laryngitis, and I practiced with it and played the voice back on tape. It was exactly what I wanted. "Now," I said, "what am I gonna do, get sick?...

"Then we were back in L.A. and we had to shoot the next day, and I still did not know what to do about the voice. So in a panic I went into a room, closed the door and started screaming until I got hoarse. The next day my voice was OK again, so I screamed while I got dressed. I screamed leaving the room. In the car I rolled up the windows and screamed all the way to the Sawtelle Veterans' Hospital....

"It was a five-hour makeup job, and every half an hour I'd stop and start screaming. I was just panicked because there was the camera and I knew no other way. After makeup I found a padded room with a mattress on the floor, and I went in there and screamed. Before I knew it, two hospital guards were looking through the window in the door, looking at this nutty old guy in a corner of this dark padded room, just screaming....Finally I got the voice."

In the immortal words that Sir Laurence Olivier is said to have quipped to Hoffman when the method actor stayed up for days to achieve the exhausted look for 1976's *Marathon Man*: "Why don't you try acting?"

Ridin' High, Wide, and Lonesome

Michael Cimino had taken home two Oscars—Best Picture and Best Director—in 1978 with his Vietnam epic, *The Deer Hunter*. Cimino was a golden boy with a ticket to ride, and he took that ticket west. Since 1970, he had had a pet script in pocket about Wyoming's Johnson County War of 1892, one of the bloodiest blots on American history. It made Shane's problems look like a picnic. The resentment of local cattle barons (in the guise of the Wyoming Stock Growers' Association) against the influx of immigrants and a rash of rustlings took a nightmarish turn when the barons imported a mob of forty-six gunmen (a.k.a. the Regulators) from Cheyenne to execute every person on a death list of undesirables (at a rate of five dollars a day plus fifty dollars for every immigrant shot or hanged). When a local posse, two hundred strong, finally surrounded the killers, the U.S. Cavalry was sent to extricate the Regulators, and because of the cattlemen's political connections, none was ever brought to trial.

Cimino tells his heinous tale through the experiences of James Averill (Kris Kristofferson), a Harvard graduate who heads for the romance of the West, a stint as federal marshal, and the romance of local prostitute Ella Watson (Isabelle Huppert). Ultimately siding with the townspeople as things get uglier, Averill comes up against his old friend and rival for Ella's affections, Nathan D. Champion (Christopher Walken), a gunman formerly hired by the stock owners to enforce their law. In a final intensely bloody scene, Averill, with the help of saloon owner John Bridges (Jeff Bridges), organizes the populace into a ragged but effective army: Champion makes a final stand for good in a burning house; Watson faces ordeals too ghastly to mention. Their charged triangle set against the epic backdrop of turmoil is the heart of the film.

What makes the movie great is the complete world of visual detail with which Cimino surrounds this heart, and which cinematographer Vilmos Zsigmond captures lovingly on camera. You can practically smell this film. It's enough to make Erich Von Stroheim (known for his Austrian directoral accuracy, down to the correct underwear for his Prussian soldiers) drop his monocle. Cimino told reporters: "Every article of clothing, every structure, every sign is based on a photograph of the period. Even when a detail is there but not seen, I still feel it contributes something to the overall texture of the completed film....It even helps the crew [who may not have shared his sentiment—they called him "The Ayatollah"]."

> **Q. What early 1980s western had a budget in the stratosphere, was so savaged by critics as a dirty example of Hollywood excess that it lasted only a few weeks at a theater near you, scared the bejesus out of most major studios to the point where they hardly made any major westerns through the decade, lives on in infamy as the most disastrous epic of all time, and yet is still a helluva movie?**
>
> **A. Heaven's Gate**

The early section depicting Averill's and Billy Irvine's (a jellied John Hurt) Harvard graduation was so period that it had to be shot at Oxford University. Cimino also put 150 carpenters to work on four different construction crews in three states, creating crucially detailed sets that would turn the clock back ninety years: the site of Two Medicine Lake at Glacier National Park became the fictional town of Sweetwater. Wallace, Idaho, had its six-block-long main street turned into Casper, Wyoming. Meanwhile, an ancient, hulking locomotive from Denver was sent rolling around the country trying to find tunnels big enough to allow it to get to Montana. A 100- by 40-foot (30.4 by 12.1m) old-fashioned roller-skating rink, complete with a 7-foot-tall (2.1m) wood-burning stove, was built in Kalispell, Montana (production headquarters), where nearly 2,500 locals were put to work as extras and $14 million was pumped back into the economy. Cimino himself bought 156 acres (62.4ha) of land nearby.

Verisimilitude extended to the cast. Classes were set up for actors and extras on everything from wagon driving to roller-skating to bullwhipping to waltzing. A former Green Beret gave lessons in safe handgun use. Isabelle Huppert spent three days as the guest of an Idaho bordello. The effort to create what producer Joann Carelli called "a moving documentation of the era" was not lost on the actors even if it was lost on the critics. As Christopher Walken said: "For me a character comes from the outside in. Once I put the hat on, I've got part of the guy. If I know what kind of shoes he wears, I know a little bit about the way he treats his wife." All this detail didn't come cheap. When United Artists took on the project, Cimino hadn't yet decided to tack on the Harvard graduation (with its grand ballroom dance sequence), or the epilogue in which Averill, years later, ruminates over his past from the deck of his yacht, anchored in Newport, Rhode Island. Cimino admitted, "It's hard to finish a film. It's difficult to leave any experience that's that intense." But time is money. Prices escalated daily, sometimes through the extortion of local landowners who, just before filming, upped their rental fees by as much as fifty thousand dollars. United Artists considered pulling the plug but didn't.

By premier time—almost two years, 156 shooting days, and 1,500,000 feet (457,200m) of film later—Cimino had racked up a $36 million bill for the film *Time* magazine was calling *Apocalypse Next*. The first assembly of the film for United Artists' executives came in at five and a half hours. Five and a half quickly shrank to three and a half for general release, which quickly shrank to two and a half. The critics descended, a book was written on the whole debacle, and the rest, as they say, is history. But what rich (literally and figuratively) history! This is one epic you should judge for yourself.

A WOMAN'S PLACE IS ON THE RANGE (AND DON'T YOU EVEN THINK WESTINGHOUSE!)

Let's face facts: after war movies, Hollywood's biggest boys' club was the western. Of course, no banner ran across any cowtown Main Street reading FEMINIST VALUES GO HOME! But usually, hard-edged, fast-living gals like Chihuahua (Cathy Downs in *My Darling Clementine*) were chased off screen to make room for chaster, softer señoritas (in this case, Linda Darnell in the title role). Likewise, most pictures with a pants-wearing, gun-toting adventurous woman (often Barbara Stanwyck, whose favorite movies to act in were westerns) had her tamed by love and cooing in a frilly dress—or dead, if she stuck to her guns by the final frames. And you must admit, for all their guts, *Thelma and Louise* (1992) ended their wild ride by plummeting into a canyon. Still, if being strong didn't pay off for characters, it did for the leading ladies who were woman enough to tackle the roles. Most of the time, anyway.

There were upright schoolteachers (Loretta Young in *The Lady from Cheyenne*, 1941); misplaced sophisticates (Jean Simmons in *The Big Country*, 1958, and Liz Taylor in *Giant*, 1956); single-minded settlers (Conchata Ferrell in *Heartland*, 1979); savvy saloon girls (Angie Dickinson in *Rio Bravo*, 1958); iron-willed matriarchs (Jo Van Fleet in *The King and Four Queens*, 1956); tough tomboys (Anne Baxter in *Yellow Sky*, 1948); serene Indian maids (Elsa Martinelli in *The Indian Fighter*, 1955); land grabbers (Barbara Stanwyck in *Cattle Queen of Montana*, 1954); reformers (Olivia De Havilland in *Dodge City*, 1939); and even gunslingers (Mary Stuart Masterson, Madeleine Stowe, Drew Barrymore, and Andie MacDowell in *Bad Girls*, 1994).

In a land where only the strong survived, the strongest survive longest in our memories. Let's look at some of the most formidable of these portraits of frontier womanhood.

> *I did a picture once in which a woman was crossing the prairie from the East to the gold rush. She had to face a buffalo stampede, the Indian attacks, and a prairie fire. But every morning the heroine came out of the prairie schooner wearing white ruffles and her hair done up in curls. But nobody cared, because then the public accepted motion pictures only as a fantasy and amusement.*
>
> **—Edith Head, costume designer**

Hell on Wheels

There was a notion that Frank Capra had had knocking around in his noggin for some time. Some say he put it on a note and passed it over the fence to his neighbor, William Wellman. Others say they discussed it at a barbeque. This was Capra's pitch: "Look. It's 1851. Put two hundred women in covered wagons. Take 'em across hell to California. Stampedes, accidents, Indians, and sudden death." Now that was a concept Wild Bill could work with. After they had batted it around for a while, Wellman pitched it to thinking-man's producer Dore Schary at MGM, who jumped at it, and assigned Charles Schnee (*Red River*) to script it. Schnee was so enthusiastic that he knocked off a screenplay in six weeks. By the time MGM's publicists were pitching *Westward the Women* (1951), it had been boiled down to "200 Women Hell-Bent on Matrimony!"

This story of a misogynistic wagon master hired to lead 140 eligible brides from Chicago across the considerable perils of prairie, mountain, and desert to a green valley in California was anything but far-fetched. In the 1800s, the West had desperately needed women to civilize and populate it. Weddings were so scarce that couples frequently made money charging a five-dollar admission to their ceremony. In 1849, a Mrs. Farnham had issued a circular in New York City to recruit 100 to 130 "respectable women" to go west. "Respectable" was emphasized, for indeed some scams existed to dupe and dump innocents into a life of debauchery. A.S. Mercer, president of Washington Territory, had advertised in *The New York Times* for twenty young "mail-order brides" to travel to his neck of the woods at three hundred dollars a head. Was the *Times* abashed? Certainly not; it greeted the news with banner headlines proclaiming "Brilliant Prospect for the Settlers and Miners of the Pacific Slope." Fred Harvey made a business of importing women to work in his western chain of restaurants (Judy Garland served succotash with a song in *The Harvey Girls*, 1945).

Though some women opted to sail around Cape Horn rather than face the transcontinental journey, the hardy tried it—and many died along the way. As the trailboss of *Westward the Women*, Buck Wyatt (Robert Taylor), sneeringly litanizes to a hall full of prospective brides just before they rush up to a huge board covered with photos of the available men to pick their future mates: "We jump off from Independence, across the Big Blue River, the Little Blue, the Platte, the Sweetwater, South Pass over the Rockies, down to the Big Salt Lake, then the desert. It's a long, hard grind with no let-up. Rain, hail as big as eggs, breakdown, prairie fires, sand storms, dust storms, alkali water, no water, cholera, Indians, drownings, stampedes, stupid accidents. You'll pass graves everywhere, milestones along the way. One out of every three of you will be dead before you get to his [Roy Whitman, as played by John

> *Anything you can do, I can do better. I can do anything better than you.*
>
> **—Annie Oakley, Annie Get Your Gun**

McIntire] valley. So, if you're smart you'll leave by that door. It's my best advice. Follow it now! [They don't.] All right, you asked for it. You'll get it."

And get it they do—almost everything he lists and then some. There's birth in the back of a three-wheeled wagon (with one corner held up by other traveling women), lots of death (including Buck's promised execution of a trail hand who rapes one of their charges), and fistfights (woman against woman), and when the going gets really tough, the trail hands hightail it but the women keep on keepin' on.

Dusting off records from Fort Laramie and old issues of Salt Lake City's *Desert News*, Schnee found almost every nationality and walk of womankind represented in these women's wagon trains. Director and producer complied: Parisian actress Denise Darcel, originally slated for a much smaller role, won the leading role of the French firebrand, Danon (thanks to a little personal coaching from Robert Taylor). Renata Vanni, star of New York's Italian stages, was flown in to play the twice-bereaved Mrs. Antonio Marone. Hope Emerson got the plum role of Patience, a seafaring widow who hailed from New Bedford, Massachusetts, but had "decided it was time to scrape my hull and weigh anchor." Marilyn Erskine and Lenore Lonergan also left the New York boards and headed west. Henry Nakimura, a former University of Hawaii student who was of Japanese ancestry, headed east to play the trailboss' cook and thoughtful sidekick.

Actresses, actors, crew, oxen, wagons, and Wellman converged on Kanab, Utah (Schary had wanted to shoot in 850 square miles [2201.5 sq km] of virgin film territory), for the largest location company MGM had ever assembled. Four hundred folks squeezed into the motels, guest houses, and homes of the town of one thousand residents and their three telephones. Wellman hired a local bicyclist to pound on every door at five A.M. each morning for a wake-up call. Four hundred is also a lot of folks to clothe. Luckily, costumer Reggie Callow had cut his teeth on nothing less than

Gone With the Wind and was ready with a circus tent, complete with changing rooms for two hundred. Callie was also inventive enough to use 30 gallons (113.6l) of coffee as makeshift dye when the women's costumes didn't look dirty enough.

Wellman wanted his actresses to look tough and appropriately dirty, too. Mother Nature helped out with 110°F (43.3°C) temperatures in the Mojave desert and a constant dusty wind (which made the requisite wind machines unnecessary). To that end, he also forbade all makeup and limited hair-washing to once a week, though he magnanimously allowed unlimited baths and changes of underwear. He also provided a three-week boot camp prior to the start of shooting. There were bullwhip classes, horseback riding classes, fight classes, shooting classes (which came in handy, as five rattlesnakes were shot on location the first day, one of which made its first and last screen appearance), and calisthenics classes with former boxer Johnny Indrisano. By the time it was all over, the actresses could ride, mule, slug it out, shoot, and remove and replace a 200-pound (90.8kg) wagon wheel as well as any pioneer pit crew.

The actresses' seasoning showed. When the wagon train's tattered and heroic one hundred survivors reach the outskirts of Whitman's Valley, you couldn't feel prouder. They've earned their right to demand new material for clothes from town—at gunpoint—before rolling in. (In a heart-wrenching scene, they've had to dump all their possessions to lighten their load across the final stretch of desert.) And though they slip back into their former frilly duds and societal roles, it's still the women who call the shots as they finally meet their men. Hee-haw!

> *Texas is heaven for men and dogs but hell on women and oxen.*
>
> **—Anonymous housewife**

Honey, let me tell you about Texas. Rock Hudson woos his bride-to-be, Elizabeth Taylor, before taking the Maryland flower down to the Lone Star State...and plenty of dynastic trouble...in the giant **Giant** *(1956).*

Still Waters Run Deep

Womenfolk don't come tougher than those trying to hold on to their homesteads. Jean Arthur did a pretty good job of it, but then she had Shane. Jessica Lange fought the good fight with real-life and on-screen husband Sam Shepard in Country (1984). Sissy Spacek didn't shirk when it came to The River (1985). But they all pale in comparison to Jane Fonda, who delivered a performance taciturn enough to make Gary Cooper fidgety in Alan J. Pakula's highly realistic Comes a Horseman (1978).

It's 1946, and Ella Connors is trying to hold on to her Montana ranch. On her side she's got an old cowhand, Dodger (Richard Farnsworth), period. Against her she has an aging cattle baron named Ewing (Jason Robards, Jr.), who was evil enough to seduce her in her girlhood and use it as ammo to break her father's spirit and now plots to get her land, while the real power, his partner, Atkinson (George Grizzard), is looking at both their pastures as oil fields.

The film, whose title comes from the Gordon Lightfoot song "Don Quixote," evens the odds by bringing in drifting cowboy Frank Athearn (James Caan), just back from World War II, whose partner (all-American quarterback Mark Harmon, in his first film role) has just been killed by Ewing's goons. The uneasy alliance, friendship, and eventual love affair between the honest and open Athearn and the fiercely independent, unsophisticated, and weathered-looking Connors is a beautiful thing to watch unfold. So is Richard Farnsworth's (a former stuntman who had doubled for Monty Clift in Red River) natural and underplayed performance (and death). The pair's final stand against the depressed and depraved Ewing (who tries to kill them in a horrible way) is truly stirring. As the bygone West crashes down around everyone, never has such a bleak ending held so much promise for a new start.

Though many critics derided this gem for its slow pace and brooding paranoiac quality, it's just these qualities that make it so good. Fonda and Pakula's edgy collaboration on Klute (1971) had won the former sex symbol an Oscar. Ella is a world away from the worldly callgirl Bree, but Fonda here is a diamond in the rough.

Who says guns are Freudian symbols? Or is Rio (Jane Russell) just sending a mixed message in Howard Hughes' infamous The Outlaw (1940)?

Gordon Willis' crystalline photography of the Wet Valley, Colorado, location and dark interiors shafted with sunlight add to the starkness. As critic Charles Champlin insightfully said: "Comes a Horseman is, I think, intended to be about a kinship between the individual and the land that is a surpassing love affair, born of awe and respect for the beauty and the bounty of the earth."

The Breast of the West

Sex appeal has sold its share of westerns, too. Claudia Cardinale (Once Upon a Time in the West, 1969), Brigitte Bardot (Shalako, 1968), Marilyn Monroe (River of No Return, 1954), Mae West (My Little Chickadee, 1939), Jane Fonda (Cat Ballou, 1965), Raquel Welch (Bandolero, 1968), and, of course, Bo Derek (Bolero, 1984—well, she was on horseback) have all steamed up the sage.

Lust in the dust got its first big boost when eccentric aviator, billionaire, and then–executive of RKO pictures Howard Hughes revealed the anatomical assets of twenty-year-old former dental hygienist and outstanding sweater girl of 1941 Jane Russell, in 1940's The Outlaw. In a ludicrous story that brings Billy the Kid (Jack Beutel), Pat Garrett (the unlikely Thomas Mitchell), Doc Holliday (Walter Huston), and a Mexican-Irish spitfire named Rio (Russell) together, Hughes broke new ground in both sexploitation and misogyny. Once mistress to both Doc and the Kid, Rio is weighed between them in value against a strawberry-roan horse. The horse wins out with both men.

The Motion Picture Association's press release of June 14, 1946, objected to the following: "Eight of the advertisements were pen and ink drawings in which the breasts of the star were emphasized and exposed"; man and woman were depicted "in a highly compromising horizontal position" (The scene in question ends as Rio is about to cover the chill-wracked body of the feverish Kid with her own—for medical benefits.); the line of billboard advertising copy asking "What are two big reasons for Jane Russell's success?" ("Her beauty and her charm" it answers in much smaller print below) and "How would you like to tussle with Russell?"; and "Late in April, 1946, it is alleged and not denied, a skywriting airplane wrote the words THE OUTLAW in the sky over Pasadena and then made two enormous circles with a dot in the middle of each."

Well, Russell's breasts were big, but not that big. Still, Hughes made sure he got maximum use of Russell's endowments by personally designing a maximizing bra for her to wear. And when censors objected to the amount of bust revealed, Hughes sent researchers secretly into darkened movie theaters to photograph the scantily clothed torsos of other sex godesses like Lana Turner and Hedy Lamarr in other films. Armed with his engineering measurements, he refuted the censors, proving that Russell, proportionally, was just as covered as anyone else—she just had more to cover.

Whatever his motives, they worked. After three years of delay and hype, The Outlaw drew more people into Atlanta movie theaters in its opening week than did Gone With the Wind.

The Lady with the Whip

Sex appeal is sexier when it rides tandem with personality and personal power. No other leading lady exemplified that more than Barbara Stanwyck—through twelve westerns, three television series (Wagon Train, Rawhide, and The Big Valley), and induction into the National Cowboy Hall of Fame. In 1935, her first big western gave pluck and charm to a character of humble Ohio origins: riflewoman Miss Phoebe Ann Moses, better known as Annie Oakley. Headlining as "Little Sure Shot" in Buffalo Bill's Wild West Show for seventeen years, Annie could shoot holes in coins, shoot backward with mirrors, and shoot cigarettes from men's mouths. One time, she shot 943 out of 1,000 airborne glass balls.

Dowdy Jessica Drummond (Barbara Stanwyck) gives some thought to springing her baby brother, Brockie (John Ericson), from the calaboose in Sam Fuller's gritty Forty Guns (1957).

Stanwyck gave Annie innocence, guts, and sex appeal. Born Ruby Stevens, Stanwyck had come from humble origins herself, albeit New York. Orphaned at four, the Scotch-Irish lass had gone through twelve foster homes. After graduating from Erasmus High School in Brooklyn, she worked menial jobs before becoming a chorus girl, burlesque star, stage star (where David Belasco chose her stage name from an old program on the wall of his theater's green room), and finally a screen siren with brains and humor.

She dropped the innocence for films like The Furies (1950); Cattle Queen of Montana (1954), in which, as Sierra Nevada Jones, she fights for her father's rangeland; Maverick Queen (1956), in which, as a corrupt hotel owner, she dies for opposing the male code; and finally Sam Fuller's Forty Guns (1957), which The Village Voice dubbed "the most phallic western ever made."

In Fuller's film, Stanwyck plays a babe in black, "a high-riding woman with a whip," or so the song says. As Jessica Drummond, the self-made matriarch of Tombstone, she rides roughshod over all who oppose her and backs her plays with a trigger-happy brother and a hired crew of forty gunmen. The opening moments alone are enough for a Freudian field day: an aerial shot of Drummond in tight-fitting black, charging at the head of a phalanx of lusty riders, penetrating another mass of horsemen. Whew! This breakneck western is nonstop action in every sense. The symbolism is there for interpretation, too: Jessica sits at the head of a long table surrounded by men. She takes her brother Brockie's (John Ericson) guns away while teasing him about all his illegitimate children. She wants to play with cowboy Griff's gun, but he's too abashed to let her. There's sex talk in terms of guns. One scene even focuses on a woman through the lengthy perspective of a gun barrel.

Stanwyck was up to the challenge in every way. Known for her gameness when it came to stunts, she came through for a trepid Fuller. In a storm scene provided by an artificially made cyclone (huge propellers aimed right at her), not only did she not flinch under dangerously high winds, but when stuntmen balked at doubling for her—she was to be dragged from a horse's stirrup—she did the deed herself, giving Fuller three takes at 30 miles (48km) per hour before she was through.

Fuller loved her for it (he had chosen her for the role, though Marilyn Monroe had petitioned avidly) and wanted to give her an ending with as much guts as her performance. When clutched by her ne'er-do-well brother as a human shield, leaving her love interest, lawman Barry Sullivan, to choose between love and justice, Fuller originally had Stanwyck and her brother drilled with the same bullet. But the studio balked (not at the punishment for a gal who tried to rule, but at Sullivan's ungentlemanly behavior) so Barbara was spared to—you guessed it—go crawling after her hero. It's our loss that Fuller never followed through on his later idea to film the Evita Peron story with Stanwyck. She could easily have commanded a nation.

Vay Out Vest

It's ironic that Marlene Dietrich's moniker in Joe Pasternak's *Destry Rides Again* (1939) is Frenchy, the non-Germanic name that her gunslinging beau, Frenchy Fairmont, got thirteen years later in *Rancho Notorious* (1952). But that was no more ironic than the ice queen's presence in westerns in the first place: a presence so strong that Madeleine Kahn would ultimately parody it in Mel Brooks's hilarious *Blazing Saddles* (1974).

Though George Marshall's remake of Max Brand's novel—a tale of the gunless, gangly, fearless, diplomatic, milk-drinking, anecdotal son of a famous sheriff, Thomas Jefferson Destry (Jimmy Stewart, in his introduction to the genre), and his struggle to clean up the wild and wooly town of Bottleneck—is a comedy, it's

> A woman can go further with a lipstick than a man can with a Winchester and a side of bacon.
>
> —Charles Russell, More Rawhides

still one of the most action-packed, devilishly dialogued westerns ever shot. Saloon girls don't come any more classic than Dietrich. She had busted her sultry chops in *The Blue Angel* (1930) and beat out actress Paulette Goddard (former wife of Charlie Chaplin) for the chance to raise hell in one hell of a hell-raisin' town when the Destry cameras started rolling.

Frenchy—a woman who wears diamond dust in her hair to make it glitter. Who rolls her own cigarettes. Who sings ribald songs in a voice that could belong to Arnold Schwarzenegger. Who spills hot coffee in gamblers' laps—on purpose. Who stuffs jewelry down her cleavage (though the Hays Office censored the line, "There's gold in them thar hills"). Who gambles with a Russian aristocrat (a marvelous Mischa Auer) for his pants. Who clobbers the aristocrat's wife (in a fight that took five days to film and left its participants a mass of cuts and bruises). Who even rouses the womenfolk to take back the town in a scene Carry Nation would have been proud of. As character Lord Beaverbrook remarked, the sight of Frenchy in fishnets astride the stage of the Last Chance Saloon belting out "See What the Boys in the Back Room Will Have" is "a greater work of art than the Venus de Milo."

Jimmy Stewart is no slouch in the film, either. Never has his affable manner seemed more out of place—or been more effective on screen. He has an anecdotal answer for everything. Regarding his tenacity in looking for the previous sheriff's killer, he says: "You know, I had a friend once that used to collect postage stamps. He said the one good thing about a postage stamp is it sticks to one thing 'til it gets there." He also gets to take Dietrich down a peg or two: "I bet you've got a lovely face under all that paint. Why don't you wipe it off someday and take a good look? See how you can live up to it." She does...and touchingly asks Destry to wipe away her lipstick before their last kiss.

Whatever smooching Dietrich and Stewart did off-camera is a matter of conjecture. But it is said that Stewart spent all too much time immersed in Flash Gordon comic books between takes for Marlene's insatiable sexual taste. Her remedy: she had a life-size Flash Gordon doll made to order, then locked herself, Stewart, and the doll in her dressing room together. Oh, for an ear to the door of that one...

OPPOSITE: Hey, don't guys usually do this? You don't mess with Frenchy (Marlene Dietrich, with the upper hand) as we're about to find out in the fantastic fight scene from the classic Destry Rides Again (1939).

Who's in Charge Here?

Johnny Guitar (1954) has to be the weirdest western ever filmed. Ironically, it may be the best, as well. In a time when the little screen had usurped the genre from the big one, in a time when the Hollywood witch hunt for communists had neutered most films, many eagerly waited for this rash, lurid (in tone and color), estrogen-charged experiment in stretching the boundaries of the oater to go down like the Hindenburg. Instead, it flew like the Spirit of St. Louis. But it wasn't through teamwork. Never had such a group of "distinct personalities" assembled to make a movie.

Nicholas Ray was a maverick if there ever was one. A former stage director, his films were about as close to theater as Hollywood would allow. He had already had the temerity to depict American Robin Hood Jesse James as a juvenile delinquent in *The True Story of Jesse James* (1957). He had the audacity to actually

turn down Howard Hughes's offer to let him run RKO Pictures. He had never been thwarted or threatened by the House Un-American Activities Committee because he had already been investigated by the OSS during World War II and been found free of communist ties. Still, he wanted to tempt the fates and make a film about the McCarthy witch hunt, starring two women in the type of roles usually reserved for men.

At the head of his cast for *Johnny Guitar* was the notorious diva and Mommy Dearest Lucille Le Sueur (a.k.a. Billie Cassin, a.k.a. Joan Crawford). This woman, whom F. Scott Fitzgerald had

Director Nicholas Ray superbly serves up the western as a psychological love-triangle thriller noir with gender-challenging overtones as The Dancin' Kid (Scott Brady) and Vienna (Joan Crawford) watch to see just what Johnny Guitar (Sterling Hayden) will do next in the 1954 film of the same name.

once dubbed the archetypal flapper, was in a constant flap of comeback struggle. She had worked her way from showgirl to star. All but two of her first films had been with MGM, before her career had faded and then been reanimated with 1938's *Mannequin*. She had parted with Louis B. Mayer and languished at Jack Warner's studio, only to take home an Oscar for the flapless *Mildred Pierce* (1945). She would eventually become a reigning queen of horror movies. In the mid-fifties, she needed another comeback, and she was hell-on-wheels to work with.

Playing opposite her was Mercedes McCambridge, the workingest gal in radio who during the forties performed as many as fifteen dramatic shows a week. Her first film, *All the King's Men* (1949), had earned her a Best Supporting Actress Oscar. A brilliant performer, her tormented nature and excesses made her career a struggle, as well. Who else but such a tortured artist could eventually portray the voice of the Devil for William Friedkin's *The Exorcist* (1973)?

Caught in the middle was the laconic yet just as bull-headed Sterling Hayden. A golden boy who never took Hollywood seriously, he had actually joined the army under a false name to avoid the Hollywood publicity machine. He had admitted to having been a former communist—ironic considering his later role as the commie-obsessed General Jack Ripper in Stanley Kubrick's *Dr. Strangelove* (1963). Hayden ultimately abandoned Hollywood to become, of all things, a nautical explorer. Even screenwriter Philip Yordan was an anomaly: he had been a successful playwright, yet worried about all the money he was making for his screenplays.

The seas weren't smooth for long. At their Sedona, Arizona, location, Crawford tried to bully her way into coproducing Nicholas Ray's film. She wanted changes in the script and the cast. According to McCambridge, Joan had been in her trailer when she heard the crew's applause after Mercedes had flawlessly delivered a memorized four-page speech. Ray remembers that Crawford (who had wanted another actress, Claire Trevor, for the role of Emma in the first place) emptied out Mercedes' suitcase on the highway in appreciation. According to Ray biographer Bernard Eisenschitz, Joan then informed Ray, "I'm Clark Gable. It's Vienna that's got to be the leading part!" and threatened to shut down production unless Yordan rewrote the script accordingly.

Her threats may have been a godsend. What a story! Shot in ultravivid Trucolor with an opening that whips up a full forty minutes of saloon confrontations and counter-confrontations, shifting allegiances and trusts, we are immediately engaged if not intimidated. There's Vienna (Crawford), the gun-toting saloon owner whose land lies in the path of the railroad; Emma Small (McCambridge), the rabid, sexually repressed spinster hungering for Vienna's blood, land, and boyfriend; the Dancin' Kid (Scott Brady), the lithe, acidly genial, pretty-boy gang leader; Johnny Guitar (Hayden), the drifter with a claim on Vienna but no stake in her battle; and John McIvers (Ward Bond), the head of the vigilante force, all of whom are dressed in funereal black and ready to hang Vienna and torch her establishment (ironic, as Bond was one of the biggest red-baiters in Hollywood). All the way to its twisted Gothic-romance ending, this movie is a delight like no other.

A Woman's Gotta Do What a Man's Gotta Do

Sometimes it wasn't enough for a woman to be as strong as a man. As the posters for Maggie Greenwald's moving and thought-provoking *The Ballad of Little Jo* (1993) proclaimed, in the Wild West, a woman had only two choices. She could be a wife or she could be a whore....Josephine Monaghan chose to be a man.

History holds many a precedent. Emma Edmonds fled New Brunswick, Canada, at age nineteen to join the Union Army as Frank Thompson, and lived to write about it in *Nurse and Spy in*

A Little Offscreen Perspective from the Lead Players

On Johnny Guitar *we had an actress who hadn't worked in ten years—an excellent actress but a rabble-rouser....Her delight was to create friction. "Did you hear what he said about you?" she'd tell me. "And in front of a group of people!" I couldn't believe it....She would finish a scene, walk to the phone on the set, and call one columnist to report my "incivilities." I was as civil as I knew how to be.*

—Joan Crawford, on Mercedes McCambridge

Poor old rotten-egg Joan. I kept my mouth shut about her for nearly a quarter of a century, but she was a mean, tipsy, powerful, rotten-egg lady. I'm still not going to tell what she did to me. Other people have written some of it, but they don't know it all, and they never will because I am a very nice person and I don't like to talk about the dead even if they were rotten eggs.

—Mercedes, on Joan

There is not enough money in Hollywood to lure me into making another picture with Joan Crawford. And I like money.

—Sterling Hayden, on the whole thing

Raymond Chandler Goes West

The cast's delivery of Yordan's script for Johnny Guitar (1954, based on Roy Chanslor's novel of the same name) is some of the snappiest dialogue ever to grace the sage. Here are some tidbits from Vienna, Emma, Johnny, and the Dancin' Kid. Sam Spade, eat your heart out!

VIENNA: *You don't own the earth, not this part of it.*
EMMA: *You stay and you'll only keep enough of it to bury you in.*

VIENNA: *Down there I sell whiskey and cards. Up these stairs all you can buy is a bullet in the head. Now which do you want?*

VIENNA: *When a fire burns itself out all you have left is ashes.*

THE DANCIN' KID: *New York, I've been there. Stinks of fish.*

THE DANCIN' KID: *We haven't got enough silver to plug up the holes in Bart's teeth.*

JOHNNY: *A posse isn't people. I've ridden with them. I've ridden against them. A posse is an animal.*

EMMA: *I'm going to kill you.*
VIENNA: *I know. If I don't kill you first.*

JOHNNY: *How many men have you forgotten?*
VIENNA: *As many women as you've remembered.*

JOHNNY: *Could you spare that smoke, friend? Trouble you for a light, friend? There's nothing like a good smoke and a cup of coffee. You know, some men got the craving for gold and silver. Others need lots of land with cattle. Some got the weakness for whiskey and women. When you boil it all down, what does a man really need? Just a smoke and a cup of coffee.*

VIENNA: *I'm sitting here in my own house, minding my own business, playing my own piano. I don't think you can make a crime out of that.*
JOHNNY: *We've both done a lot of living. Our problem now is how to do a little more.*

the Union Army. Loreta Janeta Valasquez followed her husband into the Confederacy (wearing a phony beard and mustache), made the rank of scout, was wounded twice, and fought at the Battle of Bull Run as Harry T. Bufford. England's Colonel Victor Barker, manager of dog kennels and boxing clubs, was discovered at his death to be Valerie Aukell-Smith. Contemporary jazz pianist Billy Tipton, adoptive father of three, proved to be more than met the eye.

Greenwald's history-based film should not be confused with Doris Day's *The Ballad of Josie* (1967). *The Ballad of Little Jo* is the simple and powerful story of a Buffalo, New York, society miss (Suzy Amis), who is disowned by her parents after giving birth out of wedlock. Leaving her bastard child with her sister, she trudges west seeking a fresh start. It soon becomes apparent that to be dressed as a woman on the road means rape, slavery, or both. It also becomes apparent that most folks will believe that anything in pants is a man (since at that time it was illegal for women to dress in pants). The agonized and abused Josephine buys work duds, clips her hair, drops her voice an octave, and even slashes her face to make a nice masculine scar.

In the mining camp of Ruby City, Montana, she is grudgingly accepted by the rough and aromatic locals as an unromantic youth, a greenhorn whom they take under their paternalistic wings. Her survival and flourishing—as an isolated sheepherder (Amis is quoted as saying, "I don't care if I never have to get near another sheep again"); student of manhood under the woman-hating Percy Corcoran (Ian McKellen); neighbor and ally to well-meaning rancher Frank Badger (Bo Hopkins) and his wife, Ruth (Carrie Snodgrass); guide and friend to a Russian emigrant family; cattle company foe; and, ultimately, respected member of the community—is as human in its scope as it is stunning in its mountainous isolation.

As a man, Little Jo must experience the heartbreak of doing things she'd never have chosen to do as a woman (like killing men, and being party to the defilement of a deaf-and-dumb prostitute) as well as the joy of things she'd never have had the chance for (like building a fine homestead, voting, and smoking opium with Chinese laborer Tien Men Wong [David Chung], whom she rescues from a vigilante hanging to take on as a cook and ultimately, tenderly, as her lover).

With any luck, this first western directed by a woman will be the first of many more. By the time the jig is up for Little Jo, she has shattered preconceptions on both sides of the screen. Jane, Barbara, Marlene, Joan, and all the rest would probably agree—being a woman in the West has never been so bitter, or so sweet.

OPPOSITE: Josephine Monaghan (Suzy Amis) goes undercover and other gender to carve out a life in the West, in Maggie Greenwald's moving The Ballad of Little Jo (1993).

Chapter Six

AS THE SUN RISES SLOWLY INTO THE WEST

Clint Eastwood has a few uncomfortable facts to tell his late wife in the final moody moments of the majestic and iconoclastic film that revitalized an entire genre, Unforgiven (1992).

You could say that for some, the end of the trail is just the beginning. Since television put the B-western plot on the little screen (where it belongs), the big screen has been freed up for more realistic fare. The cowboy has been a dyin' breed in feature films for more than a few decades now, but still he won't roll over and play dead. Through countless films he's outlived his era as only a bullheaded, red-blooded, dysfunctional American icon can. Through decades at the box office, he's managed to survive wars (war movies), economic depressions and recessions (fewer movies), international espionage (James Bond movies), global consciousness (arty movies), high-tech (special effects–filled movies), and political correctness (movies that don't feel nostalgia for anything).

This survival, shaky though it has been at times, owes a lot to the fact that the whole idea of making a living from horseback—a vanishing way of life—is manna for great moviemakers. Loneliness is nobler under the big sky. Losing your independence is more emotional when your life has been spent on the move. And locking horns with a changing, increasingly impersonal, bureaucratic, and mechanized world is something that anybody who's waded through an automated telephone answering system can identify with, vanishing breed or not.

As the Wild West was tamed and tethered to make room for the civilization of the New West, its icons met their fate in startlingly different ways. Some went down in a blaze of glory, some poetically pondered their predicament, some tried to adapt, while others simply faded away. It seems only fitting that the movies that depicted those loners and their denouements are some of the finest that the western genre can claim.

LONERS

> *A man for breakfast.*
>
> **—Anonymous**

No cowboy had it much rougher much earlier (in film history) than Jimmy Ringo. Henry King's *The Gunfighter* (1950) remains a prototype for downplayed, doom-ridden portraits of the end of the Wild West. The bulk of this riveting but deliberately drab-looking film takes place in a saloon in the little New Mexican town of Cayenne. There, aging gunfighter Ringo (Gregory Peck), hunted by the brothers of the latest ambitious adolescent he has had to outdraw, waits for either the end or a new start. Haggard from having to live with the reputation he's carved out for himself, Ringo's only wish is to see his estranged wife (Helen Westcott) and the son who's never seen him.

Unfortunately, the only ones who want to see him are the little boys to whom he's a dime-novel hero, the big boys who want to best him, and the ladies of the town who want to see him strung up. It's only by the grace of an old compadre, Mark Strett (Millard Mitchell), who's traded in his rep for a sheriff's badge, that he's allowed to wait. Still, Ringo's time is running out.

Gunfighting has never been less glamorous—or loneliness more palpable—than here in this film, which has to be one of the first psychological westerns. Peck is understated, paranoid, deadly, and sincerity incarnate as he makes a final stand against the hostile world around him. To expand

> *Oh bury me out on the lone prairie*
> *Where the coyotes howl and the wind blows free*
> *And when I die you can bury me*
> *Neath the Western sky on the lone prairie.*
>
> **—Traditional song**

There's no rest for the renowned. Young gun Hunt Bromley (Skip Homeier at right) looks to make his mark with legendary Jimmy Ringo (Gregory Peck at left), as barkeeper Mac (Karl Malden) looks on helplessly in Henry King's grim **The Gunfighter** *(1950).*

the reality of the scene, Peck wore his guns (last worn by George O'Brien in Twentieth Century-Fox's *Riders of the Purple Sage*) day and night during production to get the feel of them. Director King added to the intensity, hiring historian Sylvester Vigilante to keep an eye on the production, ensuring veracity on Fox's back lot and coaching Peck on gunfighting tactics. King even put period coins in the saloon's 1870 slot machine solely for the star's benefit.

The results were worth every effort: Jimmy Ringo is as natural as the worn and dusty clothes he wears. His hard-bitten confessional scenes with the sheriff are almost too personal to watch. The bargain Ringo finally strikes with his wary wife, and his tender moments alone with his son, are the stuff that furtive, male tears are made of. After engaging in a final round of gunplay with a sneering young punk (Skip Homeier), Ringo gives the young man some parting advice, and even offers to claim having drawn first. Though it nails the coffin lid closed on gunfighting glamour, his words fall on deaf ears. The punk tells Jimmy not to do him any favors. Jimmy's response is as honest as it is chilling: "If I was doin' you a favor, I'd let them hang you right now and get it all over with. But I don't want you getting off that light. I want you to go on bein' a big tough gunny. I want you to see what it means to have to live like a big tough gunny. So don't thank me yet, pardner. You'll see what I mean. Just wait..."

> If I was worried about dying, I'd have quit this job a long time ago.
>
> —Marshal Matt Dillon, Gunsmoke

Hanging on to the free-and-easy lifestyle of the West is no picnic. There are few westerns with a more surprising beginning than David Miller's *Lonely Are the Brave* (1962). A cowboy lies high, wide, and lonesome on top of a dusty mesa, his boots crossed, his hat slung over his eyes, his horse Whiskey hobbled and contentedly cropping grass nearby. It's a picture-postcard of rustic R&R—until a rumbling disturbs the scene. As the man squints out from under his hat, he sees a jet trail plowing noisily across the sky...and we are jolted out of our rustic reverie. Toto, I don't think we're in (turn-of-the-century) Kansas anymore.

Jack (Kirk Douglas) is truly one of the last of the cowboys. Riding into Albuquerque to visit his old compadre Paul (Michael King) and Paul's wife, Jerri (the sensational Gena Rowlands), the girl who got away, Jack learns that his idealistic old chum is facing two years in the pen for smuggling undocumented Mexicans across the border. Like any good pal, Jack decides to get himself thrown into jail with him for a visit.

But Jack's no moderate—he ends up getting thrown in the tank himself. Because of his love of freedom, he has no choice but to bust out of jail. He wants to take Paul with him, but with a baby coming, his friend is reconciled to do his time rather than live life on the run.

The rest of the film follows Jack's flight on horseback into the Agua Dulce mountains, a hot pursuit by a beleaguered but not unsympathetic sheriff (Walter Matthau), and a tragic rendezvous with the twentieth century that neither of them can foresee. The film's final image of a rain-drenched road is one that will live in your memory for a long, long time.

This project was Douglas's baby from the start. The novel *Brave Cowboy*, by Edward Abbey (the literary National Parks ranger who later became a famed environmental guerrilla), had attracted the actor's attention, but it took him two years to find a studio, in this case Universal, that would let him coproduce Abbey's unusual story.

Novelist and screenwriter Dalton Trumbo was brought in to script. After being wrangled into playing the sheriff, Kirk's old drinking buddy Walter Matthau quipped, "Kirk always sends for me when he needs a cowboy." Actually, in the last film they had done together, *The Indian Fighter* (1955), Douglas had knocked Matthau cold in a fight scene. "He enjoyed it so much, he keeps calling me back," added the former victim.

Douglas dubbed the fight in this film as the toughest of his career. Jack's ticket to jail is a barroom brawl visited on him by a relentless one-armed Mexican-American war veteran who almost kills him in the process. Kirk didn't fare much better. His real-life opponent for the stunt was his pal Burt Lancaster's one-armed

> Do you realize how many fences there are getting to be? And the signs they've got on them? No Hunting, No Hiking, No Fishing, No Trespassing, Private Property, Closed Area, Stop Moving, Drop Dead.
>
> —Kirk Douglas,
> *Lonely Are the Brave*

stand-in, Bill Raisch. Although both men were covered with cuts and bruises when it was all over, Kirk emerged with a sprained wrist, which delayed filming for two weeks.

The look of *Lonely Are the Brave* is almost as powerful as its commentary on contemporary society. As the first Hollywood film to be shot in black-and-white Panavision, its sweep and subtlety achieve a perfect balance between splendor and gritty realism, what Douglas called "a social documentary with a chase." The 2-mile-high (3.2km) Sandia Mountains of New Mexico had never been used for filming and were virtually inaccessible to the crews. Consequently, helicopters had to be used to shoot some of the most intimate scenes, an ironic fact, considering that one crashes in the film itself. Even Kirk himself went the extra mile to ensure a realistic look: his wardrobe for the whole film was bought right out of a work-clothes store and cost a grand total of eighteen dollars. How's that for the glamour of Hollywood?

★　★　★

Douglas wasn't the only fish out of water in the modern West. He was in excellent company: *The Misfits* (1961), perhaps one of the most raw, eloquent, stark, and sorrowful movies ever made about the human condition. What would you expect from a film written by Arthur Miller (*Death of a Salesman*), directed by John Huston (*The Treasure of the Sierra Madre*), and starring Marilyn Monroe, Clark Gable, Montgomery Clift, and Eli Wallach?

Here, too, the enemy is the twentieth century, and the story is stunningly simple. Fate throws together four lonely strangers, each at the end of his or her respective rope, and sits back to watch the fireworks. There is Gay Langland (Clark Gable), an aging cowboy who'd rather do anything on horseback than earn "wages" on foot, but whose options are shrinking by the day. Guido (Eli Wallach) is a recently widowed pilot and mechanic with a mouthful of dreams and a heart as empty as his unfinished dream house. Add Perce Howland (Montgomery Clift), a rancher's son dispossessed after his father's death, who now has his brains knocked out for a living on the rodeo circuit. And in the middle of it all is a magnet, Roslyn Taber (Marilyn Monroe), a recently divorced woman-child whose lust for life is equaled only by her confusion and pain. For these misfits, a last roundup of wild mustangs (for less than noble purposes) in the desert outside Reno,

Kirk Douglas (center) starred in and produced The Indian Fighter (1955).

Nevada, could be a last chance for true happiness—or a confrontation with the core of what makes each of them dysfunctional and self-destructive. And if that sounds highfalutin, it only proves how high the stakes are.

Arthur Miller, then Monroe's husband, had high stakes of his own: he had never been produced on the big screen. His marriage was starting to flounder, but he set out to adapt his 1957 short story into a movie that would show the world that his wife was a great actress, not just a sex symbol. Friend and producer Frank Taylor took the story to John Huston (who had given Marilyn her first film break in *The Asphalt Jungle*, [1950]). It was far from mainstream, long on character, and short on plot—just the thing a maverick like Huston could sink his teeth into. While they were negotiating, Marilyn, who had been snapped up for the comedy *Some Like It Hot* (1959), read the script and let her husband know her dissatisfactions with her character's weak nature. The great playwright would have to do some rewriting.

High stakes were the name of this game. As filming began in July 1960, the set was rife with arguments and insecurities: Marilyn had an image to shatter. Huston was preceded by the reputation of being difficult to work with. Clark Gable, though past his popular prime, had been grabbed (after Robert Mitchum had turned the project down because he didn't like the script) for $750,000 plus 10 percent of the gross. An old-time movie star, Gable would have to prove his merit to the New York theater–steeped ensemble. Clift had a reputation of personal excess and professional unreliability to live down. The actor came on board for $200,000, saying that he liked the script because he didn't have to appear until page fifty-seven. More likely, the attraction was the confessional nature of the telephone call in his first scene, where his character tells his mother of his change since a serious accident. Clift himself had had a brush with death in a disfiguring car accident only three years earlier. Drawing on his own personal experience, he did the scene perfectly in one take—and immediately gained Gable's respect.

Marilyn's behavior was less exemplary. Convinced that Miller was beefing up Wallach's character at the expense of her own, she put more pressure on her husband, eventually driving him to seek refuge in a separate hotel room. Memorization was a problem for her, even with the shortest dialogue, and yet with Clift she pulled off a crucial five-minute scene, in which she tenderly mothers him outside a saloon, in only six takes. Monroe's addiction to sleeping pills made her hours late for the nine A.M. work calls that Gable had stipulated in his contract. Eventually she was even checked into a Los Angeles hospital during the shoot to dry out for two weeks.

> I tell you, I'm dyin' for some fresh air, and no people, male or female.
>
> —Clark Gable, *The Misfits* (1961)

It seems a minor miracle that *The Misfits* was made: it succeeded despite Monroe's pills, Clift's vodka and orange juice, Miller's loss of thousands at the Reno crap tables, and Gable's physical weariness from throwing himself into stunts he was too old to execute. More miraculous is that this clash of misfit artists resulted in such a heartfelt and unforgettable film. But the ordeal did take its toll.

Gable, having learned on the set that he would become a father, never lived to see his son: on November 30, three days after shooting his final scene, he suffered a fatal heart attack. Clift's health also continued to deteriorate after the project until his own fatal heart attack in 1965. Monroe and Miller's marriage had gone belly-up, with Miller eventually marrying a still photographer he had met on the set. And, for Marilyn, *The Misfits*. Less than two years later, sleeping pills ended her pain forever.

That Damned Antihero: Smile When You Say That, Bambino

Jimmy Ringo may have foreshadowed it. Hombres like Jack and Gay might have suspected it. But who could have guessed that in Naples, Italy, in 1929 a child would be born who would someday save the western from virtual extinction and change its nature forever. Big words, but Sergio Leone was a big man—literally and figuratively. By the time he was forty, he was the highest-paid director in world, earning an average of $750,000 per film.

Fame, however, was a long time coming. Born into a film family (his father was a director and his mother was an actress), young Sergio first apprenticed with neorealistic Italian directors, then jobbed as an assistant director on more than fifty films (including Vittorio De Sica's *The Bicycle Thief*, 1946), sometimes working under Hollywood directors shooting films in Europe. Learning American cinematic sensibilities from the likes of Raoul Walsh (*A Lion Is in the Streets*, 1954), Fred Zinnemann (*The Nun's Story*, 1958), Robert Wise (*Helen of Troy*, 1955), and William Wyler (*Ben Hur*, 1959) was good practice, as Sergio's personal taste leaned toward action films steeped in history.

> *I once shot poor Jimmy Stewart in the leg deliberately, and that was bad enough, heaven knows. But now I kill a little boy in cold blood. What am I coming to?*
>
> **—Henry Fonda, on working with Sergio Leone**

After taking over the direction on a Steve Reeves "sword picture" called *Last Days of Pompeii* (1959), Leone made his first full stab at directorship with *The Colossus of Rhodes* (1961). Then using a little over $245,000 from his success with the sword, along with leftover sets, he surprised everyone—and took up the gun.

He'd long wanted to make a western, but the Hollywood western wasn't what it used to be. Stateside studio output for oaters had dwindled drastically by the beginning of the sixties. Columbia Pictures alone, which in 1953 had made 47 pictures, 17 of which were westerns, had sunk to one western out of 35 pictures by 1960.

Following the horrors of Hitler, moviedom's day for old-fashioned heroes had gradually ended. Saintly giants like Gary Cooper (who had died in 1961) didn't walk righteously down Main Street anymore; they shot first and moralized after. It was a mean old world out there, and deadly professionals were the order of the day, as *The Magnificent Seven* (1960) so clearly showed. What was left? Violence? Passion? Mythic plots that didn't have to make any sense? This was almost the stuff of gladiator movies. Why not take western cynicism all the way to a twisted kind of opera of death?

Convinced that Italian audiences would not accept a western from a fellow countryman, Leone took the directorial pseudonym of Bob Robertson upon the European release of *Per un Pugno di Dollari* (1964), released by United Artists in 1966 as *A Fistful of Dollars*. The plot and screenplay were almost completely pilfered from (that old William S. Hart fan) Akira Kurosawa's 1961 samurai movie *Yojimbo*, which in turn owed much of its story (that of one man serving two sides to his own advantage) to Farlo Goldoni's Italian commedia dell'arte piece *A Servant of Two Masters*. (Martin Ritt had a similar idea when he adapted Kurosawa's *Rashomon* into the 1964 western *The Outrage*.)

Whatever the nationality of his recipe, Leone served up an al dente dish audiences could really chew on: a script in which an almost wordless, serape-covered, cheroot-smoking, remorselessly killing mercenary helps two factions of a western hellhole destroy each other—all the while reaping a huge profit. It was sinisterly atmospheric, megasavage, darkly comic, melodramatic western violence—Italian style.

> *Leone's version of the West is total anarchy with scarcely any room for heroism.*
>
> **—Jenni Caulder, There Must Be a Lone Ranger**

The Pavarotti of this opera, a character only known as "The Man with No Name," had a familiar name—cattle-driving good guy Rowdy Yates of the western television series *Rawhide* (1959–1965), otherwise known as Clint Eastwood. Though Leone had originally wanted Charles Bronson in the lead, Eastwood, who was frustrated with the small screen, was just what the mortician ordered. He was also willing to work for a mere $15,000.

By 1965, Eastwood's rates had gone up. *Fistful* was a popular, if not critical, success, earning $4.6 million in little over three years in the European market, and Leone quickly followed with *Per Qualche Dollaro in Più* (1965) (based on Kurosawa's *Sanjuro*, the sequel to *Yojimbo*), released in the United States in 1967 as *For a Few Dollars More*. The film cost a few dollars more, too, though its budget of $500,000 brought back $5 million in Italian box-office receipts.

For his second film, the director hired another American western veteran, Lee Van Cleef, who had graced *High Noon* and thirty-eight other oaters. In the role of Colonel Mortimer, the hatchet-faced Van Cleef became senior partner in a temporary alliance with Eastwood (now working for $50,000) against a psychotic, pot-smoking bandit named Indio (Gian Maria Volonte) and his twisted henchmen (a group that included future German film star Klaus Kinski as a hunchback).

Leone spoke very little English, but directed with such assurance, intelligence, and communication that he imparted all the information he needed to his international casts, who all spoke their lines in their native tongues. Moral pessimism, graphic violence, flashbacks, agonizing close-ups (even in daylight, actors were lit to make their eyes glint malevolently), and barren landscapes were all components of what America was coming to call the "spaghetti western."

The *New York Daily News* thought the plot was as empty as were the sets. The *New York Times* felt Leone's film glamorized violence. The *Washington Post* scoffed at Europeans' ignorance of the real West. But crabbing critics couldn't deny the box-office hold these forerunners of the action films of Sly Stallone and Arnold Schwarzenegger had on the moviegoing public.

Clint's salary quintupled to $250,000 by the time Leone completed the third of his trilogy with *Il Buono, il Bruto, il Cattivo* (1966), released in the United States in 1969 as *The Good, the Bad, and the Ugly*. Like his star's salary, Leone's films had expanded in length from 98 to 130 to 163 minutes. And the third film added Eli Wallach to the mix in a role almost reprising his Mexican bandit from *The Magnificent Seven*.

Perhaps the critical hue and cry pierced the box-office ballyhoo, for in 1968, Leone planned a serious departure from the operatic western comic book into the existential angst of the end of the old West. Leone originally wanted to symbolically kill off Eastwood, Van Cleef, and Wallach during the film's opening titles—which, incidentally, lasted longer than those of any other western up to that time. (That turned out to be impossible, as Eastwood had moved on to form his own production company, hired an old friend from *Rawhide* to direct, and made his own spaghetti western, American style: *Hang 'em High*, 1968. Filmed on a budget of $1.6 million, Eastwood's first western recovered its expenses within ten weeks of opening.)

Leone called his 1968 film *C'era una Volta il West* (*Once Upon a Time in the West*) his "ballet of the dead." Others called it an opera with arias not sung, but glared, winced, and stared. The film starred Charles Bronson, whom Leone had long wanted to work with: Claudia Cardinale, a box-office bombshell on both continents: Jason Robards, whose subtlety on stage the director admired; and Henry Fonda, to whom Leone had originally offered the role of Mortimer in *For a Few Dollars More*.

The glare, the cheroot, the stubble, the hat—it all adds up to "The Man with No Name." Ex–television star Clint Eastwood was on his way to celluloid fame and fortune by the time **For a Few Dollars More** *(1967) hit the silver screen.*

Along with cowriters Dario Argento and Bernardo Bertolucci, Leone crafted a scenario concerning a railroad land grab, a voluptuous New Orleans beauty (Cardinale) who has inherited the water rights the railroad wants, a mysterious harmonica-playing hero (Bronson) hungry for vengeance, his half-breed sidekick (Robards), and the railroad's ruthless hired killer (Fonda).

To help Leone realize what the director intended to be his tour de force, Paramount had given him a carte blanche budget. With some shots set in Monument Valley, the Italian left the land of tell-tale telephone lines and highways to build the biggest town any western set had ever attempted, on 100 acres (40ha) at the foot of Spain's Sierra Nevada mountains. The location included reconstructions of many of the buildings from Old El Paso, Texas, 5 miles (8km) of railroad track carved through a mountain pass, and earth matched to samples taken from Arizona and Utah.

For Fonda, his character was the cold-blooded antithesis of every western hero he had ever played, and he took to it like Jack the Ripper took to anatomy. Bronson's role was just the opposite of

---

Testosterissimo...or Beyond Sergio

Ol' Maestro Leone surely seemed to corner the market on sweaty, vicious, macho movie titles, but he was only the leader of the Europack. As he once said, "They call me the father of the spaghetti western. If so, how many sons of bitches have I spawned!" Other western directors from across the ocean may have never outfilmed or outfamed him, but some of the names they gave their movies were even meaner (and sometimes weirder) than Leone's odd lot. Here are a few of the more rococo—in translation, of course. So let your beard (or the hair on your legs) grow for a few days, light a cheroot, squint, and let your imagination paint the savage backdrops for these babies. You might want to down a couple of raw oysters, too.

Alive or Preferably Dead *(1969)*
And the Crows Will Dig Your Grave *(1971)*
And They Smelled the Strange, Exciting, Dangerous Scent of Dollars *(1973)*
Bastard, Go and Kill! *(1971)*
Bullets Don't Argue *(1964)*
Colt in the Hand of the Devil *(1967)*
Damned Pistols of Dallas *(1964)*
Deaf Smith and Johnny Ears *(1972)*
Death Is Sweet from the Soldier of God *(1972)*
Do Not Touch the White Woman *(1974)*
Duck, You Sucker! *(1971)*
Get the Coffin Ready! *(1968)*
A Girl Is a Gun *(1970)*
God Is My Colt .45 *(1972)*
Heads You Die, Tails I Kill You! *(1971)*
Hole in the Forehead *(1968)*
I Came, I Saw, I Shot! *(1968)*
If One Is Born a Swine *(1972)*
Light the Fuse, Sartana Is Coming! *(1971)*
Long Ride from Hell *(1968)*

My Horse, My Gun, Your Widow! *(1972)*
Prey of Vultures *(1973)*
Raise Your Hands, Dead Man, You're Under Arrest! *(1971)*
Reach, You Bastard! *(1971)*
Ringo, It's Massacre Time! *(1970)*
Seven Hours of Gunfire *(1964)*
Stranger That Kneels Beside the Shadow of a Corpse *(1971)*
Sun Scorched *(1966)*
They Call Him Cemetery *(1971)*
Town Called Hell *(1971)*
Tramplers *(1965)*
Ugly Ones *(1966)*
Up the MacGregors *(1967)*
Valley of the Dancing Widows *(1974)*
Vengeance Is a Dish Served Cold *(1971)*
Wrath of God *(1968)*

(And for all those snobs who put down Clint for eating spaghetti west of the Pecos, here's a list of other superstars who've made their bread and butter on continental fare: Dana Andrews, Carroll Baker, Brigitte Bardot, Anne Baxter, Candice Bergen, Richard Boone, Tom Bosley, Stephen Boyd, Yul Brynner, Geneviève Bujold, Dick Butkus, James Caan, Geraldine Chaplin, Chuck Connors, Joseph Cotten, Richard Crenna, Catherine Deneuve, Henry Fonda, Farley Granger, Gene Hackman, Sterling Hayden, Van Heflin, Dennis Hopper, Klaus Kinski, Martin Landau, Jean-Pierre Léaud, Christopher Lee, Marcello Mastroianni, Patrick McGoohan, Miou-Miou, Jean Moreau, Tony Musante, Joe Namath, Slim Pickens, Donald Pleasence, Anthony Quinn, Lynn Redgrave, Oliver Reed, Steve Reeves, Telly Savalas, Elke Sommer, Barry Sullivan, Robert Taylor, Adam West, and Richard Widmark.)

Gentleman cattleman Homer Bannon (Melvyn Douglas at right) just can't comprehend how his nephew (Paul Newman at left) can be such a no-good. But bad he is and bad he remains in Martin Ritt's blistering cinematic battle between the new and the old west in Hud (1963).

every western villain he'd ever played, and he was alarmingly heroic. With a supporting cast of Woody Strode, Jack Elam, and Lionel Stander, together the stars played out themes from half a dozen classic westerns, as Leone wove every familiar element and performance into something boldly new and bad-assed, something that western fans and directors alike would not soon forget. It was just the kick in the pants the genre needed.

Real Men Aren't Afraid to Be Ugly

Like Eastwood's Man with No Name, some stateside cowboys went out with neither a bang nor a whimper, instead snarlingly taking as many with them as they could (though more metaphorically than Clint). Hud (1963) was such an hombre. When Paul Newman agreed to play the title role in Martin Ritt's first western film, the actor's agent was a little nervous. Why would a handsome, affable leading man want to play the cruel, arrogant, ruthless, drunken, immoral, violent, self-pitying antithesis of everything a cowboy is supposed to stand for? Well, perhaps because the leading man was first and foremost an actor.

Antiheroes, American-style, had made scattered appearances in westerns since the days of William S. Hart, but they usually reformed by the last reel. Hud had no such intentions, but Newman was going to make us like him anyway. This antihero was based on a character from the novel *Horseman's Pass*, by *Lonesome Dove* author Larry McMurtry, and the dynastic drama of the Bannon family of Texas was scripted by the husband-and-wife team Irving Ravetch and Harriet Frank.

Homer Bannon (Melvyn Douglas) is an elderly cattleman of the old brand, tough but increasingly mystified by the modern world around him. His angry young son, Hud, who helps work his spread of land but is never allowed to run it, is much less than the apple of his father's eye. The disappointment, yearning, and resentment

> *Why this whole country is run on epidemics. Where you been? Epidemics, big business price fixin', crooked TV shows, income tax finaglin', souped-up expense accounts. How many honest men do you know? You take the sinners away from the saints and you're lucky to end up with Abraham Lincoln. I say let's us put that bread in some of that gravy while it's still hot!*
>
> **—Paul Newman, as *Hud***

between them is so deep and complex that a lifetime of family therapy couldn't unravel it. Homer's a righteous iceberg, and Hud is so hot under the collar that all his energies go to bar fights, bedding the local wives, and plotting his pappy's overthrow.

Two lives are caught in the middle of this battle between good and evil. Seventeen-year-old Lon Bannon (Brandon De Wilde of *Shane* fame), Hud's impressionable nephew, is torn between wanting to be like his cynical stud of an uncle or like his hardworking grandfather, and Lon has no idea that Hud had a hand in ending his brother's life. But, Alma (the incomparable Patricia Neal), the Bannons' earthy cook and housekeeper, sees through Hud and the crude passes he throws her all too clearly: as Hud so charmingly says, "The only question I ask any woman is 'What time is your husband comin' home?'" Recently divorced, Alma warns her suitor, "I've done my time with one cold-blooded bastard. I ain't lookin' for another one." But Hud only smiles and replies with typical cowboy confidence, "It's too late. You've already found him." The final showdown between them all comes when a series of unforeseen ranch tragedies pushes each character to show his or her deepest, truest self. And let's just say this—it ain't altogether a pretty sight.

Like *The Misfits*, *Hud* had its casting challenges. After overcoming his agent's wariness in tackling a role that Paramount

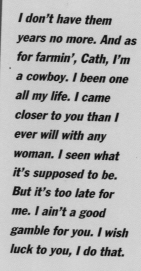

> I don't have them years no more. And as for farmin', Cath, I'm a cowboy. I been one all my life. I came closer to you than I ever will with any woman. I seen what it's supposed to be. But it's too late for me. I ain't a good gamble for you. I wish luck to you, I do that.
>
> —Charlton Heston, as Will Penny

studios would advertise as "The Man with the Barbed-Wire Soul," Newman sent a script to Patricia Neal. She agreed to do the picture only if her eight-week shooting schedule could be divided by a three-week break to return to England to her husband, the writer Roald Dahl, and their children. Paramount was leery of using Melvyn Douglas because of his heart condition, until Ritt insisted that only the slow-paced veteran actor would do for the role.

To achieve the barren, western look he wanted to reflect Hud's barbed-wire soul, Ritt enlisted the expertise of cinematographer James Wong Howe in styling a realistic black-and-white look that was as charmless as Hud was charming. As in High Noon, camera filters sucked soft, fluffy clouds out of an otherwise searing sky.

Howe spent eight sunrises alone on the film's crucial opening, establishing a sense of endless space with a shot of a truck running on an empty Texas road. Dwight MacDonald of Esquire magazine said, "The uncompromising realism is mostly in veteran James Wong Howe's photography, which does give an unretouched picture of the arid, scrubby, landscapes of West Texas, its neon squalid towns and its cheap clapboard houses, belligerently charmless inside and out."

Hud had enough charm to not only win over audiences and critics, but to win Howe an Oscar for cinematography. Newman and Ritt were each nominated, and both Neal and Douglas brought home statues of their own. What better proof could there be that nice guys finish last?

Nice guys also finished last in *Will Penny*, but with enough nobility of spirit to make up for all the Huds of this world. When Paramount released the film in 1967, it billed its protagonist as "a middle-aged cowboy with an idealistic slant on life." The first part was right; the second was pure Hollywood. There's no room for ideals on the real range. Will Penny (Charlton Heston) is a rugged, decent man in the September of his life (pushing fifty) who is just tryin' to survive, making a cowboy's paltry wages and leading the lonely and only life he knows.

Director Tom Gries' film picks up as Penny is turned loose after a cattle drive by a rancher named Ance (G.D. Spradlin, a bona-fide former Oklahoma farmhand, lawyer, electronics manufacturer, holder of a Ph.D. in history, and oil millionaire, who retired at age thirty-five and took a shine to acting). Drifting north with two compadres (Lee Majors and Anthony Zerbe speaking in

a Dutch accent) looking for winter work, the three tangle with a rawhiding, thieving preacher named Quint (a scenery-salivating Donald Pleasence) and his depraved clan (which includes a young Bruce Dern). The fight's aftermath brings Will in contact with an upright but kindhearted farmer's wife, Catherine Allen (Joan Hackett), who is being guided across to Oregon to meet her husband. It also brings him to a small town (the same Main Street used in *Shane*) where a gut-shot Dutchy (Zerbe) must rest in the care of the local doc (the character actor William Shallert) and his wife (Lydia Clark, the real-life Mrs. Heston).

Will moves on and gets a job riding line for a rancher (Ben Johnson). But up in his snow-laden line shack, Will crosses paths once again with the now-abandoned Mrs. Allen and her young son, whom he takes to calling Button. The surrogate family that they forge together in the wilderness and what happens to it after another run-in with the Quint clan makes for a truly tragic and tender story. And Heston's performance is a piece of humble and underplayed heroism if there ever was one.

Though largely panned by the action-crazed critics of the time (at least until Rex Reed gave it the boost it needed in a *New York Times* review), *Will Penny* was voted the outstanding western of 1968 by the Cowboy Hall of Fame. Now, who are you going to believe?

* * *

Rough, old cowboys in their golden years had been a precious metal mined as early as Sam Peckinpah's *Ride the High Country* (1962), an elegiac yarn of two veterans of the saddle (played by Randolph Scott and Joel McCrea) making a final trek and carrying a twenty-thousand-dollar gold shipment. The film had even been spoofed in *Cat Ballou* (1965), winning Lee Marvin an Oscar for his dual portrayal as both the elderly, alcoholized Kid Sheleen of dime-novel fame and his metal-nosed nemesis. "The last roundup" idea rounded up some fine films. Some western stars, inaccessible to finer sensibilities in their swaggering youth, mellowed with age and tapped into a well of humanity that made them even bigger at the box office.

Few managed the aging process better than John Wayne. After having battled and beaten what he called "The Big C" in the mid-sixties at the cost of a lung (apparently his doctor had been nervous about telling him he had lung cancer, leaving Wayne to learn it by chance from an intern—an experience he candidly compared to being slammed in the stomach with a baseball bat), the

OPPOSITE: Grizzled cowboy Will Penny (Charleton Heston at left) parts company with Dutchy (Anthony Zerbe at right) and Blue (Lee Majors at center) in Walter Seltzer's unblinking look at the realities of too much time spent in the saddle in Will Penny (1967). BELOW: Resurrected reprobate Rooster Cogburn (John Wayne at center) and the peaceable La Boeuf (Glen Campbell at left) pay a surprise visit to a den of thieves in the immensely popular True Grit (1969).

Perhaps I've projected something closer to my personality than other actors have. I have very few tricks. Oh, I'll stop in the middle of a sentence so they'll keep looking at me and I don't stop at the end so they don't look away, but that's about the only trick I have.

—John Wayne, *Variety*, January 29, 1976

Duke went directly back to work for Henry Hathaway (whom he called "the meanest man in the business") in *The Sons of Katie Elder* (1965). He kept on working, doing one or two films a year, and 1969 brought him the plum he so richly deserved.

In *True Grit* (1969) an orphaned girl named Mattie Ross (played by Kim Darby with a precocious sincerity worthy of Shirley Temple) enlists the aid of a fat, drunk, slovenly, foul-tempered, one-eyed reprobate of an ex-lawman, Reuben J. "Rooster" Cogburn, in avenging her father's murder. No Tom Mix–ian hero here—and that was fine with the man who had played heroes all his life. Wayne, who wanted to direct the project (he had already directed *The Alamo*, 1960, and *The Green Berets*, 1968), offered $300,000 for the rights to Charles Portis' novel. But he was outbid, by $200,000, by Paramount producer Hal Wallis, who in turn offered Wayne $1 million plus

35 percent of the gross to star and let someone else direct. That someone was Henry Hathaway.

Hathaway, true to his old-school reputation, rode roughshod over his cast, especially acting newcomer Glen Campbell and even veteran New York actor Robert Duvall. Ironically, even Dennis Hopper, whose stubborn commitment to the slow process of method acting had almost blackballed him after Hathaway's *From Hell to Texas* (1958), was now right in line with the result-oriented director. But it was Wayne who gloried in his wry role with uncharacteristic humor, profanity, and tenderness. And it earned him the one thing he didn't have: an Oscar.

When Duke got the news that he was up for an Academy Award for Rooster, he left Howard Hawks' Old Tucson set of *Rio Lobo* (1970) and flew west. Upon receiving his Oscar, Wayne said, with grit all his own, "If I'd known what I know now, I'd have put a patch over my eye thirty-five years ago." Word must have traveled fast, because when the Duke arrived back at the set, Hawks, the cast, the crew—even his horse—were all sporting that one-eyed Rooster Cogburn look.

GOING IN STYLE

Wayne mined even more deeply into his humanity in one last, great western—his eighty-ninth, to be exact. *The Shootist* (1976) depicts the final eight days in the life of the last of the great gunfighters, J.B. Books (Wayne), and seems to have as much to do with the sixty-nine-year-old Wayne as any character he'd played. Even the film's opening scenes, which chronologize Books' exploits throughout the late 1800s, use clips from old Wayne westerns as pseudo-documentary footage.

> *Cowboys are romantics, extreme romantics, and ninety-nine out of a hundred of them are sentimental to the core. They are oriented toward the past and face the present only under duress, and then with extreme reluctance.*
>
> *—Larry McMurtry, In a Narrow Grave*

Words to Live By: Part III

A. "Goddamn! I never thought I'd get killed tryin' to save an Apache."

B. "A horse will run so far so fast for so long and then he'll lie down on you. A horse lies down on an Apache, he puts a fire under his belly and gets him back up on his feet. When his horse dies, he gets off, eats a bit of it and steals another. Ain't no way you're gonna better that."

C. "I've got more lead in my carcass than that shave-tail Phil Sheridan has gold braids."

D. "That Hatchet Jack was a wild one. He was livin' with a female panther in a cave up in the muscle shell. She never did get used to him."

E. "First gettin' shot, then gettin' married—bad habits."

F. "It ain't hard gettin' shot. It's getting back up."

G. "My Daddy thinks oil is something you stick in your salad dressing."

H. "I am not a horse. I am a man."

I. "Mr. Rat, I have a writ here says you're to stop eatin' Chen Lee's cornmeal forthwith. Now, it's a rat writ, writ for a rat, and this is lawful service of same. See? He doesn't pay any attention to me. [Blam! Blam!] You can't serve papers on a rat, baby sister. You gotta kill him or let him be."

J. "Little by little, the look of the country changes because of the men we admire."

K. "'Texas is a woman,' she used to say, 'a big, wild, beautiful woman. You get a kid raised up to where he's got some size and there's Texas, whisperin' in his ear and smilin', come on out with me and have some fun.' It's hard enough to raise children any place, but if you've got to fight Texas, a mother has no chance."

L. "Leave him be. Out here by himself. No goods. Winter comin' in. He'll be a long while a-dyin' and all that time he's gonna know who done it to him. Yes sir, mighty long time. Then he'll be dead."

ANSWERS: A. Robert Duvall, *Geronimo* (1993); B. Burt Lancaster, *Ulzana's Raid* (1972); C. Edgar Buchanan, *Buffalo Bill* (1944); D. Stefan Gierasch, *Jeremiah Johnson* (1972); E. David Carradine, *The Long Riders* (1980); F. Cliff Robertson, *The Great Northfield Minnesota Raid* (1971); G. Paul Newman, *Hud* (1963); H. Richard Harris, *A Man Called Horse* (1970); I. John Wayne, *True Grit* (1969); J. Melvyn Douglas, *Hud* (1963); K. Martha Hyer, *The Sons of Katie Elder* (1965); L. Donald Pleasence, *Will Penny* (1967)

The story is simple: in the autumn of 1901, Books rides into Carson City, Nevada, where an old friend, Doc Hostetler (an equally venerable Jimmy Stewart), confirms a diagnosis of advanced prostate cancer. Trying to live out his painful last days in peace and anonymity is no cinch, though. While living as a boarder at widow Bond Rogers' (Lauren Bacall) rooming house, word of his name and fame gets out, and soon it's Jimmy Ringo all over again. The "good" want him out, the "bad" want him in a shoot-out, the press and other parasites want him to sell out, and Bond's wayward son, Gilom (Ron Howard), wants him as an out-and-out role model. Books faces the dilemma of whether to leave with a bang or a whimper, and what kind of path to steer the gun-hungry boy on.

Decisions were no dilemma for Wayne, who grabbed the role after Paul Newman, Gene Hackman, Charles Bronson, and Clint Eastwood had all turned it down. Don Siegel (*Dirty Harry*) directed (at times with unwanted help from Duke himself) a sterling cast, which included John Carradine (Wayne's old traveling companion from *Stagecoach*) as an unctuous undertaker; Harry Morgan as the most mean-spirited sheriff to ever walk Main Street; Scatman Crothers as a shrewd stable buck (a role originally intended for Yaphet Kotto); Sheree North as Books' old flame (who was supposed to unbutton Books' fly in one scene, until Wayne put a stop to it); Richard Boone (*Have Gun Will Travel*), who had also worked as an oilfield roustabout, fisherman, prizefighter, aerial gunner, artist, bartender, and writer, as an old enemy: and Hugh O'Brien (who had actually offered to do the film for free) as a faro dealer who can shoot a man through the heart at eighty feet (24.3m).

For all its machismo, *The Shootist* is a tender film. The growing father-son relationship is a theme that ironically reflects the intergenerational collaboration on the screenplay (a Hollywood first) between novelist Glendon Swarthout and his son, Miles. Wayne and Howard are a good match of aged cheddar and apple pie. Wayne and Bacall's bad man–good woman chemistry is just as touching. They had acted together twenty years earlier in *Blood Alley* (1955) and relished the reunion in their own crusty way. When asked about his leading lady, Duke growled: "She's the best thing that ever happened to Humphrey Bogart, and I'm gonna have a scene written in where I kiss her. And that will make him jealous, wherever he happens to be."

When inevitably questioned by the press as to how Duke compared to her late and equally tough husband, Bacall answered with the following sweet retort: "How the hell do I know? I've never been in bed with Duke."

Though the script dips into the cornbag now and then, the core story has tremendous heart. Books' self-knowledge in the face of his own death verges on wisdom, and his swan song at a 60-foot-

Former stagecoach-bandit turned thirty-three-year San Quentin inmate turned train robber Bill Miner (Richard Farnsworth) reflects on how times have changed in the sumptuous Canadian film The Grey Fox *(1982).*

> To a man my age, the future doesn't mean much, unless you're talking about next week.
>
> —Richard Farnsworth, as The Grey Fox

long (18.2m) bar is a masterful blend of action and acting. The six-foot-four-inch (193cm) American icon was never better, even as he battled his own mortality. Trying to drop down from a fulsome 265 pounds (120.3kg), staying on a salt-free diet (though still belting back cases of his favorite José Cuervo tequila), and breathing in Carson City's 4,500-foot (1,371.6m) altitude with one good lung while battling bronchial infections, viral pneumonia, and the Victorian flu with the other was tough enough. But Wayne had an older enemy that was getting ready for a final showdown. By 1979 "The Big C" would be the one left standing. And for many, that really was the end of the West.

* * *

The end of the trail can be sweet, too. On June 17, 1901, after serving thirty-three years in San Quentin Prison for robbing stagecoaches, Bill Miner was released into the twentieth century. Or so said the advertising copy for what can only be called the finest, and perhaps only, "northwestern" from down under

Words to Live By: Part IV

A. "I was reading about old Queen Vic. Well, maybe she outlived her time. Maybe she was a museum piece. But she never lost her dignity or sold her guns. She hung on to her pride and went out in style. Now, that's the kind of old gal I'd like to meet."

B. "Don't spill none of that liquor, son. It eats right through the bar."

C. "I was just thinking that of all the trails in this life, there is one that matters more than all the others. It is the trail of the true human being. I think you are on this trail and it is good to see."

D. "There's no Sunday west of Junction City, no law west of Hays City, and no God west of Carson City."

E. "You ornery son of a mule, you wouldn't give a bad dime to a sick kid!"

F. "Billy, they don't like you being so free."

G. "It's time I tempted fate. Let's see. Who's in here that I don't particularly like?"

H. "What kind of town is this, anyway? A man can't get a shave without gettin his head blown off."

I. "Looks like I got the plague, don't it? I guess you can't break out of prison and into society in one week."

J. "If wedlock is his aim he couldn't find a neater target."

K. "I'm no oyster picker."

L. "I myself never surrendered. But they got my horse, and it surrendered."

ANSWERS: ; A. John Wayne, The Shootist (1976); B. Walter Brennan, The Westerner (1940); C. Graham Greene, Dances with Wolves (1990); D. Gary Cooper, The Plainsman (1936); E. Jean Arthur, The Plainsman (1936); F. Bob Dylan, Pat Garrett and Billy the Kid (1973); G. Victor Mature, My Darling Clementine (1946); H. Henry Fonda, My Darling Clementine (1946); I. John Wayne, Stagecoach (1939); J. Gregory Peck, Duel in the Sun (1946); K. Richard Farnsworth, The Grey Fox (1982); L. Chief Dan George, The Outlaw Josey Wales (1976)

---

ever lensed. In 1982, Australian director Philip Borsos crafted a little gem of a movie for Canada. Kinder and gentler in tone than westerns in Hollywood or Europe, it focused on the latter-day exploits of the man credited with coining the time-honored phrase "Hands up."

The real Bill Miner was sixteen years old when he robbed the first of many Pony Express riders. By the time he was thirty-four, he had added twenty-six stagecoach robberies to his credit, acquired the nickname "The Gentleman Bandit" for his politeness and refrain from bloodshed, and been caught and sentenced to twenty-five years at San Quentin. In 1901, he was released into a new era where there were no stagecoach robberies—because there were no stagecoaches.

After a visit to his little sister in Oregon and a few futile attempts at the straight life in Washington, he robbed his first train at the age of sixty. Heading north into British Columbia, he would rob at least five more (that's almost one-tenth the total number of actual train robberies in the United States and Canada between 1870 and 1933) before he was through. Along the way, he would also stymie a Pinkerton manhunt and earn a new nickname: "The Grey Fox."

Borsos' film of the same name is bursting with lush landscapes (thanks to cinematographer Frank Tidy), catchy Celtic music (thanks to a score by the Chieftains), and a central performance as refreshing as a drink from a mountain stream (thanks to veteran stuntman and actor Richard Farnsworth). Though Harry Dean Stanton was Borsos' first pick for the lead role, Farnsworth delivers a star turn so natural and sexily underplayed it could make Paul Newman look stagey. Nor is Farnsworth simply warm and wiley: one bloody confrontation with an old friend from San Quentin proves that Bill did more than just read in prison.

There are unique pleasures here you'd be hard-pressed to find from most Hollywood fare. There's Miner's October-September relationship with a feminist photographer, played with Hepburn-esque feistiness by Jackie Burroughs. A Canadian twist on the local sheriff, in Mountie corporal Fernie, is executed with touching earnestness by Timothy Webber. Both the clear and drear of Canada's high country are rendered so well that critic Pauline Kael delighted in "the most lovingly photographed rain since *McCabe and Mrs. Miller*." And the story's ending is only as amazing as it is apparently true.

This western even contains an homage to the genre itself: Miner attends his first film, which just happens to be *The Great Train Robbery*. Along with snippets from the short's climax, we see Farnsworth's baby blues dancing with excitement at this new kind of heist—and the career prospects it opens up for an old dog. Only after the film ends and one of his fellow fans starts firing his pistol in approval does Miner reluctantly come out of his reverie. It's not unlike the way we feel after spending a pretty dreamy hour and a half in his company.

MAVERICKS: EXPANDING THE FRONTIERS OF THE MIND

In the seventies, the transition from the Old West into the New drew a few hip auteurs as well as old-time storytellers, though when it did, story may have taken a back saddle to image and character. Some audiences may have shifted restlessly, waiting for the cavalry to show up. Studio executives may have tugged nervously at their hair. Critics may have sharpened their carving knives. But time, as well as video sales, has proven that pushing the genre into the poetic, the eccentric, even the hallucinogenic has kept the western growing.

In 1971, the year that Peter Bogdanovich was nostalgically examining Timothy Bottoms, Jeff Bridges, and Cybill Shepherd's loss of innocence in a 1951 west Texas town called Anarene in *The Last Picture Show* (in which the local theater, the Royal, was appropriately featuring *Wagonmaster* and *Red River*), a rebellious Dennis Hopper was throwing western narrative to the wind. Following his successful sixties epic of young searchers on wheels (instead of horseback), *Easy Rider* (1969), Hopper created a tripped-out meditation on the innocence lost from western landscapes, western influence on other countries, and western movies themselves. *The Last Movie* (1971), which took Hopper two years to edit, follows a callow horse wrangler named Kansas (Hopper) as he remains behind in a Peruvian location after the film he was working on (with a director played by veteran western director Sam Fuller) is wrapped early because of the death of a stuntman (Dean Stockwell) playing Billy the Kid.

Kansas thinks he's found a natural paradise, Machu Picchu–style, to groove in—making love under towering waterfalls and setting up house with his Peruvian girlfriend (Stella Garcia). However, something weird is happening in town. The now film-frenzied villagers have scavenged a little leftover equipment, set up wicker replications of the rest of the filmmaking apparatus, and are making their own Billy the Kid picture (without film) full of real violence. And guess who they want to play the Kid?

This surreal film has flashbacks, flashforwards, unflinching performances of ugly Americans (including Hopper), religious rituals, James Dean iconography, soulful music (courtesy of Kris Kristofferson), lush photography (courtesy of

Laszlo Kovacs), and one of the most ambiguous narrative lines western fans have ever had to follow. Hopper's tenacity, creativity, and mind-blowing twist ending won him artistic recognition at the Venice Film Festival, but the film perturbed American critics enough so that they effectively buried his film until its rerelease in 1982. Now, of course, it's hailed as a masterpiece.

More mainstream artistic variations on the western genre have had their hurdles, too. Lovingly photographed drizzly landscapes, the piney northwestern frontier, a fine feminist role, and a man of vision are the only similarities between *The Grey Fox* and Robert Altman's *McCabe and Mrs. Miller* (1971). Altman's masterpiece of melancholy is sweet, poetic, piercing, and steeped in the turn of the century, but it's not upbeat for a nanosecond.

By 1971, Altman's incredible commercial success with *M*A*S*H* (1970) had made him a very hot, if somewhat chancy (perhaps the reason he was the fifteenth director to be offered the script), Hollywood property. True, he had reportedly been fired from the set of *The Delinquents* (1957) for the heresy of telling all his actors to speak at the same time. But a sterling track record directing television shows like *Bonanza* and *Combat*, coupled with *M*A*S*H*'s more than $40 million in domestic box-office returns, seemed to assuage the suits at Warner.

Altman had bought a script from Brian McKay based on Edmund Naughton's novel *McCabe*. The script, titled *The Presbyterian Church Wager*, told the story of a gambler-businessman named John McCabe (Warren Beatty) who rides into the rustic mining camp of Presbyterian Church, a town on the Canadian border, one cold autumn, wades through the mud to the

Is this a western or apocalypse Peru? Whatever you call it, art-meets-myth-meets-moviemaking in Dennis Hopper's visionary and controversial saga of celluloid, **The Last Movie** *(1971).*

local excuse for a bar, slaps his cards down, and announces his intention to bring civilization to this piece of wilderness by way of a high-class saloon and bordello. As he finances the new building, he also imports a cockney madam named Constance Miller (Julie Christie) to manage the ladies.

Between McCabe's grand vision and charismatic gift for gab and Miller's no-nonsense managerial skills, they turn their community into a thriving enterprise. But when a large mining outfit gets wind of their success and wants to buy them out, McCabe drunkenly blusters his way into big trouble, playing much too hard to get. The results are devastating for McCabe, Miller, and the townful of people whom we've come to know and feel for.

With a Warner Bros. budget of $2.4 million and $750 a week allotted to him for personal expenses, Altman set off at the end of 1970 for Vancouver, British Columbia, to lens his film. His crew built cabins, a sawmill, whorehouses, a bathhouse, two saloons, and a barbershop—no set pieces here, but the real thing. Altman's cameras would adjust to fit the set. He also brought his growing stable of ensemble actors, including Michael Murphy, René Auberjonois, Shelley Duvall, Keith Carradine, John Schuck, and William Devane, as well as the first "movie stars" he had ever directed, Warren Beatty and Julie Christie.

The watchword was *ensemble* as everyone took a hand in almost everything on the Altman artistic commune. Actors improvised and worked with overlapping dialogue. Beatty and Christie were treated as members of a stock company and, like the other

The dapper dude in the bearskin coat (Warren Beatty) is not half as sharp as he looks, but he sure is a dreamer to root for in Robert Altman's exquisite reflection on the dark side of Americana, **McCabe and Mrs. Miller (1971).**

actors, took part in helping Altman and McKay shape the ever-developing script. Dispensing with many unionized grips (Altman had on one occasion been severely fined for moving a prop on a union set), Altman even sneaked in a nonunion art director, Leon Eriksen.

The director's weekly personal expense account of $750 was quickly expanded to four thousand dollars and was spent on his cast and crew. For one fleeting sequence in which the town prostitutes give a party, Altman insisted that the actresses draw up their own guest list and put together a real party (using real vodka) to "celebrate." What didn't end up on film served to make a more intimate cadre of cocreators. Little got by the lens, however—Altman (perhaps as a result of his years in television) always kept two cameras rolling. Even in the background, actors never knew just when their chief would zoom in for a close-up. That made for continuous rich performances all round (which was helpful, since few characters were introduced with any exposition), and an organic feeling of real life in front of the camera.

The ensemble work succeeds. Christie and Beatty turn in some of the best work of their careers: Miller is a marvel of contradictions, as mercenary as she is ultimately maternal; and though big-thinking, big-talking, befuddled John McCabe may be about the last man you'd peg as a hero, his showdown with three mining-company gunmen (especially Dog Butler, played with bear-size, sinister suavity by Hugh Millais) would have been appreciated by Coop in *High Noon*.

Detailed though *McCabe and Mrs. Miller* is in its frontier portraits, its real power lies in intangible things. As veiled as Mrs. Miller's eyes as she sinks into an opium dream, as haunting as Leonard Cohen's voice and guitar, which well up again and again on the soundtrack, as delicate as the snow that seems to fall constantly—there is a somber, smoky beauty here unmatched by any film before or since.

That wasn't quite enough for the studio, though. Displeased with Altman's quirky product and the $600,000 he spent over budget, Warner Bros. gave *McCabe and Mrs. Miller* scant publicity and a national advertising budget of zero. Critics almost finished the hatchet job, damning the slow-paced, ambiguous film; Rex Reed called it "an incoherent, amateurish, simple-minded, boring, and totally worthless piece of garbage." It was only through Warren Beatty's muscle (he was a producer and Hollywood power broker in his own right) that it got a second release backed by an ad campaign. And though it did well enough, the film remains a celebrated sleeper to this day, as does much of Altman's work.

The pairing of Beatty and Christie was nothing compared to the next duo that hit the unconventional trail together in 1976. Who could possibly get away with asking $425,000 a week plus 2.5 percent of the gross for five weeks' work? Who else would have the spunk to dust himself off after a day of shooting, grin wolfishly, and say "Well, another day, another twenty grand"? The culprits were Marlon Brando and Jack Nicholson, and the strange, wonderful western they share is Arthur Penn's *The Missouri Breaks* (1976).

Just West of Westerns

Evolution is a funny thing. As broad as this genre is, some directors have squeezed hombres into the saddle who most real cowboys would fall off their horses just thinking about as trail companions. What's western may be in the eye of the beholder. Better behold a few of these standouts.

Film	What You Should Know
Ruggles of Red Gap (1935)	Charles Laughton as an English butler lost to a cowboy in a poker game.
Rhythm on the Range (1936)	Bing Crosby as a rodeo star riding after a runaway heiress played by Frances Farmer.
Way Out West (1937)	Laurel and Hardy dither in the dust.
The Terror of Tiny Town (1938)	An all-midget western.
The Oklahoma Kid (1939)	Bogey and Cagney don't find tommy guns in the Oklahoma land rush.
Buck Benny Rides Again (1940)	Jack Benny and Rochester head west.
The Wistful Widow of Wagon Gap (1947)	Lou Costello, super-sheriff.
The Kissing Bandit (1948)	Frank Sinatra rides the range, doing what he's good at.
Pale Face (1948)	Bob Hope plays a cowardly dentist who meets up with Calamity Jane, in the form of Jane Russell.
The Painted Hills (1951)	Lassie saddles up.
Pardners (1956)	Jerry Lewis and Dean Martin in a virtual remake of Rhythm on the Range.

Film	What You Should Know
Once Upon a Horse (1958)	Rowan and Martin as rustlers.
Flaming Star (1960)	Elvis Presley plays a Kiowa (a part originally written for Brando) to Barbara Eden's white settler.
The Singer Not the Song (1961)	Priest John Mills evades advances of gay gunslinger Dirk Bogarde.
The Outlaws Is Coming (1965)	Moe, Larry, and Curly get slapstick with a cactus.
Billy the Kid vs. Dracula (1966)	Need we say more?
The Fastest Guitar Alive (1967)	Roy Orbison spies and sings for the Confederacy.
The Shakiest Gun in the West (1968)	Don Knotts tries out Bob Hope's old dentist outfit.
The Hanging of Jake Ellis (1969)	Soft-core sex western.
Ned Kelly (1970)	Mick Jagger plays an Australian outlaw in armor.
Westworld (1973)	Yul Brynner is a deadly robot gunslinger in a theme park.
The Frisco Kid (1979)	Gene Wilder and Harrison Ford team up as rabbi and gunslinger.
Outland (1981)	Sean Connery does High Noon in outer space.

Not exactly your typical rancher-rustler scenario, the script by Thomas McGuane (who also wrote *Rancho Deluxe*, 1974, and *Tom Horn*, 1980) tells the tale of Tom Logan (Nicholson), a good-natured rustler who buys a piece of farm land from an unsuspecting rancher (John McLiam) to use as a relay station for the horses he and his cronies (including Harry Dean Stanton, Randy Quaid, and Frederick Forrest) are stealing. When the rancher's own equine stock is stolen, he hires a regulator to find and kill the varmints. The gunman arrives in the ample form of Robert E. Lee Clayton (Marlon Brando). The rest is deadly fat-cat-and-mouse, with the added complication of the rancher's daughter (Kathleen Lloyd, who was paid a mere mortal $20,000 for her efforts) falling for Logan, who is taking a surprising shine to the honest, farming life.

Simple, yes? Not exactly. When Penn hired Brando to play Clayton, little did he know that the old rebel would weigh in at 250 pounds (113.5kg) and add an Irish brogue, a dithering British accent, a Texas twang, and a flair for cross-dressing to the character description. It seemed that master actor Brando had Indians on his mind more than movies: he had supposedly signed on to the film because he needed money to fund his own film project about Wounded Knee, the Lakota's place of final betrayal by the U.S. government. He also wanted Nicholson to play Logan as an Indian. Brando was loath to memorize lines (if you watch carefully, you can see his eyes drifting offscreen to cue cards). During one scene, he reportedly asked to have his lines written on a piece of paper and attached to his scene partner's forehead. Even with cue cards, he changed his lines so often that the executive producer had to hire a secretary to transcribe the "script" in shorthand while Brando was acting.

While the rest of the cast escaped the 116°F (46.6°C) temperature of the Montana location (hot enough to wilt Nicholson's pre-planted garden before scenes could be filmed; hot enough that the crew stood in line most days to get hosed down), at the nearby War Bonnet Inn, Brando took up solitary residence in a trailer on the set, where he ate nothing but raw vegetables and fruits to lose weight, roared a Honda trail bike through the desert, picked up pieces of petrified wood, played the congas, collected grasshoppers, studied solar energy, and (according to the crew) one morning ate a live frog from a riverbank. He even stayed on after the film was over.

Though a patient Nicholson, after viewing the film's rushes, was quoted as having finally muttered, "Well, we might as well plug in an electric cord and stick it in a bucket of water, because our careers are over," the final cut, though admittedly eccentric, was quite the opposite of suicidal. Nicholson's thorough acting is perfectly countered by Brando's unpredictable playground of a ham performance (something Jack himself would take a whack at in later years).

For all his seeming laziness, Brando improvised madly, keeping everyone on their toes. After a confrontation with Lloyd's character, he might unexpectedly shout after her departing figure, "Your bloomers are showing!"—while being careful to cover his horse's ears to the vile epithet. He might solemnly praise a man

he's just flushed from a burning building—before throwing a hatchet through his head. He might comb his hair with the carrot he's about to feed his horse. He might do anything, like place a live grasshopper in his sleeping scene companion's mouth, resulting in take after take of an actor's worst nightmare. (The victim in this case, Randy Quaid, reflected everyone's bewilderment when he said, "I had no idea what was coming.")

The cinematic result is a "good guy" who's a vicious killer yet at heart a child, "bad guys" who are just trying to survive, a heroine who falls for the wrong man, and a patriarch turned victim turned psychopath; in short, more overturned western standards than you can shake a stick at. If you like your westerns rare and gamy, sink your teeth into this one.

CLINT BRINGS IT HOME

Everyone wants to pronounce genres dead. Then somebody comes along with a new one and changes everything.

—Clint Eastwood, Los Angeles Times, August 11, 1991

The end of the trail was almost the end of the trail. Before *Dances with Wolves* (1990), *Unforgiven* (1992), and *City Slickers* (1992) garnered their Oscars (and their studios' confidence), the western rode a rocky trail through the eighties. The budgetary balls-up of *Heaven's Gate* (1980) did much to veer the genre down a path of unpopularity. In *Silverado* (1985), Lawrence Kasdan nobly tried to overcome the standard, elegiac tone with new blood infused into a swashbuckling echo of Howard Hawks' buddy westerns. Even with fresh faces like Jeff Goldblum, Kevin Costner, Danny Glover, Kevin Kline, Linda Hunt, and John Cleese, the fire failed to spread. (Some actors just weren't meant to ride the range.) Similarly, Christopher Cain's *Young Guns* (a 1987 Billy the Kid yarn with a largely sons-of-movie-stars cast) turned bratpackers loose to fire up the genre, and Mario Van Peebles' *Posse* (1992) took a stab at honoring black cowboys with a largely African-American cast, but they failed to ignite older audiences. (More recently, *Bad Girls*, 1994, made a stab at retelling history with a "feminist" tale of four beautiful outlaw prostitutes.)

In the end, it took a Man with Great Name to rope the dissipated genre back into the cinematic mainstream and big box-office. Clint Eastwood had been pretty damned busy since he parted company with Sergio Leone and formed his own company. The same year that *Hang 'em High* made him the victim of a lynching who, with the help of a hanging judge (played with homey perversity by Pat Hingle), executed his executioners, Eastwood's Malpaso Company hired director Don Siegel for a lighter parable of West meets East.

Clint gets his revenge on his would-be executioners in Hang 'em High (1968), in which he escapes a lynching by the skin of his teeth.

In *Coogan's Bluff* (1968), Clint plays a western deputy at odds with New York as he tries to apprehend an escaped killer (a theme that would be recycled by both the television series *McCloud* and the 1994 film *The Cowboy Way*). The chemistry worked between actor and director. In their next collaborative effort, Eastwood and Siegel broadened the actor's romantic possibilities with *Two Mules for Sister Sara* (1969). Described by Eastwood as "kind of *African Queen* goes west," it tells the story of a drifter who saves a whore-in-nun's-clothing and aids her in helping Mexican revolutionaries battle the French. Budd Boetticher, the veteran director of numerous Randolph Scott westerns, originally intended his script to go to John Wayne and Silvia Pinal; Eastwood, however, had Elizabeth Taylor in mind for Sara. As she was unavailable, Shirley MacLaine (who had gotten her streetwalking feet wet with *Some Came Running*, 1958, and *Irma La Douce*, 1963) came to the rescue. She did so well that Siegel said, "Eastwood thinks he's leading her around, but she's leading him—he's the second mule in the title."

From there, the creative duo expanded Eastwood's image further still, placing the tough guy totally at the mercy of women in the Civil War–era, southern gothic psychodrama *The Beguiled* (1970). As a Union soldier held lovingly captive in a ladies' seminary, Clint found himself in a position that the Man with No Name would never have tolerated (but one the actor would hark back to in his first directorial effort, 1971's *Play Misty for Me*).

The seventies were good years for Eastwood. Continuing to build his macho image (and his bank account, as he was the highest-paid actor in the industry) with Siegel's *Dirty Harry* cop films, he also began to explore the world behind the camera. In his first western as a director, the supernatural *High Plains Drifter* (1972) he honored both his former mentors and struck gold (see pages 72–73).

His next at-bat, *The Outlaw Josey Wales* (1976), began a thread that he would continue to glory in 1992. This time, the killer had a gentle past. Sonia Chernus and Philip Kaufman's script (Kaufman was also director of the picture for two weeks, until he wrangled with Clint over the character of Josey) depicted a Missouri farmer whose wife and kids have been slaughtered by Union guerrillas, compelling him to become the most savage of rebel guerrilla fighters. After the war, Josey Wales makes an epic flight to Texas,

Portrait of an American icon and a true artist—the man who shot the Western into the nineties, Clint Eastwood, shown here in Unforgiven *(1992).*

By 1992, having starred in thirty-six films (ten of which were westerns), Eastwood was ready to honor his mentors, the genre, and the public with a blockbuster that could claim both a heart and a brain. *Unforgiven* (1992) had been riding in Eastwood's saddlebag since the early eighties. Written by David Webb Peoples in 1976 under the title *The Cut Whore Killings*, it had been snapped up by Francis Ford Coppola, who eventually chose not to renew the option. Unlike William Munny, the grizzled antihero of Peoples' script, Eastwood was still relatively spry, but as he said, "I figured I could age into it a little bit. I just liked the material a lot and I thought I would sit on it and think."

killing scores of bounty hunters and attracting other misfits along the way. Supported by fine performances from Chief Dan George and Sondra Locke (Clint's former longtime companion, who eventually became a director in her own right), Eastwood strikes a fine balance between good and evil.

The scales tipped back the other way in 1980 with *Bronco Billy*. The East came West as Eastwood's shoe salesman–turned–self-made Wild West show hero proved that even a little comic bumbling was permissible for an action star (something Stallone and Schwarzenegger would later cash in on). By the mid-eighties, Eastwood had directed himself in nine films. His ability to use, expand, and refract his laconic yet deadly persona had already reached a level of sophistication that few directors had achieved with other actors.

In *Pale Rider* (1985) the Leone-inspired flesh-and-blood phantom was tempered by a more traditional western script to become a savior to a group of prospectors at odds with a dastardly mining company. Eastwood's "Preacher" is a man of the cloth who isn't quite flesh and blood (often backlit as a presence rather than a mortal man), though he does manage to arouse the blood of not only a homesteader (Carrie Snodgrass) but her fourteen-year-old daughter (Sydney Penny) as well. His retribution is brutal yet leavened with sadness, self-awareness, and humor, as is evident when, after using an ax handle to club three beefy assailants away from miner Hull Barret (Michael Moriarty, in a performance almost as laconic as Eastwood's), Preacher quips, "There's nothing quite like a good piece of pine."

While he was mulling it over, real shoot-'em-up rates in America were soaring to levels even higher than those of the Old West. Some gang leaders called their cronies "posses." Even Eastwood's callously vengeful law-and-order screen persona was coming more and more to parallel the American mindset. It was time for a mainstream western to take a good hard look at its bloody bread-and-butter, and Clint was just the hombre to do it. According to Clint, "I felt it was very timely to do a film where violence not only can be painful, it's also not without consequences for the perpetrators of the violence as well as the victims. That appealed to me, because usually in westerns—and I've been in my share—you shoot a lot of nameless people off a building, it's sort of glorification and romance. In this we demythicize it." That he did. Like Josey Wales, Munny was a guerrilla fighter from the Civil War whose monstrous appetite for liquor and killing was tempered only when he became a married farmer. With his wife now dead, and he himself struggling to support his two kids on a Kansas hog farm, Munny is tempted by an offer from the whores of a town called Big Whiskey—the glamorous job: to kill the two cowboys responsible for mutilating a prostitute's face (because she had the temerity to laugh at the size of one of their members).

The money (an offer of five hundred dollars per dead cowboy) is scrappy, and so are Munny's partners: a swaggering and unfortunately nearsighted youth called the Schofield Kid (played with almost insane adolescent gusto by Jaimz Woolvett) and an old compadre named Ned Logan (played with sage humanity by Morgan Freeman). As for the ravine-faced Munny, he is girded to his task but becomes sicker by the day and guiltier by the hour over his return to one of the most notorious killing careers ever.

Together, this misfit threesome rides into town and within reach of gunfighter-turned-sheriff Little Bill Dagett (a gleefully mean-spirited Gene Hackman), who rules his little town and any itinerant gunnies (like Richard Harris as the deadly dandy English Bob) with an iron fist. With the bad townsfolk on one side, the righteous prostitutes (including Eastwood's real-life love, Frances Fisher, as the scrappy Strawberry Alice) on the other, the good bad-guys are caught in the middle. Still—when push comes to shove—honor, vengeance, and Munny's bloodlust come through with horrifying consequences.

Hackman, who had been sensitive to violence since trailer clips from Alan Parker's *Mississippi Burning* (1988) featuring his character tossing another through a mirror had grossly misrepresented his role, passed on Dagett at first. Acting violent was one thing, but starring in a film that glorified it was another. Eastwood had to convince him that this exploration of mayhem was more like *The Ox-Bow Incident* than *Rambo*. Hackman was won over—and gave no arguments when it was time to pick up his Oscar.

These myths were as human-size as the trio's jittery need to embellish on the injury that had been done to the woman they were steeling themselves to avenge. The film's most romantic figure, English Bob, meets an iconoclastic end, while Dagett spews myth-shredding truths about gunfighting to sycophantic dime-novelist W.W. Beauchamp (a veritably oozed performance by Saul Rubinek). Like the fame-hungry Schofield Kid, Beauchamp learns a humbling, humanizing thing or two before the final frame.

Eastwood shot in locations in Sonora, California, and in the Calgary area of Alberta, Canada, for eleven weeks. (Among the snippets that landed on the cutting-room floor were Eastwood's octogenarian mother, Ruth, as an extra stepping down from a train, and Fisher's own home movies of the murderous Munny kissing his horse on the lips and snuggling with his pigs in the mud.) It had taken almost eleven weeks for production designer Henry Bumstead (an Oscar winner for *To Kill a Mockingbird*, 1963, and *The Sting*, 1973) and other designers to build the town of Big Whiskey. Eastwood himself wrote the haunting guitar theme that opens and closes the film. And as the credits rolled by, as the guitar serenaded, as the sunset framing Munny's silhouette deepened, four final words hit the screen: "For Sergio and Don."

This time the genre was avenged. Critics who had underrated both it and auteurs like Eastwood scrambled over one another for superlatives. *Unforgiven* made it onto 234 critics' "Ten Best" lists that year. It swept more than twenty-six major film awards, including the coveted Academy; British Academy of Film and Television Arts; Golden Globe; New York, London, and Los Angeles Film Critics Circles; National Society of Film Critics; and Directors' Guild awards. And most important (for, as we know, in Hollywood money talks and everything else walks or takes public transportation), *Unforgiven* grossed a staggering $100 million at the box office by the time 1993 was only half over.

Yessir, the western has ridden a long and ragged mile since Eadweard Muybridge took his camera down to the racetrack. True, it may never again be the all-popular genre it once was, as we

edge further and further from the time and mindset the western originally embodied. However, as a beautiful canvas where myth and morality can be savored among sweeping strokes of adventure, with history coloring it all for good measure, it has a definite future. With films like *Unforgiven* proving that mainstream shoot-'em-ups don't have to be simple, excessive, artless, or unprofitable, the sky's the limit. And on a clear day, the western sky seems infinite.

Words to Live By: Part V

A. "All I've got left are a few memories. And if Dave was sellin' guns to the Apaches, I don't even have that."

B. "It's a hell of a thing, ain't it, killin' a man. You take away everything he's got and everything he's ever gonna have."

C. "See, if I'd a had a gun, one of us might have gotten hurt and it might be me."

D. "I can see how you cleaned up Tombstone. You can start right here...and don't forget the corners."

E. "By God she reminds me of me."

F. "Whatever you learned down flat won't serve you up here. You've got some work to do."

G. (After shooting Marlon Brando in a bubblebath) "Hell, you aren't even there."

H. "If God didn't want them sheared, he wouldn't have made them sheep."

I. "I got away with it because I had a hangover. I was too mad to be scared and too sick to worry about it."

J. "I'm not trying to be a hero. If you think I like this, you're crazy."

K. "Well, sometimes the magic works, and sometimes it doesn't. Let's go home and eat."

ANSWERS: ; A. Donald Crisp, The Man from Laramie (1955); B. Clint Eastwood, Unforgiven (1992); C. James Stewart, Destry Rides Again (1939); D. Marlene Dietrich, Destry Rides Again (1939); E. John Wayne, True Grit (1969); F. Will Geer, Jeremiah Johnson (1972); G. Jack Nicholson, Missouri Breaks (1976); H. Eli Wallach, The Magnificent Seven (1960); I. Robert Mitchum, El Dorado (1967); J. Gary Cooper, High Noon (1952); K. Chief Dan George, Little Big Man (1970)

BIBLIOGRAPHY

Adams, Les, and Buck Rainey. *Shoot-Em-Ups*. New Rochelle, N.Y.: Arlington House Publishers, 1978.

Anobile, Richard J., ed. *The Film Classics Library: John Ford's Stagecoach*. New York: Universe Books, 1975.

Behlmer, Rudy. *Behind the Scenes*. Hollywood, Calif.: Samuel French Publishers, 1989.

Brownlow, Kevin. *The War, the West and the Wilderness*. New York: Knopf, 1979.

Buscombe, Edward, ed. *The B.F.I. Companion to the Western*. New York: Atheneum, 1988.

Canutt, Yakima. *Stunt Man*. New York: Walker and Company, 1979.

Christ, Judith. *Take 22: Moviemakers on Movie Making*. New York: Viking, 1984.

Dillon, Richard. *Western Quotations: Famous Words From the American West*. Tempe, Ariz.: Four Peaks Press, 1993.

Essoe, Gable, and Raymond Lee. *De Mille: The Man and His Pictures*. New York: A.S. Barnes and Company, 1970.

Everson, William K. *The Hollywood Western*. New York: Citadel Press, 1992.

————, and George N. Fenin. *The Western*. New York: Grossman Publishers, 1973.

Fox, David J. "Mopping Up After the Oscars." *Los Angeles Times*, April 4, 1994, p. 12.

Franklin, Joe. *Classics of the Silent Screen*. New York: Citadel Press, 1959.

French, Philip. *Westerns*. New York: Oxford University Press, 1973.

Garfield, Brian. *Western Films: A Complete Guide*. New York: Da Capo Press, 1982.

Halliwell, Leslie. *Halliwell's Filmgoer's Companion*. 7th ed. New York: Charles Scribner and Sons, 1980.

Hardy, Phil. *The Western*. New York: William Morrow and Company, 1983.

Hilger, Michael. *The American Indian in Film*. Metuchen, N.J.: Scarecrow Press, 1986.

Hudson, Mona. "I Saw Marlon Brando Shoot Jack Nicholson." *Vogue*, December 1975, p. 165.

Johnson, Kristina, and Michael A. Lipton. "A Clint in Her Eye." *People*, August 31, 1992, p. 83.

Koszarski, Diane Kaiser. *The Complete Films of William S. Hart*. New York: Dover Publications, 1980.

Manchel, Frank. *Cameras West*. Englewood Cliffs, N.J.: Prentice Hall, 1971.

Mann, Roderick. "John Wayne: A Natural as 'The Shootist'." *Los Angeles Times*, March 7, 1976, p. 57.

Matthews, Jack. "The Yippie-Ti-Yo Ti-Yay! File: Clint Eastwood Saddles Up Again: How Do You Say 'Make My Day' in Cowboy?" *Los Angeles Times*, August 11, 1991.

McBride, Joseph. "Wayne, Stewart and Shootist: A Sense of History in the Making." *Variety*, January 29, 1976, p. 28.

————. "Eastwood Looks West to Honor Mentor's Legacy." *Variety*, August 6, 1992, p. 23.

McDonald, Archie P. *Shooting Stars*. Bloomington, Ind.: Indiana University Press, 1987.

Meryman, Richard. "To Hoffman, the Problem Was Not the Face." *Life*, March 1970, p. 4.

Meyer, William R. *The Making of the Great Westerns*. New York: Arlington House Publishers, 1979.

Miller, Don. *The Hollywood Corral*. New York: Popular Library, 1976.

O'Neil, Paul. *End of the Myth*. Alexandria, Va.: Time-Life Books, 1980.

Parish, James Robert, and Michael R. Pitts. *The Great Western Pictures II*. Metuchen, N.J.: Scarecrow Press, 1988.

Peary, Danny, ed. *Close-Ups: The Movie Star Book*. New York: Workman Publishing, 1978.

Phillips, Louis. *Fifty Movie Questions Your Friends Can't Answer*. New York: Walker and Company, 1983.

"Picture Prospects." *Publishers Weekly*, September 2, 1974.

Place, J.A. *The Western Films of John Ford*. New York: Citadel Press, 1974.

Rainey, Buck. *Heroes of the Range: Yesterday's Saturday Matinee Movie Cowboys.* Metuchen, N.J.: Scarecrow Press, 1987.

Richards, Norman V. *Cowboy Movies.* New York: Gallery Books, 1984.

Rothel, David. *The Singing Cowboys.* New York: A.S. Barnes and Company, 1978.

Sarf, Wayne Michael. *God Bless You, Buffalo Bill: A Layman's Guide to History and the Western Film.* Cranbury, N.J.: Cornwall Books, 1983.

Seydor, Paul. *Peckinpah: The Western Films.* Champaign, Ill.: University of Illinois Press, 1980.

Shipman, David. *Movie Talk: Who Said What About Who in the Movies.* New York: St. Martin's Press, 1988.

Simon, John. "Wayne Damage." *New York* magazine, August 30, 1976, p. 78.

Sklar, Robert. *Film: An International History of the Medium.* New York: Harry N. Abrams Publishers, 1993.

"Something's Sacred." *Playgirl,* August 1976.

Stanton, Bette L. *Where God Put the West: Movie Making in the Desert.* Moab, Utah: Four Corners Publications, 1994.

Thomas, Tony. *The Films of Kirk Douglas.* New York: Citadel Press, 1972.

_____. *The Films of Henry Fonda.* New York: Citadel Press, 1983.

_____. *The West That Never Was.* New York: Citadel Press, 1989.

Turan, Kenneth. "The Man Who Shot Great Movies." *The Los Angeles Times,* July 3, 1994, p. 5.

Tuska, John. *The Filming of the West.* Garden City, N.Y.: Doubleday and Company, 1976.

_____. *The American West in Film: Critical Approaches to the Western.* Westport, Conn.: Greenwood Press, 1985.

Warga, Wayne. "Penn, Brando, Nicholson: Three for the Show." *Los Angeles Times,* August 24, 1975, p. 35.

Weisser, Thomas. *Spaghetti Westerns: The Good, the Bad and the Violent.* Jefferson, N.C.: McFarland and Company, 1992.

PHOTOGRAPHY CREDITS

Principal photography courtesy The Kobal Collection

Courtesy American Museum of Natural History, Department Library Services, negative number 19855, photograph by Edward Sheriff Curtis: 15

Archive Photos: 12, 37, 38, 75, 120

Photofest: 5, 6, 10–11, 14, 16, 18, 20, 21, 29, 35, 42, 48, 49, 51, 53, 54–55, 58, 72, 80, 99

The Bettmann Archive: 8, 13 both, 17

Acknowledgments

Cinema Center: 66; **Columbia:** 44; **Edison:** 18; **Fine Line Features:** 99; **Fox:** 23, 26–27, 80; **Goldwyn/United Artists:** 5, 9; **Hollywood Pictures:** 75; **Jack H. Harris Enterprises:** 51; **MGM:** 30, 31, 73, 104; **Mutual:** 20; **Orion Pictures Corporation:** 6, 54–55, 67; **Paramount:** 10–11, 24, 29, 35, 37, 38, 46, 48, 49, 58, 109, 110, 111; **Pathé:** 16; **Republic:** 96; **RKO:** 92; **Triangle:** 21; **Twentieth Century Fox:** 2, 53, 56, 70, 71, 76, 93, 102; **United Artists:** 32, 34, 36, 45, 50, 60, 61, 78–79, 83, 88, 107, 113, 119; **Universal Pictures:** 65, 72, 95, 115; **Warner Bros.:** 28, 40–41, 42, 43, 57, 74, 85, 87, 91, 100–101, 116, 120

INDEX